PORTRAITS
OF
PATRIOTS

PORTRAITS OF PATRIOTS

by
Sherman
Avner
"Shug"
Bledsoe, Jr.

All proceeds from the sales of this book go
towards construction of a memorial
to veterans in Atoka County, OK.

The cost per book is $14.50
(OK residents, please add 8.5% sales tax)
plus $2.84 shipping.

To order, send your check or money order to:
Atoka County Veterans Memorial
P.O. Box 637
Atoka, OK 74525-0637

Please make checks or money orders payable
to the Atoka County Veterans Memorial.

Thank you for your support!

Published by Quarry Press
P.O. Box 181736
Dallas, Texas 75218

email: quarrypress@msn.com
website: www.quarrypressbooks.com

Written by Sherman Avner "Shug" Bledsoe, Jr.
Cover design and book layout by Angie Maddox
Indexing by Jessica Cortez and Amy Zamora

Copyright 2004 by Bill Bledsoe

Library of Congress
Control Number:
20033115484

ISBN 0-9714058-4-X

Dedicated to
the Patriots
of Atoka County,
Oklahoma

Acknowledgments

I would like to thank a few people for their help in getting these articles ready each week for the last 16 months.

First, Ron and Linda Linscott, Foster and Louise Cain, Kenneth Hamilton and his staff at the Atoka County Times; Alice Withrow with the Atoka Library; my former platoon leaders, Lon Robert Fink and Scott Wells; Jesse Wayne Phillips and Tinker Ray who "walked on egg shells" while the story of "Winkim, Blinkim and Knod" was being written; "DAS" Ditters Cole who spent a great deal of his time helping me to research various articles; Connie Zalenski, who gave her time for all of the computer work; to each of you who gave us encouragement each week about the articles. And finally to those who with either getting the interviews or helped with information about each of our subjects.

I can't say thank you enough to each of the men or women we have written about. I would remind you that over 1,500 from Atoka County have served in the military of this country, that in excess of 100 of these were killed and 20 plus were taken as prisoners of war.

I hope that someone will pick up from here and continue to write about our patriots or else they will be swallowed up by history and forgotten.

Thank each of you for your time each week and may God continue to richly bless this country with freedom and those willing to give their lives for each of us.

Shug Bledsoe
March 5, 2000

The Atoka County Veterans Memorial

In the year 2000 Sherman "Shug" Bledsoe envisioned a veterans memorial in Atoka County that would honor its veterans.

Shug spent endless hours in the court house, looking through newspapers, on the phone, talking to friends, and any other sources he could access to find names of Atoka County veterans.

He came up with a list of over 2,000 names from the Spanish-American War through Operation Desert Storm. Shug worked with *The Atoka County Times* to publish the list of those named. Since then to the present (2003), people have called in the names of approximately 700 more veterans.

Shug arranged for several veterans to take a trip to Stuart and Tishomingo, Oklahoma to look at those city's veteran memorials. This gave us some ideas of formulating the design.

The Atoka County Veterans Memorial will be on a 50-foot square slab. A 4'x6'x6' granite stone embedded with the seals of the five branches of service will sit at the front. Behind it, 22 granite stones will sit in a 37' diameter circle. Both sides of each stone will display names of Atoka County veterans. A flag pole will stand in the center of the circle.

The Atoka City Industrial Authority has leased to the Veterans Memorial Council of Atoka County, Inc. two acres of land for $1 per year on a 50-year contract. The two acres are on the north side of Highway 3, just east of the new community building in Atoka.

Glenn Norton, Adjutant,
Veterans Memorial Council of Atoka County, Inc.

All money derived from the sales of this volume will go toward the construction of this memorial. See page 4 for information on how to order.

Introduction

Portraits of Patriots is a collection of columns that appeared in the *Atoka County Times* for 16 months, starting in late 1998 and concluding in March, 2000. The author of these columns was my older brother, Sherman Avner Bledsoe, Jr., of Lane, Atoka County, Oklahoma, known to most people as "Shug." About a year after writing the last column, Shug went on to be with the Lord; he was about a month shy of his 68th birthday.

What prompted Shug to write "Portraits of Patriots," a weekly column about men and women who had distinguished themselves in our country's armed forces?

The roots of his interest probably go back to World War II. Born in 1933, Shug was a just a young boy when our country took on the Axis powers which were bent on dominating the world and changing our way of life. He had a vivid memory of our grandparents, Bill and Roby Cartwright, proudly displaying six stars in her window, one for each of their children or spouses who were serving in the armed forces. They had nine children (eight surviving) altogether, and those who were not in the service, like our father who was too old to join, were active in war-related activities. Our aunts and uncles in the service weren't heroes in the traditional sense, but they were heroes to Shug.

Shug followed in our family's tradition when he joined the National Guard in Atoka at age 15. Soon after he graduated from Atoka High School, his unit and many of his classmates were called into active duty with the 45th Infantry Division. His army unit bade farewell by marching through the town of Atoka, then went to Ft. Polk, La, for basic training as military policemen. In a few months he was sailing on the U.S.S. Gen. Hugh Gaffey troop ship through the Panama Canal and on to further training duty at

Hokaido, Japan. Soon thereafter, Shug found himself on the front lines in Korea along with many of his friends from high school. He survived a Jeep crash and a terribly cold Korean winter.

His commanding officer, Col. Scott Wells, would later write about Shug: "He was always cheerful and upbeat. No person should have expected more of him. In Korea during the coldest winter on record, he was stationed at the top of Double X Hill, which was two miles up a narrow mountain road. Sometimes when I visited his post, he looked like an Eskimo frozen with snow, sleet and rain. Never a complaint. I am proud to have served with him."

Shug was hospitalized with frozen feet, which continued to trouble him for the remainder of his life.

Between the patriotism of his own family and his own personal sacrifices for his country, Shug ended up with a special place in his heart for war veterans. Many of them shared with him their own, often painful, experiences; often these were things so gruesome they had not told even the closest members of their families.

Another motivating factor for Shug writing his columns was the sheer number of men from Atoka County who gave their lives for their country. I recently read a book which called the Civil War "a rich man's war, a poor man's fight." I pondered this, thinking about what Shug told me about the number of men from Atoka County who had served, been wounded or had died. Upon hearing this large number, I remember crying, and so did Shug.

Shug's faith in God gave him the mettle necessary to survive horrifying experiences of Korea. Yet at the same time it gave him empathy for his fellow human beings—no matter what their income, ethnicity, education or military rank.

Shug and I were brought up going to church. In fact, our parents, Sherman Avner Bledsoe, Sr. and the former Ollie May

Cartwright, were instrumental in establishing a Church of Christ congregation in Lane, meetings which were originally lit by kerosene lamps. Shug followed in our father's footsteps as a song leader with a bounding voice. He was an ardent student of the Bible, an excellent teacher and preached when necessary. Later, he became an elder at the Lane Church of Christ, which is noted for its local benevolence and mission works in Romania, Africa, Cuba, Mexico and Guatemala.

Shug attended grade school at Lane and graduated from Atoka High School. After service in Korea, Shug graduated from North Texas State University (now the University of North Texas) in Denton, Texas, with a degree in business management. It was there he met his future wife, Thelma Lamb from San Angelo, Texas, a descendant of Gen. George Armstrong Custer. In college, Thelma won the honorary title "Dreamgirl of Pi Kappa Alpha," Shug's fraternity.

After graduating from college, Shug worked in Dallas at American Airlines, Western Electric, and was a manager at Pollock Paper Co. before forming his own insurance agency. But his heart was always in Atoka County, which is where he wanted to raise his family.

In 1970 Shug, Thelma, and family moved back to Lane, Oklahoma, where he lived the rest of his life. They had two children, Bryan Allen and Tonya Alene, and five grandchildren, Matt James, Wendy Barton, and Melissa, Scott, and John Bledsoe.

Back in his native county, Shug was a special investigator for the Oklahoma Crime Commission, was vice-president of Bledsoe Energy Corp., owner of Bledsoe Land and Cattle Co. and operated Bledsoe's Diner in Atoka. He also wrote a book, <u>Lane and Its Neighbors</u>.

Shug died of heart-related problems on April 3, 2001. As a

final tribute, people came to his funeral in Atoka from at least four states. There was not enough room in the church to seat everyone; a very close friend drove from near Houston, Texas and had to stand in the street with many others.

That tells you about the author of these columns. But this book is not a tribute to Shug, and he would not have wanted it that way. This book is a tribute to the brave men and women from Atoka County who have defended this country. The heroes are the people named within these pages. When you read their stories, you'll understand why Shug proudly called them patriots.

Bill L. Bledsoe
Dallas, Texas
July, 2003

Atoka County, Oklahoma: A Brief Background

Written by Bill L. Bledsoe with liberal quotations from articles written by Gwen Walker, Marie Wilson and Mel Phillips in *Tales of Atoka County Heritage*, Atoka County Historical Society, 1983.

Atoka County is located on the edge of the Jackfork Mountains of the Ouachitas in southeastern Oklahoma, formerly known as Indian Territory. Two major geological features, the Choctaw Fault and the Ti Valley Fault, thrust northeastward across the county, dividing the rocky outcrops of the north from the rolling hills and fertile soils to the south. Two pristine lakes, Atoka Lake and McGee Creek Lake, provide excellent attractions to sportsmen for boating and bass fishing and the low mountainous areas and valleys shelter abundant wildlife for hunters. The main rivers are the Muddy Boggy and the Clear Boggy, both flowing southeastward through Atoka County before merging to join the much larger Red River, bordering Texas.

The Atoka area has a long history of nomadic Indian life; the Caddoan and Plains Villagers hunted and lived in the area from 700 A.D. to as late as 1500 A.D., as evidenced by the continuous findings of arrowheads, spear points and other flint tools in their ancient campgrounds.

About 1800 A.D., Indians continued to roam free, hunt, and inhabit the big country, wonderfully untouched by barbed wire and fence posts. The lush, fertile plains and valleys abounded with large spacious tracts of grazing lands covered by the native blue stem grasses. Virgin forests were not yet scathed or scarred by saw, axe, or timber roads. The same geological fault structures trapped the great herds of buffalo grazing in their migration routes out of the western prairies and were regularly converged upon by

Indian hunting parties from the Great Plains.

Indian Territory (the present state of Oklahoma) was included in the Louisiana Purchase of 1803 and became part of the United States of America. Soon thereafter, explorers crossed the land surveying and mapping the new addition to America.

The five civilized tribes of Indians - Chickasaw, Cherokee, Choctaw, Creek, and Seminole - who occupied land east of the Mississippi River, were moved by the U.S. Government in the famous "Trail of Tears" to the newly acquired land known as Indian Territory. The Indians brought their own culture, alphabet, language, schools, religion, laws, and traditions.

The onward tide of white civilization caused tremendous change and demanded that the Indians be subject to the laws and customs of the new inhabitants. The Indians fiercely resisted but eventually yielded and entered into treaties with the United States. The 1830 Treaty of Dancing Rabbit Creek promised the Choctaw Nation land "for as long as grass grows and water flows." Atoka then became part of the Choctaw Nation and was generally settled by the Choctaw Indians of Mississippi.

The Choctaw Council of 1850 named the area Shappaway County, which included parts of Atoka, Coal, and Johnston counties. An Indian Chief named Rtoka was a member of the Shappaway Council and the county was named after him. The "R" in the Choctaw language has the same sound as "A" in English; thus, the name Atoka. The word "atoka" means "a place of much water."

Soon came the waves of military men, traders, home seekers and pioneers who blazed trails and settled across the land. In 1857 the U.S. Congress awarded a contract for a stagecoach and mail route to the Butterfield Overland Mail Company. The Butterfield Stage route would swing south and southwest from St. Louis, Mo., through Indian Territory, Texas, west across New

Mexico into southern California, and then north to San Francisco; this was the longest stagecoach route in the world and it covered some 2,800 miles. One passenger wrote: "The stage reels from side to side like a storm-tossed boat, and the din of the heavy iron wheels in constant contact with the rocks is truly appalling." The Butterfield Stage had three stations in the Atoka area: Waddell's, Geary's, and Boggy Depot. The stage line was the first transcontinental overland mail service in America and continued to operate until the outbreak of the Civil War.

After the end of the Civil War, the nations of the five civilized tribes consented to the construction of two railroads across Indian Territory; one from north to south and the other from east to west. In 1872 the Missouri, Kansas, and Texas Railway began operation with a train depot located in Atoka. The railroad was credited with causing the greatest growth and development of Atoka County, which soon became the cultural and educational center of the Choctaw Nation.

The Choctaws accepted the new settlers. They became close neighbors, traded together, worshiped together, married together, schooled together, and fought together in wars against mutual enemies. It was easy for the Choctaws to be well liked in school because they were generally magnificent athletes, especially in track and field; they were usually the quickest, fastest, most enduring, with amazing natural abilities, insights, and intelligence.

The white men in Atoka County soon outnumbered the Indians, but were not allowed to vote, hold office, or own land unless they were married to an Indian woman. A white man who married an Indian woman became an adopted member of the tribe and was called an "intermarried citizen." The number of people in this category increased so rapidly that very strict laws were made in regard to the marriage of Indian women to white men. The cost of a license for intermarriage was made high; in the Choctaw tribe it could cost as much as $100.

White men coming into Indian Territory to work were required to buy a license or permit from the tribe; the price varied according to the type of work proposed.

The Curtis Act of 1898 abolished the Indian tribal courts and all tribal laws were done away with. Indians were placed under the white man's law, and all citizens were then allowed to vote and hold office.

On April 4, 1905, one of the largest crowds ever amassed in Atoka (about 5,000) witnessed the arrival of the MK&T "Katy Flyer" at the new depot with President Theodore Roosevelt aboard. He stopped on his way to attend the Rough Riders Reunion in San Antonio, Texas. The President's handsomely decorated train proudly displayed the U.S. flag painted on both sides of the tank, along with the figure of the rough rider above the headlight. Other patriotic designs and bunting illuminated with electric lights were all over the engine and beneath the boiler.

The Katy Flyer stopped in Atoka just long enough for President Roosevelt to make a short speech expounding "what a fine country this part of Oklahoma is." The cheering crowd, including school children, waved flags, banners, and slogans while the band from the Murrow Indians Orphans Home played music appropriately honoring the President.

In 1907, Indian Territory became the state of Oklahoma. At that time, the population of Atoka County was 11,824. In 2000 the county had a population of 13,879; of this total, 11.4% were American Indians.

CHAPTER 1

"Whites Eyes" Witnesses the Choctaw Cry

This past summer, my life long Choctaw friend, James Nelson, and I were doing some repair work on my house. We were talking about the "old days" when we grew up at Lane and during our conversation some young Choctaw "bucks" came by and could not believe what they were hearing about the "CRY." We thought that maybe some others might be interested in how as young boys, we remembered the *yaiya* (cry).

It was the summer, at the end of my second grade at Lane school, when it became time for the *impa chito* or *chepuleci*. This is what we "white eyes" would refer to as a festival or summer camp meeting. As far back as I could remember, we heard the church bell ringing every Sunday morning calling the locals to worship at the Chish Oktak Double Springs Presbyterian Church, which had been in Lane since right after the Civil War. This time of year, however, the bell was ringing to gather the Choctaws for their annual "cry."

Not many whites ever attended the *yaiya*, and the only reason that I went was because I was invited by three of my best school friends, Joephene Allen, David Allen, and Ben Carnes. All were full blooded Choctaw, and each was about three years older than me. Our fathers "bucked slabs" together at the Haggard-Cotner sawmill. No one dared to bother me at school or my friends would take care of them. This year I was invited by my Indian friends to go see just what happened at their annual gathering - something that shall never be forgotten or regretted.

When we arrived at the church grounds, there were Choctaws from all parts of the country coming by *isuba* (horseback), *ita chanalli* (wagon), hitch-hiking, walking, or by any means to get to Lane for *yaiya*.

There were Indians camped out in wagons, some camped on open ground, some were able to have use of a brush arbor, and some stayed with friends or relatives. Food for the occasion was all cooked outside on open fires in kettles, spits, or on hot rocks placed in holes dug in the ground. They would barbecue *wak ushi* (calf or beef), *shukha* (hog) would be cooked on a spit and in pots, *akanka* (chicken) cooked in pots, *ta-fula* (hominy) being cooked in big iron kettles, *tanchi* or *nipaslia* (corn or roasting ear on a stick) and *pask alwasha* or *paska* (fry bread) was baked on coals of fire. No one went away hungry as there was always plenty to eat.

After the big meal, the Choctaws were called to church for the beginning of the service of the *yayai* or "funeral cry." The whole family would attend, but men and women sat on opposite sides of the church house. Something else was very unusual in that no one talked during the service except the preacher or the one in charge of the meeting.

The speaker would preach a funeral sermon for all who had died in the past year, then friends and relatives would accompany the wife or mother to the grave site of their beloved for a crying period. Once they reached the grave, they would sing and pray with the women crying and moaning over the deceased; occasionally you could see tears gently moving down the cheeks of some of the men.

They would go wherever the new grave sites might be whether in the area of Ray Sheffield's pasture, behind the home of John Nichols, the Double Springs Church cemetery, or in the tree line of the property now owned by the U.S.D.A. Wes Watkins Research Center, or just isolated graves out in the woods. Usually, people were buried near their homes.

Graves were marked in different manners with some having a mound of dirt piled over the grave, some were marked by a flat rock, and some had a boxed trough built over the top of the site. Many times some personal articles were buried with the deceased. Usually before mourners departed the grave site, they would leave colorful objects as decorations, such as glass marbles, colored trinkets, or you might see glass fruit jars painted in bright colors intermingled with black.

After the final cry at the graves, each participant would return to the church grounds for a final meal with each other and leave for their homes. The "cry" was a moment of sadness. It paid respect to those who had gone on but it was also a joyous occasion because families go to visit with each other and old friendships were renewed.

You no longer hear about the "Choctaw funeral cry" being a part of the Choctaw community tradition, I guess it's just *taha* (gone or finished). My three school friends that were previously mentioned are no longer here. They each have gone on to meet their maker without ever having a "cry" over their resting place. It is with much thanksgiving that my buddies took me to an event that very few "white eyes" have had the honor and privilege to witness.

CHAPTER 2

He Helped Capture Subs That Attacked Pearl Harbor

The Japanese bombing of Pearl Harbor on December 7, 1941 was called by President Franklin Roosevelt "a day of infamy." We would like to give you a portrait of a man raised at Harmony and Atoka, Chief Gunners Mate Leroy Blackburn, who was a survivor and a participant of this historic day.

Leroy became a member of the U.S. Navy on January 3, 1940. He was trained as a torpedo striker aboard the minesweeper U.S.S. Chandler, built in 1919. The ship subsequently became a destroyer escort.

Two days before the bombing the Chandler was operating off of Hawaii as a plane guard for the aircraft carrier U.S.S. Lexington. As the ships lined up going into dock at Pearl Harbor, it was discovered that the officer on the bridge had gotten the Chandler in the wrong position, causing the ship to become dead in the water; it was within 100 yards of the Lexington's flight deck and the mast of the Chandler was directly in the way of any landing or takeoff of aircraft.

All at once the Chandler was given instructions to leave the harbor and to work with the U.S.S. Minneapolis. On that fateful morning as the Minneapolis and Chandler were waiting to go into Pearl Harbor, Leroy had the deck watch and was in charge of the depth charges rack. He noticed these unusual airplanes, Japanese Zeros, beginning to dive from the sky and beginning to strafe the US Army B-17 bombers on the ground at Hickman Field. All at once, he saw smoke, fire and various buildings being blasted to pieces and then the word came that they were being attacked by the Japanese.

A call came that a Japanese submarine had been located at the mouth of the harbor, and the Chandler was to search out and destroy the vessel. The Japanese sub was sunk and yet the zeros still came in hordes, attacking any and all ships plus trying to blast a rock point at the mount of Pearl Harbor to block all entry or exit. The smoke became so dense they could no longer see the attacking planes or their targets.

That afternoon, the Chandler managed to get back into the harbor and began to see the devastating results of the sneak attack. As they sailed past battleship row, they could see parts of the sunken remains of the U.S.S. Oklahoma, U.S.S Arizona, U.S.S California and several other vessels that had been hit.

The bodies of men who'd burned to death were floating throughout the harbor. The oil and debris were some six to seven inches deep on top of the water. It took nearly a year for the surface to clean itself.

Leroy said they tied up the Chandler to a coal-loading dock, and he watched as they brought the bodies from the Oklahoma down a rope to be placed on a 50-foot motor launch and carried to shore.

Later in the afternoon of the 7th, sonar picked up the sound of another submarine. The Chandler was dispatched to drop depth charges, and it was discovered that a small Jap sub had been run aground on the harbor beach. Needless to say, they captured this sub and notice was received that another sub was close to the beach. The navy immediately strung a net between two ships and began trawling for the sub like you and I would try to get fish bait. They were successful in netting the sub and managed to get it hoisted on to a dock.

By the way, some of you may be old enough to remember in the late summer of 1943, a War Bond Drive was conducted nationwide and they brought one of the two captured small subs to Atoka for us to see the prize. Leroy was part of the crews that helped capture these subs.

On Monday, December 8 at 11 a.m., sonar picked up the sound of another submarine outside the harbor. The Chandler was dispatched to destroy the vessel. As they approached, the sub fired a torpedo which missed when it went under the bottom of the ship.

The skipper ordered Leroy to fire 16 depth charges to explode at 125 feet, but these all missed the target. Another run was made over the sub, and Leroy fired five charges to explode at a depth of 75 feet. Shortly, the crew of the Chandler saw a white swirling of water rising up followed by an oil slick, debris and finally bodies of Japanese sailors coming to the top. The crew cheered. The Chandler's skipper was awarded the Navy Cross for this action. He and his crew were subsequently involved in their defense of the north side of the island at a place called Kaneoha Bay Harbor.

Leroy was later transferred to the U.S.S. Dennis, a destroyer escort, and they took part in the Battle of Leyte Gulf in the Philipines. During this naval battle, the Dennis took four hits by the Japanese yet managed to stay afloat. There were 13 American ships in the battle group and five were sunk. One of those sunk was the aircraft carrier U.S.S. St. Lo; from the gulf waters the crew of the Dennis picked up 435 survivors that had been aboard the carrier.

During the battle of Iwo Jima, Leroy was notified that his brother, Sgt. Houston Blackburn, had been killed at the battle of Leyte while serving as a U.S. Army medic.

Leroy was discharged January 3, 1946, having been involved in nine different Pacific naval battles. He was awarded the following: the U.S. Presidential Unit Citation, the Philippines Unit Citation, Philippine Liberation Medal with one star, American Defense Medal, Asiatic-Pacific Theater Medal with nine battle stars, Pearl Harbor Medal, Navy Good Conduct Medal, and the Victory Medal.

This December 7 you will hear "remember Pearl Harbor," which we should, but also remember a local patriot who was an eyewitness, a survivor, a defender, who was willing to lay his life on the line for you and this country. Chief Gunners Mate Leroy Blackburn is truly a great patriot.

CHAPTER 3

An Empty Stomach Prevented an Enemy Bullet from Being Fatal

This portrait is of a former McGee Valley resident, a one-fourth Chickasaw Indian, Cpl. Charles F. "Bud" Williamson. Bud was one of many area 18-year-olds who happened to be in the right age bracket to be drafted into World War II. He went into the U.S. Army on November 17, 1943 and reported for training at Ft. Sill, Oklahoma; later he was assigned to Ft. Ord, California for advanced infantry training. In late 1944, Bud was put aboard a troop transport bound for a port in England.

Bud was assigned to a Replacement Company in the British Isles for a while, then the first part of February, 1945 he was sent to Europe as an infantryman replacement reporting to Co. B, 318th Infantry Regiment, 80th Infantry Division. His new company was located across the Rhine River in Germany.

Bud had been in combat for 13 days but he and the men in his outfit had not eaten in three days. A supply truck carrying food rations caught up with them, and the infantrymen gathered around the vehicle to acquire their rations. They were ordered to "move out" and to eat later. Bud grabbed an arm load of ration boxes and ran to catch up to his squad when all at once he found himself on the ground with a tremendous amount of pain and a lot of bleeding from the area of his lower stomach. He tried to get up to walk but could not get his legs under him. Again he tried to stand but the pain grew greater and it was then he realized that he was badly wounded. There was no help for him as his squad had moved on and the pain grew so intense that Bud passed out.

Unknown to Bud, he had been shot by a German sniper's bullet that had entered just above his left hip, traveled across the lower part of his stomach and exited just above his right hip. Hours passed as Bud lapsed in and out of consciousness. To make matters even worse, it started to rain.

Later, a tank drove near where he was lying. For some reason the driver stopped, came over to look down at him and said, "Sorry, buddy." He then drove off, leaving Bud alone.

He does not know how much time passed, but the tank driver was able to notify medics of his location. The medics treated his wound the best they could and then transported him to an aid station. The doctors believe that what saved his life was his stomach being practically empty from not having eaten for three days.

Bud was sent to a major medical surgical unit for surgery on his digestive tract and to repair tendon damage to his legs. Several operations were performed and on more than one occasion, he was almost at the point of death. In all, he had over 40 major surgical procedures performed to try and repair the wound from one sniper bullet. The last time he had surgery he was told they could do nothing else for him.

Bud was discharged from the army in 1947, being declared as totally disabled. His wound has caused him to be in pain for over 53 years with severe stomach problems and a very noticeable limp when he walks.

Here is another young man that was willing to give his life for you and his country. A patriot, I think Bud Williamson is at the top of the list.

CHAPTER 4

Booby-Trapped Body Haunts Veteran

This portrait is a full-blood Choctaw Indian from Lane by the name of David Allen. David joined the Oklahoma 45th Infantry Division in August, 1950. He made the decision to "go with the boys you know" after Claud Tidwell and I recruited him to join the local 45th MP Co. He realized with all probability that he would be drafted and assigned to some unit where he knew no one; he mobilized with the Atoka unit and motored with the rest of us by convoy to Camp Polk, Louisiana. Later he was assigned to Co. C, 1st Battalion, 279th Infantry Regiment.

I never saw David from December, 1950 until I happened to meet his unit moving to the line at Chrowon, North Korea in April, 1952. Our meeting was very unusual in that Hershel Eastridge and myself had just completed an assignment from Double X Hill and were riding back to our company area. David's company had been in reserve and was moving to a position on the front to replace another unit of the 279th. We met these two columns of infantry sloshing through shoe-top-deep mud, with one column on each side of a dirt road, when we noticed David and Joephene Allen as a part of this unit. We stopped and the two Choctaws fell out of rank and talked to us for a few moments before running off through that mud to catch up with their company. That was the last time I ever saw Joephene. However, some years later I would see David.

I was living in Garland, Texas and was on my way to Lane to visit my Grandma Cartwright. While going through Durant my

attention was drawn to a familiar face of an old friend.
Immediately, I found a parking space off Main Street and a search was made to locate my boyhood buddy. Finally, David was found just outside of a hamburger place on the old square. As I approached this individual, he looked much older than his age, yet I was certain that it was my friend. We walked towards each other, and I called his name; He was stunned at first but then called my name. As we stood there talking, you could hear a loud growling stomach of hunger so I suggested that we go around the corner and share a meal together at the White House Cafe.

We ordered the Blue Plate Special. We began to eat when all at once tears streamed down David's cheeks, and he started sobbing. I had known him all my life, knowing him to be a tough guy, but had never known or seen him cry. I tried to comfort him and asked what was wrong. Finally, he said "I can't forget."

"David, what can't you forget?"

Here's what he told me: "In the spring of '52 we were on an outpost on the front when one night the Chinese attacked and over-ran one of our squads that was manning an outpost; a firefight ensued, and all the men except three were able to leave the area when the shooting subsided.

"The next morning we moved out to retake the outpost and received no resistance. We advanced out on the point, and I could see the three men lying face down; another soldier and I went to remove the body of the first G.I. When that other soldier rolled the corpse over, there was a huge explosion. The Chinese had booby-trapped the body so that any movement would cause the explosion.

"Shug, I can't forget."

Finally, I got David to control himself, and we left the café. We were both too upset to finish our meals.

That was the last time I saw David but every time we went through Durant, I was always trying to see if my friend was on the square. Some years later, I happened to be at Lane and asked a mutual friend about David. He told me David had died.

I am thankful for having had David as a part of my life and now I can't forget, either.

I mentioned Joephene, Claud and Hershel in this story. They, too, have all gone to meet their Maker.

CHAPTER 5

His Ability to Plan Saved the Lives of Others

This portrait is of Major Robert G. "Bob" Cates of Atoka, who fought in World War II. Bob was raised in Atoka and later attended the University of Oklahoma where he was a member of the Army ROTC program. Upon graduation, he received a commission of second lieutenant in the Army Artillery. Bob came home and joined Co. B, 180th Infantry Regiment, 45th Infantry Division as a platoon leader. He was mobilized for federal service with the rest of the division making training assignments in Louisiana, Fort Sill, Oklahoma, Camp Barkley, Texas, Camp Pickett, Virginia, Pine Camp, New York, and Fort Devens, Massachusetts. He then went aboard ship to North Africa. During all of the training periods, Bob had been promoted to captain and was given command of Tulsa's Co. L, 180th.

Their convoy dropped anchor in the harbor of Oran, Algeria, on June 8, 1943. After a short training period of landing operations, they boarded ship and were told they were going to make a landing in Sicily. Bob's company was to be in reserve to support the 1st Battalion, and they were to land about one-half mile east of the Acrate River, just east of the town of Gela.

Before the landing, on July 10, 1943, the Mediterranean winds began to kick up and the sea became full of rolling swells; the landing craft were on the point of becoming capsized. After the men finally got into the small boats, due to naval error they were erroneously landed in wrong places. Bob's Co. L landed as far as 6 miles south of Red Beach to 5 miles north of their designated area; this was due to failure of the Navy boat crews not knowing the right beaches and the landing zones not being properly marked. It wasn't until 8 p.m. that they were able to become a fighting unit.

Co. L and the 3rd Battalion conducted a successful flanking attack and played a big part in the capture of Biscari Airport, Sicily. Up to this point, this was the toughest and most vicious fighting for the 180th, and they were successful in defeating the German counter-attack launched to retake the airport.

By July 27 Bob's Co. L was overlooking the town of Castel di Tusa, having arrived under the cover of darkness. He immediately disbursed scouts and patrols, and they located two companies of Germans. His men, though small in number, made the enemy think they were a much larger force. Without firing a shot, Bob and his men caused the Germans to withdraw and give up their very valuable high ground.

One of Bob's men, S/Sgt. Franklin Adams of Marlow, Oklahoma, was awarded the Legion of Merit Medal for exceptional meritorious conduct for service in Sicily and Italy as a squad leader from July, 1943 to January, 1944.

The 45th Division started its landing on the Anzio, Italy beach-head on January 30, 1944. Bob was now assigned to the 180th Regimental Command Post area performing the duties of Assistant Regimental S-3. He had earlier been S-3 of the 3rd Battalion for seven months, and he was considered by his superior officers to be an excellent planner and leader of men.

Lt. Col. Bill Whitman, retired former B Co. exec and commander of several companies in the 180th, stated, "Ol' Bob was brilliant and gave his job all that he had to give. There are a lot of soldiers who returned home safe and sound from the war because of the diligence he gave to planning."

During March, 1944 at Anzio, Bob was at the Regimental CP when shrapnel from a German shell hit outside the dugout area. Bob was wounded in one of his eyes. It was necessary that he be removed from the field of battle. Later, Bob would be promoted to the rank of major and would be decorated with the Legion of Merit. His medal and citation are at the Atoka Museum.

Bob came home to Atoka and has been very successful in business and is very active on the political scene. Bob deserves our everlasting gratitude for his giving of himself for each of us and his country. He is a great patriot.

CHAPTER 6

"Cactus Jack" Gave It All

This portrait is of Tech Sgt. Curtis W. "Cactus Jack" Garner of Lehigh, Oklahoma. He had gotten the nickname "Cactus Jack" due to Vice-President of the United States at the time being "Cactus Jack" Garner of Uvalde, Texas, serving with President Franklin Roosevelt.

Curtis was a member of Co. B, 1st Battalion, 180th Infantry Regiment, 45th Infantry Division, one of the guard units from Atoka.

Curtis was awarded every medal for bravery that this nation could bestow on a soldier except the Congressional Medal of Honor, and he was recommended for that one.

Part of Curtis' story has been told in "The Story of the 180th Infantry Regiment," written in 1947 by Col. George Fisher, 45th Adjutant General, which is as follows:

"In the ever-moving headquarters of Co. B, Captain Philip J. O'Jibway, Bacone, Oklahoma, conferred from time to time with leaders of his platoons and squads, as this reserve company was about to be committed into the battle which raged on this first day of June. Into the headquarters came Technical Sergeant Curtis (Jack) Garner, Lehigh, Oklahoma, who for the 23rd time since his company had landed on the coast of Sicily, had taken command of a platoon during emergencies on the field of battle. Yes, 23 times Garner had been called upon to take over as a leader fell or was taken to the hospital due to illness during crucial times.

"Aside from a few days in October, 1943 when he was absent in the hospital suffering from fever, Garner had participated in every hour of combat which his company had undergone since that historic morning on the south coast of Sicily. Garner was one of the original national guardsmen inducted with his company on September 16, 1940, when Capt. Robert C. Dean answered the call for federal service with a fine group of boys from Atoka, Oklahoma.

"One by one, in the course of combat, Garner had seen the Atoka boys go down. Most of them were noncommissioned officers. There had been the bloody initial fight on the estate of Count of Massera in Sicily, Biscari Airport, Bloody Ridge, Oliveto, Telese, Vanafro and Anzio. These places had taken their toll, but Garner, always in the thick of things, had come through.

"As the drive from the beachhead progressed, word was received from the First Battalion that Garner would be recommended for battlefield appointment to grade of second lieutenant. Preparations were made for the completion at the recommendation for such appointment, and it was planned that it would be sent forward from the regiment. German shells crashed into and around the Co. B positions on this morning of the first, but preparations for the final assault on the German positions went ahead. Suddenly, a German shell crashed into the company headquarters and when its smoke cleared away, this man, who upon 23 occasions had been called upon to perform the duties of an officer in combat, and who, on each occasion had responded in a most credible manner, lay dead.

"'It just can't be true. They couldn't hit that fellow. I saw them throw everything they had at him at Venafro, and he went right on up after them.' This was the statement made by one private first class upon hearing that Garner was dead. This private had followed Garner since the trying days of November on Mount Croce and Mount Corno.

"Strangely enough, many men in combat showed a tendency to develop a confidence in leaders who proved themselves extraordinarily brave to such an extent they convinced themselves that such leaders could not be killed and that as long as they were with the leader, they could not be. This made for very closely knit and efficient work within platoons and squads, but, upon several occasions, the recoil from such a degree of confidence was difficult to cope with when the leader fell.

"Men like Jack Garner, Tilden Roark and the many others described in this account, by their personalities, absolute fairness and bravery, made their men idolize them. They did not have to cajole their subordinates or drive them. They led."

Jack Garner was another "Immortal Sergeant," and in his passing Lehigh, and Atoka, Oklahoma, had the memory of a man, who along with such fellows as Anderson Jim, William D. Franklin, John Bennett, James L McElroy, Wilbern Beard and J.D. Clark, gave his all in order that the soil of those little communities deep in the heart of the Indian Territory, might be forever the free land of a free people.

One can get some idea as to the sacrifices made by the men of the Atoka area when he takes into consideration the fact that after the fighting was over in June, 1944, two Atokans remained in Co. B; they were Corporal Scott Wells, nephew of First Sgt. McElroy and the smiling and game little Indian, Private First Class Ellis Jackson.

The same shell that killed Technical Sergeant Garner gravely wounded Captain O'Jibway and he was later evacuated to the United States.

"Cactus Jack" was killed on June 1, 1944, in what is referred to as "The Anzio Breakout" in Italy. I believe that you would have to agree with us that he truly was a patriot.

CHAPTER 7

A Highway Bears the Name of This Patriot

This portrait is of Cecil B. "Bud" Greathouse, a native son of Atoka County. He spent his first years living in the Crystal community, just south of Lane, where his father ran a grocery store and was the postmaster. Many of us fondly remember "Ol' Bud" as a long, tall drink-of-water known for his ability as an outstanding first baseman with a very accurate throwing arm. He was good enough to earn a contract with the Shreveport Sports of the Texas League, but he never made it to the big league.

World War II found Bud as an infantryman serving with Co. A, 1st Battalion, 3rd Infantry Regiment, 3rd Infantry Division (The Railroad Sign Patch). He served in Sicily, Italy, France and Germany, having fought alongside America's most decorated World War II hero, Audie Murphy from Farmersville, Texas.

Bud himself was highly decorated, having been awarded every medal this country gives for bravery with the exception of the Congressional Medal of Honor, and on two different occasions he was recommended for that distinction.

In 1949 Bud joined the Oklahoma National Guard Atoka Unit as a member of the 45th Military Police Co. He would mobilize with the rest of us and report to Camp Polk, Louisiana, later serving in Japan and Korea. Bud would try to volunteer for the Army to serve in Vietnam but was told his age would not allow him to once again go to combat in defense of this country.

Bud rarely talked about his combat experiences, but he did mention his baseball throwing ability gave him the accuracy to throw hand grenades through the opening slots of machine gun nests where the barrel of the protruding weapon could be seen.

He was personally decorated by General Charles DeGalle, the President of France, for bravery and even had a picture showing President DeGalle making the presentation and then kissing Bud on both cheeks. Brick "Hammerhead" Dashner said there was a second picture showing Bud responding by kissing President DeGalle on the mouth. Hearing that, Bud would roll his eyes, grind his teeth and start cussing "Hammerhead." Then I would join in and swear that I had seen both pictures.

When Bud put on his dress uniform, it was something to behold. He took a great deal of pride that all of his decorations were arranged in order and in a straight line, the razor crease in his trousers were very straight and they were bloused over his boots just right. His boots would have the best mirror shine I have ever seen. "Hammerhead" and I would accuse him of having three pairs so that he could always have one pair in the mail back to Casey Thomas, the shine man at Bob Choate's barbershop, in Atoka.

He would get all bent out of shape and start in on us. One time we prepared a package for Bud. While "Hammerhead" was getting ready to deliver it, I was gathering some of the men around by telling them that it would appear that he had gotten some homemade cookies. When he opened the package, much to his chagrin, there was one of the worst looking pair of worn out boots you have ever seen. Brick immediately stated, "I guess ol' Casey gave up on polishing this pair."

There are a lot of stories about Bud, but probably the one that all of us liked best is as follows: Once during an inspection by a major general, we were all standing at attention when the general passed through all of our officers, walked directly up to our good friend and said, "How are you doing Bud?"

Bud answered, "Just fine, dummy." We all like to have passed out but the general smiled and told him, "If you need anything let me know." The general knew Bud personally and was aware that he called everyone "dummy." However, the one exception was Brick Dashner whom he had for years called "Hammerhead."

When former members of the 45th MP Co. get together, some way, somehow the conversation will get to Bud Greathouse, then we start telling things that we each remember about him.

Just last week, Lefra Stackhouse dropped by the Diner, and he stated that he will always remember Bud saying, "I'll be standing on high, when they bring your body by." We all admired, respected and deeply loved Bud. In our talks with each other, the men in the company will tell you they don't think he was afraid of anything. At his funeral you couldn't find a dry eye among those with whom he served.

We were all so pleased when the City of Atoka and the Oklahoma Department of Transportation complied with our many requests that the new four-lane highway by the high school and 45th Division Park be named Greathouse Drive.

When patriot is mentioned in Boggy Bottom the first name that comes to mind is Cecil B. "Bud" Greathouse.

CHAPTER 8

He Saw Combat Action in Two Wars

This portrait is of Chief Warrant Officer Wesley W. Sherrard, U.S. Army, Retired, who lives in Lane, Oklahoma. Wes was originally from Dallas, Texas and after graduating from high school, he became a member of the 49th Armored Division of the Texas National Guard. In February, 1950 he joined the regular Army and was sent for basic training at Fort Riley, Kansas. After basic, he went to Fort Benning, Georgia for non-commissioned officer school. This was followed by paratrooper training and by Ranger training.

In September, 1950 he was transferred to the 187th Regimental Combat Team, Airborne Unit known as Rakkasana (which in Japanese means "falling umbrella"). He was a member of the Security Platoon of the RCT Service Company being landed at Kempo, South Korea. This unit would be in heavy combat duty and in October, 1950, they fought their way to Pyongyan, the capital of North Korea. It was Wes's outfit that made military history at Sukchon when they successfully air dropped a 105 mm artillery cannon howitzer out of a C-119 air transport.

Wes stated that the two worst battles that he was involved in were Wonju, South Korea, in February, 1951, (his unit was awarded the U.S. Presidential Citation,) and at bloody Inju in May 1951, (his unit received the Korean Unit Citation.) It should be noted that from September 1950 thru May 1951, four of his fellow troopers were awarded the Congressional Medal of Honor.

The following is a story of "Butch," a little Korean boy, that was written by Wes:

Butch

"Early one cold morning in the month of February, the year, 1951, a small lad wandered into our area of combat, in the mountains, north of Wonju, Korea. The only item of clothing he was wearing was a U.S. Army OG-108 wool shirt. He did not have any shoes, socks, underwear, pants, gloves, coat or hat, only the wool shirt.

"Looking back on that morning, I would say that the temperature was somewhere between zero and five degrees with a 15 to 20 mile-per-hour north wind blowing across and through the mountains. Believe me, it was cold!

"My platoon, more or less adopted this little lad at first sight. We took him in and thawed him out by wrapping an army wool blanket around him and taking turns holding him. When he was warm enough, we fed him a good ol' can of GI C-rations (ham and lima beans with a hot chocolate drink), gave him a real good an' hot GI sponge bath, and last but not least we gave him a name, Butch. The platoon sergeant sent for the regimental translator and we were told by the translator that Butch's parents had been killed during the night by elements of the North Korean Army. The platoon sergeant took up a collection and sent a young trooper to the nearest town (Wonju) to buy Butch some clothes.

"We kept Butch until October at which time the 187th Airborne Regimental Combat Team was rotated to Japan to receive qualified airborne replacements, training and new equipment. Before the regiment departed Korea, we located an orphanage in Teague, Korea, which agreed to take Butch. During the next four years, the men in the platoon supported the orphanage by sending money to the chaplain's office in Teague.

"While Butch was with us, he had approximately 35 fathers looking out for his well being, and you can believe this old trooper when I tell you that the day we turned Butch over to the nuns at the Orphanage, there were tears in one helluva lot of old combat harden airborne troopers' eyes. Butch was a scared little seven year old when he found us in February, and by the time we left him in October, he had matured one heck of a lot."

~ ~ ~ ~ ~ ~ ~

Let me add something to the "Butch story" for the men of the 45th MP Company by asking them to remember the spring of 1951 when Chaplin Bill Pharr from Atoka asked us to give a one-time donation to a Korean orphanage. Remember? This is the orphanage that we all chipped in to help. Small world isn't it?

The 187th RCT made two combat jumps during the so-called "Korean police action," and Wes made the last jump at Munsan-ni on March 23, 1951. In December, 1950, his outfit was noted for their delaying action of holding off the North Koreans and the Chinese with fire fights, by blowing up bridges and other installations while the U.S. 8th Army retreated from Pyongyan, North Korea. They were going towards Seoul, South Korea to the main supply route and the Texas line. Wes was slightly wounded in this action but did not require any hospitalization.

In June, 1951 he left Korea for Camp Chickamauga, Japan then in October, 1951 to Fort Campbell, Kentucky. In June, 1952 he was again assigned to Japan and in October, 1953 he was allowed to re-join his old outfit, the 187th Airborne RCT, at Camp Wood, Japan. In July, 1955, he and his family were transferred to Fort Bragg, North Carolina, then from 1956 through the first part of 1958, he was again stationed at Fort Campbell to help reactivate the original 101st Airborne Division.

In 1958 Wes was sent back to Korea, back to the states in 1959, then from 1963 till 1966 Wes was a part of the 3rd Armored Division Intelligence Unit at Frankfort, Germany. In 1967 he went to Cu Chi, Vietnam as a part of the 2nd Battalion, 27th Regiment, 25th Infantry Division. While in Cu Chi he was promoted to warrant officer junior grade, having served from the rank of recruit through master sergeant and now commissioned.

In 1968 Wes was promoted to chief warrant officer. It was during this period of time that he was the re-supply officer and had motored up to Tay Nikn on August 5, 1968 when his driver took deathly sick, they had to call for a medivac chopper to airlift him back to Cu Chi. Wes was now driving his own vehicle when it ran into a Viet Cong road ambush. The enemy blew out the right side of the windshield while wounding him with shrapnel and glass; somehow he managed to get through the ambush and back to his base.

It was February 23, 1968 during the Tet Offensive when he was recommended for and received the Bronze Star with Valor for having played a big part in turning the tide of the battle. Wes was observing the Viet Cong launch a rocket attack onto their position when he called for mortar fire on top of his location, stopping the attack. At the conclusion, they went out to see how many enemy were in the attack but all they found was streams of blood on the ground where the Viet Cong bodies and wounded had been pulled back into the jungle.

He came home from Vietnam but was sent back in 1971 to Da Nang until 1972. He was scheduled to go back to Nam in 1973 but decided to retire to his place at Lane.

When he got his family all settled in their new home, he went to work at the Mac Alford Prison for the Oklahoma Department of Corrections and retired from the state after 21 years.

Wes made 187 parachute jumps during his military tenure and has been awarded the following decorations:
    Master Jump Wings
    Ranger Emblem or patch
    Bronze Star with Valor
    Purple Heart
    Meritorious Unit Citation
    Army Commendation Medal
    Vietnamese Service ribbon with 1 star
    Presidential Unit Citation
    Combat Infantryman Badge
    Good Conduct medal with 5 loops
    Army Occupation with the Japan Bar
    United Nations service
    Korean campaign with 4 stars and 1 arrowhead
    National Defense Glider Badge
    Vietnamese Unit Citation with Palm leaf

When you stop and think that this soldier made 187 jumps from a C-130, C-119 and C-47, and he was always waiting to hear the jump master say, "We are about to get the green light, stand-up, hookup, check your equipment, shuffle and stand in the doorway." Then waiting to be tapped and told to go. I can visualize now him going out the door of the aircraft with the wind hitting his face waiting to feel the sudden jerk of the parachute harness on his thighs, groin and chest looking up to see that his chute had opened. Rakkasana, trooper. This is a patriot.

CHAPTER 9

Surrounded by Nazis, They Shot Their Way Out

For this portrait let us take a look at an area soldier, Lt. Herman Rhodes, from Savanna, Oklahoma, who served as an enlisted man with Co. F, 180th Regt. the Hugo, Oklahoma Unit and lastly as the Company Commander of Co. B, 180th Infantry Regiment, 45th Division, the Atoka Unit.

The 180th Regimental History records for you the bravery of Herman Rhodes and some of his fellow soldiers when they were surrounded by a Company of Nazis. The following is the recorded story:

"On the night of February 13th, 1944, Staff Sgt. Herman L. Rhodes, Savanna, Oklahoma, Private First Class Edward E. Pagen, Detroit, Michigan, Sgt. William C. Rush, Ashboro, North Carolina, and Tech. Sgt. Claude A. Carpenter, Hugo, Oklahoma, were members of a patrol of Co. F which was operating far out on the flat ground northwest of Padiglione, Italy.

"Despite the extreme caution which the patrol exercised while moving through the darkness, the Germans found it; the Nazis pressed in company strength with their fire concentrated on the little bank which did not number more than a dozen. For a few minutes the patrol held its ground and exchanged fire with the Germans. It was then realized, however, that the Germans were gradually surrounding the position and Carpenter ordered a withdrawal. The Germans, in a giant horseshoe formation, were moving in ready to close the two prongs of their trap. The situation looked hopeless.

"It was then that Staff Sgt. Rhodes demonstrated the qualities that he had often shown before, which eventually resulted in his appointment on the battlefield as a second lieutenant and which made him one of the outstanding company commanders in the history of our regiment. For 30 minutes he blasted away at the Germans with his sub-machine gun as his comrades slowly withdrew from the trap. Many times the Germans tried to close in but each time they fell back before his blast.

"As some of the men crawled through the escape gap, a German machine gun began to sputter, covering the gap with a band of fire. Toward the gun with his fingers digging into the cold and wet mud for traction, slithered Private First Class Pagen. He got very close to the machine gun, pulled the pin from a hand grenade, held it until it seemed that it must go off in his hand and then quickly threw it into the German position, killing two members of the gun crew and wounding a third.

"They knew that Sgt. Bill Rush was good before, but they never knew it before as well as they did on that night as he laboriously pulled himself through the mud to the side of a wounded comrade and pulled the fellow back to safety through the escape gap.

"Rhodes and Carpenter with their automatic weapons attacked separate jaws of the trap, as the last of their comrades passed through to relative safety. Two machine guns and many rifles were firing at these two brave Oklahomans, but they did not waver until the last of their men had gotten through. Fighting every bit of the way, they managed to join the remainder of the patrol as it made its way back to our lines.

"Rhodes, Pagen, Rush and Carpenter were each awarded Bronze Stars. Yes, this was 'mere patrol activity'."

A word for Herman L. Rhodes. When Herman was inducted

with the 45th in 1940, he had only completed two years of high school. Since his discharge, he has finished high school and a year in the University of Oklahoma. Despite a severe chest and abdominal wound which he sustained while leading Co. B in Germany, he still expressed a willingness to join the new 180th of the Oklahoma National Guard if he was needed. I believe you would agree that Rhodes was truly a patriot.

CHAPTER 10

Patton Awarded Him the Silver Star

This portrait is of First Sgt. James Tilden "Jabo" McLeroy of Atoka, Oklahoma. He was a member of C. B, 180th Infantry Regiment, 45th Division, having joined the Oklahoma National Guard while he was still in high school.

James was always a leader, having lettered at Atoka High for four years in football, baseball, basketball and track while maintaining a straight "A" average in his studies. His school records indicate that he completed all 12 years of schooling without missing a day.

James enlisted as a buck private and rose through the ranks to become the company first sergeant. He was mobilized with the Atoka Unit into federal service in September, 1940. At this time the 1st Battalion commander was Maj. Wylie Turner, Co. B's commander was Capt. Robert "Doc" Dean, executive officer was 1st Lt. Charles Dunn, and the platoon leaders were 2nd Lt. Robert "Bob" Cates and 2nd Lt. Paul Hayes all of Atoka.

After some three years of training in the states, the 45th received orders to board transports, and the ship's anchor was dropped June 22, 1943 at Oran, Algeria. Around July 1, 1943 the 1st Battalion re-embarked aboard the U.S.S. Calvert (APA-32), where they were informed they were going to the island of Sicily for an amphibious landing called "Operation Husky."

By the time of the landing in Sicily, the officers had been changed with the battalion commander now Lt. Col. William "King Kong" Schaeffer, the B Co. commander was Capt. Robert

Fleet, executive officer was 1st Lt. Bill Whitman and one of the platoon leaders was 2nd Lt. Robert Brown. This was just a few of the many officers who would become a part of James' military experience.

The morning of July 10, 1943 began with de-embarkation at 2:15 a.m. for what would later be called the "bloody laboratory." Numerous things went wrong for this landing. The normally calm Mediterranean Sea became rough to the point of capsizing some landing craft. Some of the men got sea sick bobbing around on the rough waves, while flaming shells and tracers filled the sky. To make matters worse, the naval landing party did not know their landing assignments and the 180th Regiment was put in the wrong area. Instead of a 3,000-yard beach for their assigned position, they were strewn along a 12-mile sector of the landing zone.

James' landing craft was unloaded in another company's area so he and his men joined up with another outfit for the initial fighting. By the way, it took Lt. Col. Rowe Cook, the beach master from Atoka, some 48 hours to get the Regiment assembled back like it should have been.

It was during the first day of the invasion, July 10, 1943, near Biscari, Sicily that "James" was awarded the Silver Star Medal for gallantry in action. The citation reads, "When elements of his company were trapped by heavy enemy machine gun and sniper fire; in order to effect the withdrawal of his men to more secure positions, First Sgt. McLeroy, armed with a Thompson submachine gun, advanced towards the enemy, keeping up such a heavy fire on the enemy positions that he caused their fire to cease temporarily. Not until all his men were safe did he crawl back and rejoin his men. The courage and complete disregard for personal safety displayed by First Sgt. McLeroy reflects the highest traditions of the armed forces."

When General George Patton, Seventh Army Commander, pinned the Silver Star on James' chest, he stated, "I would like to have 10 divisions of men of your caliber." Not only for this brave action, but for always being out front leading his men in some furious battles, they nick-named him "Gung-Ho."

After the Battle for Biscari Airfield ended on July 14, 1943, James would report to the B Co. Executive Officer, Lt. Bill Whitman, that of the 200 men and officers of Co. B, that went down the cargo nets of the U.S.S. Calvert for the landing, only 68 men had made it through the battle.

James would learn that William D. Franklin of Atoka, though mortally wounded, seized several hand grenades, pulled the pins and threw himself underneath a large German tank which was coming down on B Co. Also Sgt. John "Cue Ball" Bennett, of Atoka, and his squad of 12 men would be found dead. (They included Michael Ouriel, Salvatore Miccoli and George Morgan, all of Atoka.)

He also learned that some of the following men with the 45th had made it through the first battle. They were Scott Wells, Billy J. Harris, Robert "Doc" Dean, Robert G. Cates, Charles G. Weaver, Gus Henry "Speed Ball" Miller, Olen Curry, Bill Goforth, Bill York, Anderson Jim, Wilbern Beard, Curtis "Cactus Jack" Garner, Ellis Jackson, James Winslett, Bob Chick, Herman Barton, Hicky McCasland, Leonard Garside, Linnon Dobbs, Robert Merritt, Clifton Mills, John Musler, Calvin Robinson, Carl Lovinggood, and Roy Mead. These are all that I could think of at this time, however, there were others. Bud Greathouse and Paul York of the 3rd Division also survived. Some of those listed would later be killed in action in Italy.

After the Battle of Biscari Airport, Gen. Patton would write the following in his book, War As I Knew It: "On the field south of Biscari Airport, where we had quite a fight, I could smell the dead enemy while driving for at least six miles along the road."

Patton also announced the capture of Sicily by August 17, 1943, and that his Seventh Army in 21 days had killed or captured 87,000 enemy soldiers, destroyed 561 cannons, 172 tanks, 928 trucks and 190 airplanes. His green Army Troops had their first baptism of fire and had defeated Hitler's best army, the Hermann Goring Unit know as "Hot Mustard."

On the morning of September 14, 1943, the 45th Division would storm the beaches of Salerno, Italy. Within a week B Company fought its way up to Oliveto, Italy, which was to be labeled as "The Battle of Blunders." It was here that James and Sgt. Wilbern Beard of Atoka crawled behind some large rocks and boulders to attempt to locate German guns that had been shelling the company. Artillery fire became very heavy and these two Oklahoma men were both killed by the same round that hit their observation position.

The Second Session of the Oklahoma Legislature, Resolution No. 91, February, 1989 voted to honor James by naming the south-bound lane bridge of Highway 69 across Muddy Boggy River, just north of Atoka, the First Sgt. James Tilden McLeroy Bridge. The next time you drive into Atoka from the north, slow down, take notice of the sign with the Thunderbird on it and say to yourself, "Thanks, James, for giving your life so that I can be free." Another patriot who made the ultimate sacrifice.

CHAPTER 11

This Football Star Had a Premonition Before Leaving for Vietnam

Of all the stories I've written through the years, this one has been the most difficult for me to write. This patriot is SP/4 Benny Joe Lewis, the son of Bob and Neoma Lewis of Atoka. I have had the pleasure of knowing this outstanding family all of my life.

My feeble attempt will be to document Benny's story by using factual information as to his life until the day of May 18, 1968. We can prove where he was, why he was there, his combat assignment, his living conditions and we think we know what happened that day in May. There was supposedly a soldier that was there when they found Benny, but I understand that he moved to either Idaho or Wyoming, leaving no forwarding address.

This story is a composite of meetings with several Vietnam veterans who were combat infantrymen serving in the same area as Benny, so I owe each of them a debt of gratitude for helping fill in some of the blank spaces during Benny's combat service.

Benny Joe was an extremely well liked young man who seemed to be able to be the very best at whatever he set out to endure. He was a very avid coon hunter and would seldom miss an opportunity to help turn the dogs loose to run for a good night of "legging it out" (and listening to the dogs tree).

He was an outstanding athlete at Atoka High School but was known best as number 45, the bruising fullback and linebacker, for the Wampus Cat football team. The other day, Ron McGue and I were at the diner talking about Benny when he mentioned that when they played football together, Ron was a defensive nose guard and Benny played middle linebacker right behind him. He told how Benny would get behind him, put his hands on his rear and push him in the hole so one of them could get the tackle. I wish you could have seen the admiring expression on Ron's face while he talked about his friend.

By graduating time in May of 1966, Benny had been given a full scholarship to play football for the Eastern Oklahoma A&M College Mountaineers. During the fall of 1966 he wore number 32 running fullback for Eastern. By the end of the semester, he was just in the right age group to be drafted for military service in Vietnam. Benny thought they would draft him in a month or so but they called him to enter the Army on June 14, 1967. Two other local boys, Flint Sutton and Larry Farris of Coalgate, were drafted at the same time Benny was called.

Benny was sent to Ft. Bliss, Texas, for basic training and became a member of Co. A, 2nd Bn., 2nd Infantry B.D.E. He was given some advanced training then was allowed to come home on leave. While at home, he spent a lot of time with a very close friend, who just happened to be the preacher at the Southside Baptist Church, Monroe McNally. Benny had something heavy on his heart and by talking with "Ole Mac," he thought it might ease his thoughts and mind a little. You see, Benny had a premonition that he would never return alive from Vietnam; he had also told others this same thing, including Ron. They all tried to assure him that he would be okay, but he was serious in his belief that he would die on the field of battle.

Once he returned from his leave, he was airlifted to Ohau, Hawaii, for advanced jungle warfare training. He became a member of the 2nd Squad, 1st Plt., Co. D, 4th Bn., 21st Infantry of the 11th Brigade. He enjoyed his stay in Hawaii and he was stationed there until the middle of April, 1968. Part of the 11th Infantry Brigade had already left Schoefield Barracks, Hawaii and had joined the Americal Division headquartered at Chu Lai, Vietnam. Benny's unit would be going in a few weeks.

The year of 1968 opened with an unwarlike quietness because of the New Year truce, even though some army units were still finding rice caches and some small amounts of arms and ammo. All across the rest of Vietnam, civilians and military were supposedly planning family reunions and celebrations for the three-day holiday starting the last of the month. Firecrackers were exploding with happy anticipation of the Buddhist New Year. Family gatherings were held everywhere without suspicion, and this was exactly what the Viet Cong (VC) and NRV Army needed as they smuggled in arms, rice and some 70,000 men who were moved in by trucks and sampans.

Food and weapons were carried to cemeteries inside coffins in mock funerals. They even hid grenades and ammo in flower pots and by January 30, they used their newly made arsenals to start the TET Offensive. Due to the sudden increase in activity throughout South Vietnam, there was a need for increasing replacements to various units. The call for more men was heard at Ohau, Hawaii and was answered with Benny's unit, 2nd Sg., 1st Plt., D Co., 4th Bn., 21st Infantry, 11 Brigade ordered to be a part of the Americal Division at Chu Lai.

Benny's unit was airlifted by transport after the 20th of April, 1968 and landed at Da Nang; then they went by helicopter to the Americal Division base camp. After a short rest period they once again boarded helicopters and flew to an outpost in Quang Ngai Province to a hamlet called Duc Pho. Their duty post was on the top of a hill that had the jungle cleared off so they could have a clear view of the jungle behind them and were able to observe the bend of the S. An Lao River just off the front of their location.

Their job was called "Interdiction Observation," which meant they were to search the waters of the river for sampans carrying ammo, rice and men downstream to enemy units. At one time units had observed a large sampan flotilla in the area, and their helicopter gun ships sank 31 vessels in one week. Later, they would sink 98 more.

This outpost was a valuable tool in trying to make a dent in the enemy supply line, so the VC had to try to eliminate the observation point. Sometime during the early morning hours of May 18, the VC cut loose on the outpost with rocket fire and mortars. We think Benny was on guard in a trench area overlooking the backside into the jungle, and the VC managed to get into the trench and took Benny prisoner. The unit held the rest of the hill, but Benny was dragged into the jungle. When help arrived from Chu Lai base, Benny was not found, and he was reported "missing in action." His family was notified May 20 that he was missing, then three days later they received notification that he had been killed in action. We believe that he was taken prisoner, taken in the jungle just off of the outpost perimeter and executed by being shot in the head.

Within three weeks from the time Benny arrived in Vietnam, his corpse started the long trip back home.

When Benny's body was first discovered, it was placed in a black body bag, and flown by helicopter to graves registration for preparation of sending his body home for burial. His body was escorted back to Atoka by Larry Capps of Tushka. Benny's service was conducted by the very man, Monroe McNally, who only a few months earlier had prayed with Benny and heard his premonition that he would not return alive. It was one of the largest attended services ever held in this area, giving a loving tribute to Benny and the Lewis Family.

They carried his flag-draped casket to Green Meadows Cemetery for burial. The flag was ceremonial-folded, and the man in charge handed the tri-angled banner to the Lewis family and told them that this was from a grateful nation. Having known Uncle Bob all of my life, I could readily see the hurt, but inside I knew that he was saying "Son, I'm so proud of you."

Benny was not a coward; he was not a draft dodger; he was not a peace marcher; he was not a hippie; he was not immoral nor a shack rat; he was not a draft card burner, he did not shirk his duty and run away to Canada, or go to England on protest or have part in burning the America flag in Russia for the TV cameras for all of the world to see. No, he was a proud young American called upon by his country for duty, and he never wavered but answered his nation's call. This man gave his all; the ultimate sacrifice that he could give, his life. This is a patriot. His family was cut to the quick yet inwardly proud.

I went back to Green Meadows this week, walked past my father's grave where he had been laid to rest some two months earlier, and four graves down from my father is Benny. I stood at the foot of his grave, with the toes of my shoes touching the military marker that reads:

SP/4 BENNY JOE LEWIS
January 9, 1947
May 18, 1968
VIET NAM (PH)
CO. D, 21ST INF. AMERICAL
DIVISION

I stood there for a moment, took one step backward, gave a hand salute then wiped the tears from my eyes. All at once there were no more tears and a passage from the New Testament Bible came to mind; the scripture is John 15, verse 13, where Christ says "Greater love hath no man than this, that a man lay down his life for his friends."

Taps has been played for a patriot.

CHAPTER 12

Even Facing Death, This Soldier Remained Unselfish

This portrait has an additional author helping to document the story. I wanted to write a story on another young soldier who lost his life in Vietnam, so I asked his older brother to assist. This brother, Eugene Swindell, was a classmate of mine; we played football together, served three years in the 45th Division together, and he is also my brother in Christ. Eugene and I spent some time together, and this is the story we submit to you.

On December 1, 1941, one week before the infamous bombing of Pearl Harbor, Bobby Dale Swindell, the third child of Ovel and Zetta Swindell, was born. His first 11 years were spent in Atoka, then he moved with his parents to Dallas then on to south Texas. The next several years were spent attending school and helping his dad on the farm.

In late March of 1964, Bob was drafted into the U.S. Army with an expected 24-month tour of duty. Fort Polk, Louisiana was the location for his basic military training. Almost immediately, Bob's leadership qualities and his military knowledge gained during six months in the Texas National Guard, made him a standout in the group of new recruits. Due to a shortage of non-commissioned officers, Bob was given the temporary rank of sergeant which he held all through basic training. After eight weeks of this grueling physical and mental toughness conditioning, he was sent to his new duty station in Alaska.

During the next 21 or 22 months in Alaska, Bob earned the

permanent rank of sergeant E5 and his life was filled with a lot of fun, excitement and sense of duty. His duties as a member of an infantry unit were to patrol the Russian and Alaskan border and to perform Arctic rescues, which were many. The fun came as he was the soloist and guitar player in a combo group that performed for homesick GI's.

His unit was slated to ship out for South Vietnam in March, 1966. This was the time of the large build-up of troops in that country. As a draftee, Bob was required to spend only 24 months in service but as he told his mother, by a letter, he felt obligated to go with the men he helped train. He was allowed to extend his enlistment for six more months.

Normally, men in service are given home leaves before shipping out, but this time they could not let everyone go so they had a drawing for this coveted pass. Bob was one of a few lucky ones to draw one of the winning numbers. One of the men in the unit was very disappointed that he had not gotten the chance to go home to see his new son for the first time. Bob unselfishly gave up his pass to this friend. After two or three weeks in Hawaii and arriving in South Vietnam, Bob wrote his mother saying he was apprehensive about the next six months but was glad to be in a warm climate and have a chance to thaw out after being in Alaska so long. He was made a part of Co. B, 4th Bn., 23 INF, 2dBde, 25 Infantry Division being assigned to the southern area of South Vietnam.

The unit wasted no time in sending out patrols to make contact with the enemy. On May 17, 1966, his 19th day in Vietnam, Bob was on a mission in the vicinity of Cu Chi when he was hit by fragments of a VC anti-personnel mine. Sniper fire kept his unit pinned down, and they were unable to render immediate medical help for Bob. He died that day in the service of his country. A Bronze Star Medal was awarded to him posthumously for bravery. The following is the order issuing the medal:

"The President of the United States of America has awarded the Bronze Star Medal to Sergeant E-5 Bobby D. Swindell, US 25975255, United States Army for Outstanding Meritorious Service during the period 28 April, 1966 to 17 May, 1966 in connection with ground operations against a hostile force in the Republic of Vietnam. Through his untiring efforts and professional ability, he consistently obtained outstanding results. He was quick to grasp the implications of new problems with which he was faced as a result of the ever-changing situations inherent in a counterinsurgency operation. The energetic application of his extensive knowledge has materially contributed to the overall effort of the United States in Vietnam. He was a motivating example to all with whom he came in contact. His devotion to duty, loyalty, and meticulous attention to detail are in keeping with the finest traditions of the United States Army, and reflect great credit upon himself, his unit, the 25th Infantry Division, and the military service. Dated 13 September, 1966."

Harry Norris, Bob's good friend, was with him on that fateful day and wrote a letter to the family. A portion of that letter follows:

"Our brother was on a 10-day operation. Early on the third day our company was leading the Battalion and our platoon led the company. The day that I'm talking about was bad from that morning until that afternoon. Anyway, we came under sniper fire, my squad moved against the sniper and received three casualties. But we killed the sniper.

"As we moved out, the third squad, which Bob was in, led out. As we moved, we came to an area that was very thick with bamboo. The only way through it was cut our way through or go around. Going around meant going down a trail so they sent us down that way.

"The first and second squads and a squad from another platoon moved down the trail into an opening and as the third squad moved down the trail, they started into the opening. Bob was the third man through in his squad.

"Just as they came into the opening Charlie (Viet Cong) set off an electric detonated mine. The man in front of Bob and Bob himself never knew what hit them.

"Charlie kept us trapped there for two hours. Our platoon took 22 casualties that day.

"To me Bob was very brave because he did live for awhile afterwards, but he didn't yell for a medic because I feel he knew that if a group were to form around him and the others, another mine would go off. But the medics got to him as quickly as they could, but there was nothing they could do. He received head and leg wounds. I'll tell you, Gene, I cried that day. Bob was the closest to being a brother to me as any person I know. We were together just about every waking moment in Hawaii. I'll never forget him."

The Swindell family was notified on May 20, 1966 that their son had been killed in action. His body was shipped home for burial, and his service was held at the Atoka First Baptist Church on May 24, 1966, and the burial was at Green Meadows Cemetery.

Here lies a truly great patriot and one of the first local boys to die in combat in Vietnam.

CHAPTER 13

This Uncle Sam Landed at Normandy

This portrait is of First Lt. Samuel F. Cartwright of Lane, Oklahoma. Sam finished high school in Atoka and then attended East Central College in Ada. He earned a teaching certificate and was employed at Coal Creek when he became a member of Co. B, 180th Infantry Regiment, 45th Division, Oklahoma National Guard.

He was teaching school when his unit was called up on September 16, 1940. The 45th first went to Louisiana, then to Fort Sill, Oklahoma, and on to Camp Barkley at Abilene, Texas. After months of training, he was allowed to come home on leave.

On the return trip to Abilene, just south of the Tushka railroad overpass, Sam was driving and his best friend, Tom Rounsaville, was riding with him when he tried to straighten out a curve and wrecked his car in a swampy area. Sam's neck was broken, and Tom saved his life by holding his head out of the water until help came. Needless to say, Sam was in a cast for a few weeks.

After Sam had recovered from his injury, the call went out for men in the 45th that would like to apply for Officer Candidate School (OCS). Sam along with others, including Tom Rounsaville, Jesse B. "Slick" Cartwright, Marion "Chunk" Haggard, Leo Williams, Willie Bowman and Standford Downs were accepted to Infantry OCS, while Vincent Howard and Bill Soules went to the Army Air Corps OCS. They would all be commissioned as second lieutenants, but none would return to the

45th Division for service. (There may have been others that went to OCS, but I can't remember any more.)

Sam received extensive training in desert warfare in California. Once he received a leave from Ft. Ord, he returned to Abilene, Texas to marry Daisy Brown. He, Tom Rounsaville and Scott Wells had met her during their stay at Camp Barkley. His new wife would accompany Sam back to his post in California.

In the first part of 1944, Sam received orders to report to a port of embarkation in New York where he boarded a troop transport bound for England. Upon arriving at his destination, he was assigned as a platoon leader of a mortar unit of the Heavy Weapons Company, 359th Infantry Regt., 90th Infantry Division, to train with the men he would lead into combat. Their unit, like all others in England at that time, would train, train and then train some more.

Finally, on the morning of June 6, 1944 they were loaded on to Naval APAS with landing crafts dangling off of the side of the ship. They were to be a part of the Allied "Operation Overlord," the invasion of Normandy. Sam's unit went in on D-Day plus one, the 7th of June. He would long remember the men he saw: the dead still on Utah Beach, all of the devastation that comes with battles, the intensive fire that the Germans were still laying down towards the beach, the wounded being attended to and all the while remembering their mission to get off of the beach and help the other units to push the enemy inland. Their mission was accomplished.

On June 15, Sam was moving his platoon out of a very dense hedge row when he happened to round the corner of one of the rows, and all at once he and a German soldier spotted each other. The German had a "potato masher" grenade in his hand and threw it at Sam about the same time that Sam raised his carbine and killed the German. The grenade hit in a tree branch in front of Sam, knocking him to the ground and the concussion from the blast caused blood to come out of various openings of his body. The medics treated him and sent him to division rear for medical treatment; he was released from the field hospital and was allowed to rejoin his company in about a week. Incidentally, this blast would later cause him to lose one lung and badly damage the other.

The 90th Division would be a part of the breakout of Normandy hedgerows, having suffered tremendous casualties. Their division's orders were to fight towards the town of Saint Lo. They reached their objective in August, 1944, fighting their way through heavy German resistance and intensive artillery fire.

On August 17, 1944, Sam's company commander needed his platoon to clear a sector of snipers, to locate a forward artillery observer and put him out of business. They had almost completed their mission when the Germans made a last ditch effort to hold that part of the city by firing a very heavy barrage of 88 "Screaming Meammies" artillery. (This engagement was known as the Falife Gap.) One of the rounds hits close to Sam, resulting in a shrapnel wound in his leg and once again concussion of his lungs. The medics evacuated him to a hospital in England, then he was sent to Walter Reed Hospital in the states and finally to a hospital for lung disorders in McKinney, Texas.

Sam was discharged in 1946 and returned to Atoka with his wife and son. He would later become the safety officer at McAlester Naval Ammo Depot and in 1970 became the safety officer for the entire 4th Army Area with headquarters at San Antonio, Texas. During all of these years after his discharge, he would be in and out of military hospitals with breathing problems. In the spring of 1972, the lung disorder finally caught up with him, and he died at the Fort Sam Houston Military Hospital.

He was brought back to Atoka and buried at Green Meadows Cemetery. Sam was 53 years old when taps was sounded over his body.

Lt. Samuel Fulton Cartwright was 13 years older than me; he was always my idol, my hero and truly a patriot. Sam was my favorite uncle and my best friend. Rest in peace, Sambo, your family is very proud of you.

CHAPTER 14

This Decorated Trucker Kept the Supply Line Moving

This portrait is about a highly decorated truck driver veteran from Lane by the name of Pfc. Walter Maxoe Zinn, Jr, commonly referred to as "Mac."

He served some 44 months in the U.S. Army during World War II with 32 months overseas. Mac was with Quartermaster Trucking Companies and served in the 12th Air Force during the African Campaign. He was then involved with the 34th Infantry Division as a part of the invasion of Gela, Sicily, Salerno, Italy, then at Red Beach, D-Day, France. At times he was assigned to the 5th Army and the 7th Army.

During his tenure in combat he was wounded seven times and was decorated for bravery. He was part of an organization that was responsible for getting ammo, food, water, gas and medical supplies from the various seaports to the front lines. At times he hauled POW's and American dead back from the front. He and his fellow truckers were constantly being swooped down on and strafed by German fighters. They endured mines placed in the roadway to blow up their vehicles or anything else the Germans could do to stop the allied supply line; they rode with sandbags in the floor boards of their trucks.

At one time, he was part of the famous "Red Ball Express" that in the summer and fall of 1944 was responsible for keeping the rapidly advancing American Army supplied as it steamed across France towards the German border. In the first few weeks after the Normandy D-Day invasion, the Allies made little progress against the disciplined and stubborn German Army and the GHQ planners were afraid that unless they could breakout, there would be a return to the trench warfare of WW I.

But in late July, 1944 the German front would crack and the race was on to take France. There were some 28 allied divisions moving across France towards Belgium and Germany. Each of these divisions ordinarily required 700-750 tons of supplies a day, a daily total of about 20,000 tons. These supplies were coming from England into the ravaged seaports on the French coast that had been captured by the invasion. The French Railway system had been destroyed by air attacks and artillery fire, so the only way to get the needed goods to the front was by trucks.

At first, lengthy convoys were formed driving day and night, running under blackout conditions, looking like a massive group of cats with their eyes snaking down the roads at some 25 miles per hour. There were some 6,000 trucks used in this operation and before long the driver learned to strip their trucks of governors so they could get up more speed and power to work in some of the areas they were required to drive.

Once these convoys started, the civilian population was quick to learn how to slow down or stop the convoy of trucks on small or winding streets and at times kill the drivers and steal their load of supplies to be sold on the black market. It became necessary to give a general order that the trucks were to stop for nothing, in fact to run over anything that got in their way, including civilians. These supplies had to reach the front, no excuses. Some of these drivers would have those scenes to haunt them for the rest of their lives.

There were times when Mac and other drivers drove up along side stranded Sherman tanks that had run out of gas and would pass jerrycans (5 gallons gas cans) of gas to the crew while the enemy was within shouting distance. Some of these drivers remember hauling back the bodies of soldiers killed in action, a very dreadful task and the pervasive odor of death that took days to dissipate. They would have to hose down their trucks but regardless of how thorough they washed, the blood and grime would remain in the cracks of the floors of the truck beds.

Later organized were other trucking companies with names of the White Ball Express, the Little Red Ball Express, the Green Diamond Express, the ABC Express Route and the XYZ Route. Mac would also drive for some of these outfits.

Mac was discharged on August 29, 1945, having accumulated 185 points towards his separation from service. He would return to his family and friends at Lane. Mac had seen and went through enough in 32 months of combat to last several men a lifetime, however; he was always proud of the part that he had in helping to defeat the Axis in Europe and received 11 Battle Stars.

Mac was buried in New Zion Cemetery on Boggy Depot Road, having passed from this life June 22, 1974 at the age of 66 years. Here is another patriot who was willing to lay down his life for his country. Taps has been played.

CHAPTER 15

He Went from the Lane Laundromat to Guarding a Famous Prisoner

This portrait is a soldier from Lane, Oklahoma, Pvt. Gordie Gene Linscott. He was born in Texas and his family moved to the Butler community, just east of Lane, before he became of school age. They moved to Lane for his second year in school and have continued to live in our area for over 50 years.

Gordie and I grew up together and were extremely close friends. All of us young bucks admired him for his mechanical ability and the fact that he got the first bicycle in our area didn't hurt him any either, as he was good enough to let us take a spin on his two-wheeler.

His mother and father put in a help-yourself laundry across the road from where Coben's store is now located, and the building lot is now part of the Lane Baptist parking lot. The laundry washing machines had gasoline motors, requiring a lot of mechanical attention. Gordie got to know those motors inside and out.

I remember what a genius we all thought he was when he took one of the motors and installed it on his bike making himself the proud owner of Lane's first putt-putt. All of us boys became very close. In fact, we spent numerous nights together in his mother's, "Aunt Fannie" to us, cellar while dining on her canned peaches that she kept under the bed. There are a lot of great memories of those get-togethers.

While attending Lane school, he became a part of "Miss

Nannie Lou's Country Boys Quartet." Gordie sang a mean first tenor. We all wore overalls to school, so she went out and bought each of us a white shirt so we could all be dressed alike. Now this was during World War II when gas and tires were rationed but somehow Mrs. Dodson found a way to take us to sing on the radio at Durant, Oklahoma, the station at Paris, Texas, and numerous BPW and teachers' meetings. She would have Gordie always start the program with his tenor introduction of a classical song, "Night From Lebistrom," then we would do at least three pop songs of the period like "Praise the Lord and Pass the Ammunition," "Coming in on a Wing and a Prayer" or "Don't Fence Me In." We always had a couple more for an encore. Seriously, she had made us a pretty good group of singers.

    The Korean War broke out, and Gordie was drafted into the army in 1953. After basic training, he drew a duty station in Alaska. For some unknown reason, all at once he was assigned to duty in West Berlin, Germany, inside of Communist Germany. He would become one of a very few soldiers to become a member of the Elite Constabulary Force Of Berlin.

    The duty was at Spandau Prison, located in the Allied sector of the Communist-held city, for those sentenced in 1946 for war crimes. This prison had only seven captives and the most famous was Rudolf Hess who was known as Prisoner No. 7; he was captured by the British in 1941 as a result of an air crash. Hess was supposedly Hitler's number-one deputy.

    At the end of the war, in 1946, Hess was tried and convicted at the famous Nuremberg War Crimes Trials and over the objection of the Russians, he was sentenced to life in prison.

    The guard arrangements were the Americans would be in charge of the prison every four months, the Russians, the English and the French had the same assignments. Gordie spent part of the time right outside of Hess's cell; occasionally he worked inside the cell run and also drew the duty of entry guard at the Spandau gate. Hess would outlive all of the rest of the prisoners and if memory serves me correctly, just a few short years ago he died at the age of 91. Spandau prison has since been torn down.

Something else out of the ordinary happened to Gordie while at his duty station at Spandau. One weekend, while off duty, he managed to stumble into the Communist Sector of East Berlin and was taken prisoner by the Communist Police. They took Gordie to an upper room and interrogated him and they finally realized that he had no knowledge of what they wanted to know. Before they turned him loose in the Allied Sector, they gave him a very unusual punishment by blindfolding his eyes and placing a coal bucket over his head. For several hours, they would hit the side of the bucket with some sort of metal object right where his left ear was located. The constant banging of the metal damaged his hearing so that if you watched him closely, he would turn his head to the left so that he could use his right ear to understand.

After his honorable discharge from service, he would come back to Lane, get married and go into the trucking business. In April, 1985 he developed a nose bleed. Gordie was taken to the doctor in Atoka where they packed his nose to stop the bleeding and returned home. The nose began to once again bleed and before they could stop the hemorrhaging, he bled to death. He passed away on April 18, 1985 at the age of 52. He is buried at New Zion Cemetery on Boggy Depot Road along side other members of his family.

I have a lot of fond memories of "Ol' Gordie" and thought that part of what I have written was not previously known by members of his family. He was quite a guy and definitely a patriot. Taps for a great friend.

CHAPTER 16

This Patriot Rose to the Rank of Colonel

This portrait is of a Standing Rock-Wards Chapel, Oklahoma soldier, Col. Lon Robert Fink, retired, U.S. Army and Oklahoma National Guard.

Lon graduated from Atoka High School and was inducted into the armed service of his country on June 25, 1943. He reported to Camp Walters, Texas, for basic training and in a few months found himself landing at the French seaport town of Cherbrough as part of a replacement company that was assigned to 121st Infantry Regimental Combat, 8th Infantry Division; his first combat was at Brest, France in August, 1944. Later his unit would join the 84th Infantry Division for the Battle of Saint Lo and the push toward Germany.

After the Battle of Saint Lo, his unit was part of a drive towards Luxembourg and Belgium to split the German army fighting into the Ruhr Valley. The infantrymen were riding on the top of tanks into Luxembourgh when the tank Lon was riding took a hit on the gun turret. The shrapnel fragments struck Lon from his left knee all the way up to behind his left ear; in fact, he is still carrying some of those fragments in his body today. He was wounded in mid-April, 1945 in the area of the Ruhr pocket at a town of Nepham.

Lon would later rejoin his unit for more intense fighting for lengthy periods. He went so long with his feet being wet that he developed trench foot in November, 1944. His feet were so bad that at one time they talked about amputation.

Also, they were lucky if they got a shower and change of clothes every three weeks.

Lon's unit would walk 86 miles from Duhan to Cologne, Germany. Everything was hurry, hurry to beat the Russians to an area outside of Berlin. They reached a Nazi concentration camp for political prisoners and Polish civilians near the town of Schreen.

The revelation of the findings inside of this concentration camp were not anything that Lon was prepared to deal with during all of his ten months of combat. He had been in many vicious fire fights, saw men wounded, watched some of his own men killed in battle, been hungry, spent lengthy time without sleep or rest, wet for days on end, cold, needing to just shave and shower, but this was nothing in comparison to what he was about to witness.

When his unit entered the prison camp, they saw a row of dead bodies stacked like cord-wood some 200 yards in length. There were dead all over the compound, the stench of death was horrible.

The eyes of those who were still alive were sunken back in their heads. They begged for food, but they had to wait for the medics to help them. Some of the prisoners died just as the Americans were entering the camp. These prisoners had been starved, beaten and worked to death. The scene was so bad that the division commander, Gen. Green, ordered that every soldier and German citizen in the area would pass through the camp to see the atrocities committed by the Nazis. This was May 3, 1945.

Lon came home in mid-July, 1945 for leave and was on his way to the Pacific theater when the war ended. He was discharged at the rank of sergeant.

In 1946 he was offered and received a direct commission as a second lieutenant in Co. H, 180th Infantry, 45th Division. He served with that unit until 1949, when Co. H became a part of the 45th Military Police Company that had been transferred to Atoka.

Lon would travel to Camp Polk, Louisiana with the rest of us for federal mobilization, leaving Atoka on September 1, 1950. There was an incident at the end of that month that some of us will never forget. Lon was to take 11 men (including me) and four Jeeps to accompany a division finance vehicle some 75 miles to Alexander Air Force Base. When we arrived, we were told to guard while they unloaded an aircraft. We were then to escort the finance vehicle with two Jeeps in front and two behind back to Camp Polk. It was after our arrival that we learned we had brought back and guarded over a two million dollar division cash payroll and not a one of us had a single round of ammunition. Kind of scary, isn't it?

The next month you can be sure that we were locked and loaded as Lon and Bud Greathouse had secured ammo for all of us. This detail of the same men went on for three months. (All of us were from Atoka).

In March, 1951 the entire division would move by train to the Port of Embarkation at Camp Leroy Johnson in New Orleans. We left the mouth of the Mississippi River for a trip through the Panama Canal, finally arriving at the Port of Otaru, Japan where part of our unit went to Camp Crawford in Sapparo, Japan. The balance of us, under the command of Lt. Lon Fink, went to a tent city erected at Chitose, an airfield that had been used to train Japanese Kamikazi pilots.

In November, 1951, Lon and selected division staff officers were secretly flown into Korea to make plans for the 45th to replace the First Cavalry Division. We made an amphibious landing at Inchon, South Korea on December 5, 1951 and then moved up to the Jamestown Line in the Yonchon-Chorwon section in North Korea.

The 45th was ordered to defend the existing front and limited to attacks necessary to strengthen the MLR and establish outposts. There were continued patrols, ambushes, raids and an occasional fight for varied outpost positions. This remained the pattern of combat action for the division for the first part of 1952, and one of our worst battles was against the intensively cold North Korean winters.

Lon rotated home in the very late spring of 1952 to become a part of the new 45th, which was not on active duty. Before long, he was made company commander of the MP Company and later would become the division provost marshal.

Gen. Hal Muldrow, who served with the 45th in WW II and Korea, became the division commander. He was looking for the right officer to become the director of the Division Officer Candidate School and the head of Military Support of Civilian Authority. Knowing Lon's record and his ability of handling men, his professionalism as a soldier and the respect he had from his fellow Thunderbirds, he was asked to become the head of this dual project. He said that he would accept the assignment for one year but stayed 21 years until he retired and moved back to Atoka.

While heading the Military Support Unit, on two separate occasions he was responsible for the protection, care and safety of President John F. Kennedy and his staff. Lon has a personal letter from the President thanking him for protection while in Oklahoma. Also, he was in charge of security around the capital for the inauguration of Governors Geary, Edmondson, Bellman, Bartlett and Hall and on each occasion escorted the first lady to the inaugural stand.

Lon retired in 1978 having completed 34 years of military service. In looking back over that period of time, there were over 350 men from the Atoka area who have served with and under Lon's command. Having served with him four years of that time and knowing the men that he commanded, I know of no one who would not speak very highly of his leadership, his loyalty to his men and his ability to make the best of any situation that arose. He has proven himself time and time again to be a very brave man in the face of the enemy.

In closing, all of us men could hardly wait until he would report the platoon or company so that our eyes would all be on him to see him at attention and deliver the sharp salute that he was known for by everyone. No one could imitate his reporting delivery.

Col. Lon Fink, for all of us who served with you, we want you to know that we are very proud of you and wish for you continued good health and longevity. Here is a real patriot.

CHAPTER 17

He Survived the Bataan Death March and Three Years as a POW

This portrait is a young man raised in a sawmill camp in Lane, Oklahoma, by the name of Capt. Clyde A. Coats, U.S. Army. He was born July 16, 1920 at Lane and entered the Army on March 14, 1941 in Oklahoma City. After completing basic training in April, he was transported to Manila, Philippines, arriving on May 8 and becoming a member of Co. A, 31st Infantry Regiment, Philippine Division.

Clyde's combat experience began on December 29, 1941 in the Battle for the City of Manila, when Japanese invasion forces entered the Lingayen Gulf of Luzon and began pushing Allied troops down the Bataan Peninsula. Losses were heavy on both sides, and Bataan became a battle of savage hand-to-hand fighting in the underbrush.

It was in this type of fighting that Coats was wounded in the left shoulder on Valentine's Day, 1942. He was sent to a field hospital, but before long any wounded man who could shoulder a weapon went back into the thick of battle.

The Japanese kept fresh reinforcements coming in, and the weary Bataan defenders were under constant shelling both day and night.

Our forces were doing their best to hold the peninsula. They were promised that reinforcements, ammo, food and medicine were on the way; however, the promise never came to fruition.

For several weeks each man was trying to subsist on only 15 ounces of food a day. Exhausted, outnumbered by both men and material, they were finally pushed back.

Finally, on April 9, 1942 Gen. King was compelled to surrender. Bataan had fallen, but the noble defenders had written an imperishable page in history. The humiliation of defeat was bad enough, but the worst was still to come with the death march and the unspeakable atrocities of the Japanese prison camps.

The Japanese rounded up the defeated men and put them in groups of 1,000 each. The first part of the march was about 60 miles to San Fernado Pampanga, which was a continuous march day and night. It was pure hell because the first thing the Japanese did was take away all of their clothing except what they had on. Some were, in fact, naked. Medical supplies were confiscated as were canteens, head coverings, mess kits and any personal belongings.

These men were forced to walk in the boiling sun on the plains of Luzon during the hot season for up to 20 out of 24 hours each day without being fed, while being subject to all kinds and forms of brutality. Those who were sick or physically unable to continue the march were killed by either being shot or bayoneted.

When and if they were given rest periods was in open rice paddies and they were not allowed to use any of the water, leaving thousands of thirst-crazed prisoners even in more torment. During the march, if the prisoners crossed streams or muddy creeks and one tried to reach down to get just a small taste of water, he was killed.

Once they reached San Fernado, they were herded into railway boxcars and transported to Capan in the province of Tarlac. They were taken out of the boxcars and marched seven more miles to Camp O'Donnell, arriving on April 14, 1942.

About 12,000 Americans and 64,000 Filipinos had surrendered at the fall of Bataan. Over the next three months, some 26,000 of those who started the march were dead from the brutality of their captors, starvation, disease and horrible living conditions.

Clyde was reported missing in action on May 7, 1942. By this time the rainy season had started, and the wind and rain of the tropics were very miserable. It was cold and wet and about one-third of the men at Camp O'Donnell had not one stitch of clothing nor one single blanket to shelter them from the elements. They were forced to sleep on floors of split bamboo, as there were no bunks or beds. Food at the camp consisted of about three cups of rice gruel and water weeds which the Japs called greens. Between 30 and 50 men died each day.

Water was still scarce, and they were allowed one canteen per day for drinking, bathing and any other necessary use. It was during this time that the Japs would use any fictitious reasons for taking men and torturing them openly for 48 hours before executing them. Some prisoners would beg that they go ahead and kill them, but they were claiming to be setting examples for those who broke their rules. At one time, they took 12 officers, in the presence of the whole camp, forced them on their knees and beheaded them. Occasionally, men were used for live bayonet practice, then killed. Clyde was beaten several times with rifle butts and four-foot bamboo poles.

We do not know how he managed to do it, but Clyde kept a sort of a diary that his captors never found. He started it on December 8, 1941. It showed some men from Oklahoma who were prisoners with him. Those named were Chaney Calvin of Tuskahoma, Joe Blackman of El Reno and Wayne McHenry of Tulsa. Incidentally, it is reported that at the time of the starting of the fighting in the Philippines, there were somewhere between 500 to 900 Oklahomans serving in the area. Clyde's diary would also reveal the prison camps where he was sent. He arrived at Camp O'Donnell on April 14, 1942, Tyabys on May 12, Bilibid on July 29, McKinnely on December 2, Nellson on January 29, 1943, Ziablin October 23, 1943, Bilibid again on August 20, 1944 and then to Japan on a slave ship September 4, 1944 and was in the same prison camp as Gen. Jonathan Wainright, who had surrendered the Philippines to the Japs.

The reason he was always being transferred from one camp to another was for varied work assignments. In Japan, he was given extra rations for painting boats.

When the Americans started bombing various Japanese towns, the older guards at their prison in Japan were replaced by very young boys who were constantly leaving. Clyde and a couple of other men managed to get to a Japanese tailor shop and had an old man to make a rough U.S. flag that flew over the prison in order to keep the Allied planes from bombing the camp.

Clyde was released from captivity in September, 1945, having spent some 37 months as a prisoner of war. At the time of his release, he weighed less than 100 pounds. He was placed on a hospital ship on October 1 and arrived at San Francisco 16 days later. It was then that he was flown to Borden General Hospital at Chickasha, Oklahoma for further treatment. Members of his family were allowed to go to the hospital to see him.

When Clyde was allowed a short leave to visit Lane, I can remember as a 12-year-old boy how sorry that I felt for him. He appeared to me as a bag of bones and very sickly. They asked him what he would like to eat and he answered "one of Gus Miller's pool hall hamburgers." They came to Atoka and got several hamburgers and brought them to Lane. Clyde ate three or four bites but could not hold the food on his stomach. A few months later, Clyde would get to enjoy several of Gus Miller's hamburgers.

Clyde was discharged from the army in 1946 but he re-enlisted in January, 1946, for one year. He returned to civilian life in 1947, but his health was gone. He moved to California and on November 18, 1978, he passed away at age 57. He is buried at Forest Lawn in Cypress, California.

For his service he was awarded the Purple Heart, Combat Infantryman Badge, Asiatic-Pacific Ribbon with one bronze star, Philippines Defense with one bronze star, American Defense, Good Conduct, Prisoner-of-War medal, Philippine Unit Citation with Two bronze stars, the Victory Medal and Marksman Badge.

Here is truly another great American Patriot. He endured an awful lot for his country and had the willingness to live for another day. Taps for Clyde Coats.

Writer's Note: Our research shows that there were three men from Atoka who made the Bataan Death March. They were Coats, Pfc. Walter E. Bohannon (who we know nothing else about) and a soldier who we have misplaced his name but he is mentioned in the book Never Plan Tomorrow by Joseph A. Petak. (We know that this soldier went to the mines working in Manchuria and did survive the war.)

If you would like to know more about the men held captive by the Japanese in World War II, there is available through the Atoka County Library the book Prisoner on the Rising Sun by Oklahoma Supreme Court Justice William A. Berry who is a survivor. But let me warn you in advance that you better have a strong stomach.

CHAPTER 18

This Hero Served in WW II's "Jackass Brigade"

This portrait is of a home-grown "boggy bottom boy" who at the age of 16 years enlisted in Co. B, 180th Infantry Regiment, 45th Division as a buck private and rose thru the ranks to become a lieutenant colonel. I'm pleased to write about one of my closest and best friends, Walter Scott Wells.

Scott had barely started shaving when his unit was called to active duty on September 14, 1940. He made the entire round to Louisiana, Camp Barkley, Ft. Sill and all other training stops, then made the trip to North Africa, invasion of Sicily, invasion of Anzio, invasion of Salerno, the fall of Naples, the crossing of the famed Volturno River, spent the winter of 1943-44 in the German Winter Line, the liberation of Rome, the invasion of Southern France and was part of the push towards Germany. He spent all of this time as a combat infantryman, and he along with one other Atoka boy were the last to leave the original outfit to rotate back to the states.

The story that I wish to relay about "Ol' Scottie" is something that most were not aware had happened since the old days of the cavalry and the claiming of the west.

After the American VI Corps had taken Naples on October 1, 1943, the 45th Division was deployed with two other divisions to move inland to press the Germans back towards the Volturno River. The 45th was pushing north to cross the river, however, the Germans withdrew in good order and were digging in for resistance using the mountain passes, deep gorges, the downpour of rain with swollen rivers, and the bridges for crossing, which had either been washed out or blown up.

Regardless, the river had to be crossed as it was a milestone on the road to Rome. The 45th was on the right flank and met severe opposition but pressed on the high ground north of the junction of the Calore and Volturno Rivers. The Germans had established "The Winter Line."

Co. B's position was above the town of Venefro on a high mountain range just across the river. The mountains had a steep incline of about 90 degrees and the trail to the top zig-zagged back and forth and was very rocky. In military terms the hill was referred to as Hill 470. Incidentally, some of these mountains were over 6,000 feet in height, and the terrain was so rugged that the only way to supply the troops was by foot. Someone came up with the idea of using pack mules, so VI Corps began to get some of the small Italian burros. Unfortunately, they could not handle the loads, so the army brought in mules from Fort Reno, Oklahoma.

I'm going to let Scott tell this part of the story...

"These mules were big, sixteen hands in height, weighing around one thousand pounds and were they ever ornery. To get a halter on them you had to twist their ear and bite on it with all your might. Pliney Reiger from Atoka was the Chief Mule Skinner, and there was never a braver soldier. Night after night we would follow Reiger's lead up the narrow, rocky, curving footpaths with the mules being loaded with food, ammo, water and anything else that the company might need.

"I had a sorrel mule called 88, because he bucked and kicked all the time I was trying to get a pack on him. So I would try to get cases of ammo or mortar shells on him to weigh him down. The reason we named this mule 88 was the Germans had a rapid-fire cannon that they could light a match stick at a thousand yards. We used to sing a song "these 88's are breaking up that old gang of mine." Ask any tanker about the 88 MM.

"We traveled only at night, and we would wrap the mule hooves with burlap because the Germans would shell the trail with mortars if they heard any noise. All GI's know that on Thanksgiving and Christmas, the army always had turkey and all the trimmings and this year was no exception. The food was placed in mormite cans to stay hot until served and these cans were easy to stay strapped on the pack mule. Again, we always went up the mountain after dark and the rain, fog and snow made it very difficult to keep your footing while pulling on the mule's reins.

"This one Christmas night I will never forget as halfway up, the Germans began shelling the trail with mortars. A shell landed about 20 feet from us, and we were all trying to reach cover behind a rock when old 88 began to buck and bray. All of us were frantic so I just pulled out my 45 caliber pistol and shot 88. Cans of food were flying everywhere. We brought up a tamer mule and in the dark gathered up the cans and by daylight we had made our delivery.

"We would bring the dead back down the mountain, but they would have to place the body in a mattress cover and wrap it good in a poncho so the mules could not smell the blood. Needless to say, the wounded had to be hand carried down the mountains. One of the wounded carried down was Sgt. Bill "Buffalo Bill" York of Harmony, Oklahoma."

Previously, I wrote about Curtis "Cactus Jack" Garner, one of Scott's closest friends. Scott said that "Cactus Jack" had a Thompson machine gun that he had filed the shear pin off so it would fire full automatic. Curtis would crawl through the barbed wire at night, tearing his shirt, but he could be heard quite a distance away shooting at the Germans.

Curtis had told Scott that when they entered Rome in about a week, he sure would like to have a shirt to replace his torn, worn out one that he was wearing. When Curtis was killed, Scott had just found him a shirt to wear to enter the city of Rome.

Scott and B Co. entered Rome on June 5, 1944 less than a week after "Cactus Jack" had been killed.

Scott has kept this shirt for 55 years, and this May he will present to the Anzio Museum the shirt with the Thunderbird patch on the left sleeve that Curtis would have proudly worn as he and the other Atoka boys entered triumphantly into Rome. Scott will also pay tribute to the 26,000 American soldiers, ages 19 thru 26 years, that are buried there.

Scott saw a lot of horrible things happen to the men in the 45th and was there when his uncle, First Sgt. "Jabo" McLeroy was killed.

Scott came home and was discharged August 31, 1945. When the 45th was reorganized, he became a member of Headquarters Co. Special Troops and held the rank of sergeant.

In February, 1948, at the age of 14 years, I joined the guard and Scott was my sergeant. Later, we became a part of the 45th MP Company, and he became my platoon leader. He went on to serve in Japan and Korea with all of the rest of us and be sent home in the late spring of 1952. Again, he would join the Guard and worked his way towards college degrees from Southeastern Oklahoma University and the University of Oklahoma. He taught school at Lane then moved to be the principal of Thunderbird School in Atoka for 14 years. A new position was offered in the Edmond School System, so he and his family moved to the Oklahoma City area.

Meanwhile, he stayed with the 45th and was promoted to the rank of lieutenant colonel and provost marshal. He retired in 1983, having served a total of 43 years of active duty and national guard service, having fought in World War II and Korea as an enlisted man and an officer. The amazing thing is that the entire 43 years were served with the 45th Infantry Division. He is extremely proud to wear that Thunderbird on both shoulders.

Scott has been called on many occasions "a foot soldier's soldier" as he was always looking out for the best for his men. I can truthfully say, that if I had it to do over again, I would want "Ol' Scott" to show me the ropes as he has the experience to make the right decisions regardless of the situation. In short, he knows how to soldier.

I could tell you a lot of interesting things about Scott, but space is limited, so I will close by saying they had "Ol' Scott" in mind when they coined the word "patriot." Quite a guy and a great leader.

CHAPTER 19

Aviator Survives Exploding Plane and Nazi Capture

This portrait is of another soldier from Lane, Oklahoma, First Lt. Bill Soules. Bill's family lived about one-half mile northeast of us at Lane. His sister, Claudene, was one year older than me. As children, she and I met almost on a daily basis at her home to play.

It was at this young tender age when I first became acquainted with her older brother—this tall, blonde young man who answered to Bill. It was really neat going to the Soules' home to visit as Bill had joined the men of Co. B, 180th Infantry the last part of 1939. He was good friends with my two uncles, Sam and Slick Cartwright, who were part of the same Atoka unit.

One of the biggest thrills a kid like me could have was when Bill brought home his military uniform and let me put on his campaign hat. Also the Soules' grandfather, Pat Murphy, lived with them, and he had a big tent in the yard where Claudene and I were allowed to play. Incidentally, if memory serves me correctly, Murphy was the first sheriff ever elected in Coal County.

In September, 1940, Bill and the rest of the men of the 45th Division were ordered into active service, eventually reporting to Camp Barkley just south of Abilene, Texas. Soules was a leader and had managed to be promoted to the rank of buck sergeant. When the army needed experienced men to test to go to officers candidate school, he was chosen.

Bill had some mixed emotions about leaving his running

buddies, including Sam Cartwright, Slick Cartwright, Scott Wells, "Cactus Jack" Garner and Tom Rounsaville to become an officer candidate, but Bill had always wanted to fly and felt this was his chance to become a pilot. He was chosen by the Army Air Corps. and reported to Blackland AAF, Waco, Texas, where he became a member of flight class 43-H 221.

By August 31, 1943, Bill's dreams came true as he proudly stood at attention while his fiancé, Miss Evelyn Garner of Lehigh, Oklahoma, pinned on his silver wings as a pilot. Just a little later it was announced that Bill was given the Award for Merit for having been judged the best all-around cadet of his class in flying, ground school, athletics, military discipline and attitude. (It seems that some of his 45th training had come to the forefront.) For having been chosen the best, Bill received a headset for radio-equipped aircraft.

Within a month, half of the men of his class were fighter pilots overseas in combat, but Bill was chosen to go for additional training as a bomber pilot. He was sent to Kelly AFB in San Antonio, Texas, for bomber pre-flight, then to Brady, Texas for Flying Training Detachment, Basic Flying School at Waco, Texas, Advanced Flying School, then finally to AAF Fort Worth, Texas, for B-24 and B-17 bomber transition. He completed all of this training and on April 10, 1944, he was assigned to the 457th Bomb Group, 8th Air Force at Glatton, England. Bill immediately started flying bombing missions in the famed B-17 Flying Fortress Bomber, riding in the co-pilot seat for the first few runs over Europe.

On April 25, 1944, Bill flew his first mission as captain and with his crew of 10 men, they were to be a part of a night bombing mission that involved 1,000 bombers and fighters to bombard three German airfields located in Nancy, Metz, and

Dijon, France.

Bill and his crew reported for briefing and were taken in the dark to their waiting bomber to prepare for take off. He made his final cockpit checks and while a mechanic stood on the ground with a fire extinguisher ready, carefully, one by one, he started each of the four engines. He listened to the motors as they rough idled, watching the hot red exhaust as it danced across the wings.

Satisfied that they were ready to get underway, Bill gave the thumbs-up signal to the ground mechanic that he was ready for take-off. He eased the throttles forward and the bomber started to shudder, then he flicked off the brakes and the B-17 began to roll.

The tail lifted off and the bird wanted to fly, but Bill held the nose down, got more speed for his weight of bombs on board, he then coaxed back the stick and climbed slowly into the dark night sky to join the rest of his squadron to head for his assignment of Metz, France.

Reports indicate that they would receive no German fighter opposition. However, when they got close to their target, all hell broke loose, and anti-aircraft flack became very thick and his aircraft began to take hits. Bill reached his objective and had a successful bombing run when all at once his plane took a bad hit, catching the aircraft on fire. Bill saw that the situation was hopeless, so he ordered his crew to bail out, while he tried to keep the aircraft in the air long enough for everyone to jump. When it came time for him to step out into the night sky, the airplane exploded, causing him to receive a shrapnel wound in the back and burns on his neck and back. Momentarily, he felt the air go into his chute and felt the sudden jerk on the straps from the jolt on his legs, letting him know that his chute had opened.

Despite not knowing the terrain of the countryside, he was able to escape the German ground troops and was fortunate enough to be taken in by a French family. They tried to attend to his wounds and gave him some civilian clothing. The Germans searched out the area the next day and captured Bill. Since he was wearing civilian clothes, they treated him as a spy, placing him in a extremely filthy Gestapo prison. Bill could not lie down before being immediately covered by fleas and other insects.

Each day they would blindfold him and take him out in front of a firing squad. The officer in charge would give the order, "Ready, aim, fire." But then none of the soldiers would shoot. They pulled this maneuver on him several times and when they decided that he was not going to break down and give them secret information, they handled him in another way. First, he was stoned by civilians. Then they took Bill with some 30 other officers and put them in a small box car, locked the door and transported them to an Airman's POW Camp, Stalag Luft III, near Poland (Saigon), Germany.

He was placed in a camp with about 1,500 other prisoners to wait out the duration of the war—at least so they thought. The rations at Stalag Luft III consisted of an 11-pound Red Cross package that was supposed to last a week. However, the supply on hand dwindled at an alarming rate, so the Nazis cut each prisoner to one-half of the original rate and later would decrease that amount. The men's resistance to fight off any disease became weak. Bill developed a bad cough like he had a chest cold. Their sleeping accommodations were bottom-rung with 12 men sleeping in a room measuring 12 feet by 12 feet.

One night about midnight, the German guards told the prisoners to get their belongings and blankets together because they were being moved. The prisoners marched out into the cold for an unknown destination. This march was fatal to some of the prisoners. They walked until about 8 a.m., when they reached a small village. Some were allowed to enter a small building for about three hours. They were forced to continue to march in the snow, and some of the men began to lose their minds.

They ended up in a boxcar for four days and two nights and finally arrived at one of the worst prisons in Germany at a place called Nuernberg. The lice and fleas took over, plus they almost starved to death as they had to depend on the Germans for food, which was mostly a soup made from dehydrated vegetables and a small amount of bread.

The prisoners were moved from Nuernberg just in the nick of time as the allied bombers destroyed the industrial section and the prison they had just left. They were marched to Mooseberg, and in about 10 days they were liberated. It was April 29, 1945. Bill weighed 129 pounds, and one of the doctors asked if he was always that thin.

Bill returned to the states on May 29, 1945 and married Evelyn. Little did he have any idea in 1941 when he first met Evelyn that his close friends of Cactus Jack would become his brother-in-law and Tom Rounsaville would become his cousin by marriage.

The cough that Bill developed in the POW camp turned out to be tuberculosis. He began to try to get some financial help from the Veteran's Administration, and finally, by August 3, 1955, they decided that his illness was caused from being a POW. Bill was granted 100 percent disability and was under medical care. He entered the hospital on July 31, 1964 and passed away August 3, 1964.

First Lt. Bill Soules is buried at Coalgate, Oklahoma and was definitely an inspiration to all that knew him. Here is truly a patriot who gave his all and died at a young age of 44 years. Taps for Bill.

Writer's Note: The following men from Atoka turned up in my research as having been German Prisoners of War: Alfred "Cotton" Turner, Charles Dunn and Jesse Franklin who all had been members and mobilized with Bill Soules as members of Company B, 180th Infantry; S/Sgt. Herbert Goss; PFC T.J. Heard; Pvt. Jess Dodson; James I. Williams; Lt. Claude E. White; S/Sgt. Floyd E. Maloy and Lt. Bernard G. Morrow. There may have been others that I am not aware of and did not show up on my research. This certainly is a large number of soldiers to have been German POW's from Atoka county.

CHAPTER 20

This Female Patriot Carried Military Secrets to Her Grave

This portrait is of a retired Lane school teacher affectionately known as "Shanks," whose full name was Knolly Ann (Cartwright) Hoffelt.

She was the fourth of nine children born to William Davis and Roby Isabella Cartwright; she was also the only child not born in the Atoka vicinity. Shanks had to drop out of high school, but she managed to finally get her high school diploma at the age of 25. She then went to East Central Oklahoma University to earn a teaching certificate and continued to work towards a college sheepskin. Shanks taught at Limestone Gap and Webster, Oklahoma before entering the service. Little did she know that her enlistment into the Women's Army Auxiliary Corps, later to be known as WACS, would result in her being a participant in the now famous "Manhattan Project," the super secret development of the first atomic bomb.

In May, 1942, the WACS began recruiting women to heed the call to arms in the nation's hour of need, and some 13,000 women stormed registration centers across this country. One of those answering the call was an Atoka County school teacher, Knolly Ann "Shanks" Cartwright, who upon being accepted into service was the first woman from Atoka County to become a member of any branch of the U.S. Military.

Shanks was inducted in July 1942, and sent to Ft. Oglethorpe, Georgia, for basic and other training. In September, 1943, she was selected as a potential candidate for a secret assignment. She was to undergo extensive background investigation and in the fall of 1943, various government agencies visited Lane to inquire about her and her family. Needless to say, we were all puzzled at all the attention being given to Shanks as we had no idea what was going on. When the investigation was completed, she received top clearance and was assigned to the project.

The last of September, 1943, she was placed in charge of other project assignees, and they left by train to Santa Fe, New Mexico. Upon arrival, they were met by a convoy of trucks and taken to a newly constructed base at Trinity, New Mexico. Once they had reached their new base, they were taken by security personnel and told that they were under strict security; they could not tell anyone what they were doing. They also learned that when they left the area for any reason, they would be under close scrutiny and any violation would cause charges to be filed against them. All of their letters both incoming and outgoing were censored. When she came home on leave, the Cartwright grandkids were terribly upset at their Aunt Shanks when she would not and could not mention what part she was playing in the war effort. Even to this day, she will say very little concerning the development of the Manhattan Project.

The arrival at Trinity in the fall of 1943 resulted in her being assigned to the U.S. Atomic Energy Commission at Los Alamos and little did she know what the next 33 months would hold in store for those associated with the Manhattan Project. She would meet the now famous Dr. J. Robert Oppenheimer and General Leslie Groves who together were the major part of the leadership and intellect behind the final development and testing of the world's first atomic bomb.

Shanks said they were all on pins and needles the day the first test blast was scheduled as it was raining, and they really did not know how it would affect the fruits of their labors. During the early morning, the rain stopped and at 5:30 a.m. on July 16, 1945, the bomb was detonated at the test site. Doctors and nurses, some five miles from the test site, were told to lie down on the dirt and not to look in the direction of the blast site. Those closer to the detonation had to use protective visors, special clothing and were behind various types of barriers for their protection.

Shanks was back at the base and could see the flame, fire, hear the rumble and felt the after shock and said, "It was a frightening moment, yet a very thrilling feeling to know that we were successful in our experiment and knowing that it would end the war."

The first A-bomb was dropped on August 6, 1945, being a 9,000-pound bomb named "Little Boy." It was dropped from the bomb-bay doors of a B-29 nicknamed the "Enola Gay," with the target being Hiroshima, Japan. The bomb killed some 70,000 people with an explosion equal to 20,000 tons of TNT.

On August 9, 1945, a second A-bomb known as the "Fat Man" destroyed Nagasaki, Japan, killing some 36,000 people. This was a different type of bomb and weighed some 10,000 lbs.

Needless to say, the massive destruction of these two bombs brought the Japanese government to surrender unconditionally.

In the fall of 1946, Shanks was discharged from military service and was awarded a Meritorious Service Award for having played a part in this project. She says that she was happy to have been chosen as one of the limited personnel to be a part of this nation's history and has no regrets.

I can remember how proud Grandma Roby Cartwright was when one of the service organizations in Atoka came out and presented her with a cloth flag with four gold stars showing that she had four children serving her country.

Shanks returned home and started teaching again at Pittsburg and Lane, Oklahoma. After her retirement she continued to do private tutoring.

The last six years of her life were spent at the Oklahoma Veterans Center at Talihina. The center had a newspaper contact her for a news story about the atomic bomb, and some of the questions she would not answer as she said that over 50 years ago she was sworn to secrecy.

Shanks passed away January 9, 1997 at the age of 88 years. You cannot believe how proud her family was of her accomplishments. I believe you will agree that my "Aunt Shanks" was definitely a patriot. She rests in Green Meadows Cemetery in Atoka, Oklahoma.

CHAPTER 21

He Helped Liberate a Nazi Concentration Camp

This portrait is of a 17-year-old young man from Lane, Oklahoma, Pfc. Roy Mead. In September 1940, he accompanied other men of the 45th Division, initially as a member of Co. B, 180th Infantry, then transferred to Co. D, 120th Medical Regiment, and later attached to the 157th Infantry Regiment.

Roy and the other members went to Louisiana, then a pup tent city at Ft. Sill, Oklahoma, yet another tent city at Camp Barkeley, Texas, then to Ft. Devens, Massachusetts, and to Pine Camp, New York. Yet another move to Camp Picket, Virginia with 44-below-zero temperature and waist deep snow, and finally to the division embarking point of Newport News, Virginia.

On June 8, 1943, the 45th sailed from the coast of this country for a landing on July 2, 1943, near Oran, North Africa.

Prior to landing in North Africa, Roy had been reassigned as a medic to the 157th Infantry Regiment and served the balance of the war with that unit. He was involved in the landings of Sicily, Salerno, Anzio, Southern France, and the drive to the Rhineland.

Roy stated that he was aboard an English transport named the Wm. T. Bittle for the trip to Africa and that at Sicily he waded ashore on the 4th invasion wave. According to the various historical military writings, his unit was one of the first allied companies to step foot on German soil when on December 15, 1944, (following a fierce battle) at about 1 p.m., the unit broke through the famous French Maginot Line at Wingen, Germany.

The 45th fought its way into the Rhineland and then to Central Europe and on April 29, 1944, they liberated some 32,000 prisoners (mostly Poles, French and Russians) from the horrors of Dachau Concentration Camp.

This April 29, 1999, will be the 54th anniversary of Company I, 3rd Battalion, 157 Infantry Regiment, 45th Infantry Division scaling the walls of the German Dachau Concentration Camp, located some ten miles from the town of Munich, Germany.

Munich was loved by most Germans as it was the birthplace in 1918 of the Nazi Party and was the town where Adolph Hitler gained his power in 1932 and 1933.

The Nazi Party needed a prison camp for those who were not part of the new government and at Dachau, in 1933, they built one of their first concentration camps. These camps eventually became known as "extermination camps" for Jews and political prisoners and were well known for brutal medical experiments performed on more than 3,500 people. Thousands were starved to death, thousands were executed, thousands died of diseases, some were beaten to death as an example to their fellow prisoners and many died in the gas chamber and were cremated in the coal fired ovens.

At the time that the troops of the 45th entered Dachau, they encountered opposition from the hated SS Troops. After the fighting ceased, there were some 32,000 prisoners still alive behind the walls and locked gates of Dachau. Roy Mead was one of the first to enter. He remembers very vividly the Liberation Day of April 29, 1945.

Upon entering the camp, he saw some 35 to 40 railroad cars on the siding that looked as if they were filled with prison clothes, yet they were full of dead bodies stacked like cord wood. Roy saw an open space with wooden beds made like cattle feed troughs that were built five or six high and were used for beds. The stench and smell was something else. A brick building that had gas showers where they would make the prisoners strip naked, gas them to death, move their bodies to a trench to bleed them, and then deliver them to the crematorium.

Roy said, "I saw a hole in the ground where they poured the ashes and small bones from the crematorium; they found some Jewish women that were stripped naked and had been knocked in the head but had not yet been cremated. Many of the prisoners were so weak they could not walk. For quite a while all they had to eat was weak potato soup. We were told not to give them food as their bodies could not absorb food for some time, but some of us gave them little pieces of candy and cigarettes."

One writer described the 45th's arrival at Dachau in this way: "Counting 39 open-styled railroad cars standing near the walls; at first glance the cars seemed loaded with dirty clothing, then one saw the feet, heads, and bony fingers. More than half of the cars were full of bodies by the hundreds." The information they were told was the trainload of prisoners had stood on the tracks for several days, and most of the prisoners had starved to death. This grisly spectacle was viewed by Roy and other members of the 45th, including Atoka's Co. B, 180th Infantry.

Roy Mead came home in July, 1945, a man not quite 23 years of age, who had spent a total of 5 years, 10 months with the 45th with 25 months of this time engaged in overseas duty, and he had spent 511 days in combat with the division. Somehow, with all the firefights he was involved in, his only wound was from glass shattered by mortar rounds.

These men of the 45th would all readily agree with the article written by Bill Barrett in the 45th Division News printed in Germany May 15, 1945, with the headline reading, "Dachau

Gives Answer to Why We Fought."

April 22, 1990, was a special day for the Tulsa Jewish Community as they dedicated Liberators Memorial Park on the grounds of the Tulsa Jewish Cultural Center at 2021 E. 71 Street. This park is to honor those Oklahomans who fought and died liberating the survivors of the Nazi Holocaust. Members of the 45th Infantry Division were invited to attend as they were the first allied forces to enter the Dachau Concentration Camp.

Roy was invited to be a part of this dedication. However, due to health reasons, he had to decline.

Roy returned to Lane and worked as a game ranger for the Oklahoma Wildlife Department until his retirement. His health worsened and death took yet another patriot on January 24, 1998. Taps was played for Roy at his burial in the Butler Cemetery.

CHAPTER 22

Honoring Those Who Died in Vietnam

Let me digress and submit to you a copy of my letter to the editor of November 11, 1982, entitled "Lest We Forget." The reason I would like to reprint it is for my old friend, Scott Wells, who visits the Vietnam Memorial every time he is in the Washington, D.C. area. He is particularly interested in four whose names are inscribed on that wall. You see, of the 57,693 of our young men who died in Vietnam, Ol' Scott had taught these four.

Following is my letter to the editor:

I started this past Sunday morning, in what is a usual fashion for me, by watching the CBS morning news report prior to going to worship and while watching their commentary one of their stories hit me like a ton of bricks. This particular report concerned a war memorial dedication to those from the State of Vermont who lost their lives in the fighting in Vietnam; this was followed immediately by the national news story of the Vietnam Veterans Memorial to be unveiled and dedicated this week in our nation's capital. This new memorial is to be part of the observance for Veterans Day is of black granite, being a pair of 200 foot-long sloping walls that join to form a V-shape and these walls have inscribed the names of all 57,693 Americans who fell in battle in Vietnam between the years of 1963 through 1973.

Beginning Wednesday, the 10th of November, from the National Cathedral in Washington, D.C., will begin around-the-clock reading out loud each of these names listed on the black granite wall; it is estimated that some 1,064 names will be read each hour, taking some 56 hours to complete the reading of our country's newest heroes.

On this piece of granite and this reading of names will be 985 brave men from the State of Oklahoma with the following being some of those that you and I know from our area: Dean Edward Armstrong, Atoka, Larry Neal Boatman, Caddo, Sam Webster, Stringtown, Randy Wayne Derrick, Lehigh, Forbes Pipkin Durant, Jr., Atoka, Danny Leo Evans, Atoka, Jimmy Don Hyde, Caddo, Turner Coleman Johnson, Caddo, Benny Joe Lewis, Atoka, Derwin Brooks Pitts, Boswell and Bobby Dale Swindell, Atoka.

Supposedly the first Oklahoman to fall was Capt. Lavester L. Williams of Oklahoma City, and the last Oklahoman killed was Master Sgt. Donald J. Hall of Stroud.

The Veterans Administration says some 130,000 Oklahomans served in Vietnam. I also understand that the average age of those who served their country in that remote part of the world was 19 years.

As the CBS television camera slowly encompassed the length and breadth of the two black glistening upright slabs of stone, reflecting the names of those thereon inscribed, a heaviness developed inside of me and yet a sudden flashback was triggered allowing me to remember my childhood fellow classmate, an all around athletic part-Choctaw by the name of Dean Armstrong of Harmony who became what was known as a "Gunny Sergeant" who had fought in the Korean War and was either on his 3rd or 4th tour in Vietnam when he was killed. I remembered another young man just out of high school who was as fine a person as one would ever want to meet, a student well thought of by all and a great football player by the name of Benny Joe Lewis.

Yet there is still another in a young first lieutenant by the name of Collen Lamb, the son of Robert Lamb of Boise, Idaho, who was surveying the battle area of supposedly victory that had been concluded, was an Aide to General Westmoreland's staff, was killed when his helicopter was shot down. Robert was my wife's first cousin.

I hope that on the 11th day on November, this coming Thursday, that each of us will remember all those of all wars that fell on the field of battle so that each of us could have this day our freedom.

You know, supposedly, that the original holiday set aside to honor our veterans was following World War I; it was to be the war that ended all wars and many a sonnet has been written concerning the men of Flanders Field concerning the row after row after row of white crosses to mark the fallen. Wake up, America and be grateful, for without those who were willing to die, you would not be here and free today.

CHAPTER 23

A Grenade Ended His Tour of Duty in the Pacific

This portrait is of S/Sgt. Neil G. Cole of Bentley Oklahoma. In order to really show you a part of Neil's life, I have asked his son, Ditters Cole, to co- author this article.

Neil was living in Vera community, Knox County, Texas, working as a farm hand in a cotton patch when he decided there was surely an easier way to make a living. Neil had always loved horses and thought he might become a cavalry soldier, so on March 25, 1941, he volunteered to become a member of the U.S. Army.

He was assigned for basic cavalry training at Ft. Bliss, Texas, becoming a member of the Wprns Tr., 7th Cavalry, 1st Cavalry Division. After completing his initial training, he received extensive training as a heavy machine gun operator. It was shortly after finishing this training that he needed to go home. But due to his having been in service just a short period of time, he was turned down for leave. It was then that Neil made the mistake of deciding to go AWOL. The authorities soon caught him and returned him to Ft. Bliss. Neil's punishment was six months in the post stockade.

He was not long behind the barbed wire fence when he was made a trustee and assigned to do personal work for General Mudge. (These two would see each other again at Antipolo, Luzon, Philippines.)

Neil's unit, along with their mounts, were assigned to load on a special train bound for Ft. Riley, Kansas for an extensive training period during the winter of 1942. The entire command was returned to Ft. Bliss for advanced infantry training. They were ordered to a port of embarkation at Camp Stoneman, California, to join the Pacific theater of operation. His unit, the 7th Cavalry, sailed from San Francisco on June 26, 1943, aboard the U.S.S. Monterey, a liberty ship, arriving in the port of Queensland, Brisbane, Australia on July 11, 1943.

Once in Australia, they were encamped at Camp Strathpine and received an unexpected visit from Gen. Douglas MacArthur. Strathpine became the headquarters of the 1st Cavalry Division with the entire command to undergo extensive jungle and amphibious training through the fall of 1943.

Early in 1944, the 1st Cavalry completed a movement from Australia to Oro Bay, New Guinea. Being ready and impatient for immediate combat service, they were disappointed when they were first assigned as labor troops to unload ships.

The long-awaited time for the men of the 1st Cavalry came in February, 1944 when they became a part of the Admiralty Campaign with the major islands being Los Negros and Manus. The invasion came on February 23, 1944. The ensuing battles for the Admiralty were concluded as of May 18, 1944, with the 1st Cavalry receiving high praise from Generals Kreuger and MacArthur. The division had killed 3,317 Japanese while losing 290 men killed, 977 wounded and 4 missing.

Incidentally, another Atoka soldier, Lt. Tom Rounsaville, a team leader of the famed Alamo Scouts, was in charge of the recon mission landed by a Catalina flying boat on Los Negros to survey the area as it was thought there were only a few Japanese on the island. Rounsaville immediately reported "the island is lousy with Nips." As a result of the scout report, the landing was moved up from April 1, 1944.

Neil's unit stayed encamped on Manus Island until they made the initial assault on October 20, 1944 for the Leyte-Samar-Campaign, landing at Tacloban, Leyte, Philippines. The 1st Cavalry landed at White Beach with the assignment to capture the town of Tacloban and then commence a two-pronged drive to the north and the northwest. Their mission was accomplished by November 2, 1944.

Meanwhile, the Sixth Army developed unexpected problems when the Japanese managed to land more that 20,000 troops on the west coast at the port of Ormoc. The 1st Cavalry was called upon to battle through the mountains separating the Leyte and Ormoc valleys which has been described as the outstanding achievement of the Leyte campaign.

By December 27, 1944, the 5th, 7th and 12th Cavalry mopped up the remnants of the "Yamashito Line" as they pushed towards the western shores of Leyte Island. By January 2, 1945 the 1st Cavalry engagement ended having killed 5,937 Japs and capturing 52. The Cavalry's losses were 241 men killed, 856 wounded and 2 missing.

The next assignment for Neil's division came on January 27, 1945 when they made an amphibious landing in the Mabilao area of the Luzon Gulf. The 1st Cavalry unloaded in record time and concentrated initially in the vicinity of Urdaneta, then they were called upon to take Santo Tomas Internment Camp in Manila.

On February 3, 1945, a 1st Cavalry tank named the "Battling Basic" crashed through the prison gate and some 3,700 emaciated and tattered men, women and children who had been prisoners of the Japanese during the three long years following the fall of Manila were freed. This daring attack became known as "the 100-mile flying column" as they smashed through the middle of Jap-held territory to make this liberating drive.

On February 20, 1945, the 7th Cavalry spearheaded a drive eastward across the Maraquina River to what was called "the Shimbu Line" at Antipolo. The enemy defenses had taken full advantage of the series of sharp ridges that comprise the Sierra Madre Mountains. Each ridge was honeycombed with systems of interconnecting caves and tunnels. The Japs held the ideal positions as the battle was all uphill for the 7th Cavalry.

Neil was constantly moving his machine gun's location as ground was taken. They were in the process of setting up one of the machine guns when Neil saw four enemy soldiers on the horizon; he got his carbine and killed three of them. He saw the fourth one, an officer, run to another location. Neil positioned himself on his left leg to stabilize his upcoming shot at the officer. All at once, Neil saw that the enemy had thrown a hand grenade, and he thought that it had gone over him. Instead, the projectile rolled under his right hip and exploded.

Neil was picked up by the medics and rushed to a regimental aid station where they performed the first surgery on him. He had lost the biggest part of his right hip and most of the right leg, making it necessary to amputate the right leg; his right arm was just dangling uselessly, and they had to remove the third, fourth and fifth toes on his left foot. Neil had shrapnel penetrating wounds all up the right side of his body. This all happened on February 23, 1945.

Remember, earlier we mentioned that Neil worked for General Mudge at Ft. Bliss? The general was brought in the same tent with a belly wound.

Neil was transported to the states to a hospital at Temple, Texas and then was transferred to the Percy Jones Hospital Center at Ft. Custer, Michigan. It was at Percy Jones that he shared the same hospital ward with a Lt. Bob Dole of Kansas, later to be a

United States Senator and Presidential candidate. Both Dole and Cole had the same type of injury to their right arms. As a result of his wounds, Neil was declared 100% disabled.

By the way, for the four campaigns of the 1st Cavalry, they killed a total of 24,097 Japanese, and took 1,365 prisoners; Cavalry losses were 680 killed, 2,334 wounded, and 3 missing in action.

Neil was discharged from the service the July 16, 1945, having served three years, five months and eight days with one year, 10 months and nine days overseas. He was awarded the following decorations:

    Combat Infantry Badge
    Purple Heart
    American Defense Service Medal
    American Theatre Ribbon
    Asia-Pacific Campaign ribbon with four Bronze Stars
    Good Conduct Medal
    Philippine Liberation ribbon with two Bronze Stars
    World War Victory Medal
    Presidential Unit Citation

Neil Cole passed away at age 67 and is buried in the Bentley Cemetery.

Before this article is complete, I have a burr under my saddle blanket. When Neil passed away, the family contacted the military authorities for an honor guard to fire a volley over his remains with taps to be played, and they were told there were no units available, and besides that, it was too far for them to come anyway. Wonder what would have happened when Neil's country called for him, and he told them it was too far and he was not available?

Neil Cole, you are a great patriot. Rest in peace.

CHAPTER 24

He Kept Open the Rivers of Vietnam

This portrait is of another man from Lane by the name of Jimmie Goodson. He graduated from Atoka High School in the spring of 1959 then proceeded to college at the University of Oklahoma. Upon entering O.U., Jim applied for and was accepted as a part of the Naval ROTC program and in May, 1963, received a commission as an ensign in the U. S. Navy. He reported for active naval duty on June 1, 1963 at Pensacola Air Station in Florida.

Once arriving at his duty station, Jim began pre-flight training to become a fighter pilot. He had always wanted to fly and loved the time when he was airborne. However, after four months he went to the squadron commander telling him that he was just not cut out to be a fighter pilot. To be a top-notch fighter flyer for aerial combat, you supposedly have to get the feel of your aircraft. Jim said though he tried to get that feeling, it just wasn't there. So he asked to be reassigned.

The Navy assigned Jim to a Mine Force Welfare School in Charleston, S.C., where he underwent two years of extensive training learning about demolition and underwater mines. In 1965 he was sent to Coronado, California for six weeks of Counter Intelligence and Guerrilla Warfare Training, then on to Whidbey Island, Washington for POW Training.

Jim and other members of his class were submitted to the type of torture techniques that some of our men were already receiving by the Viet Cong. They were introduced to the black box where you can't stand up, lie down or get comfortable in any position. They went without food and water for a short period, their hands and arms were tied behind their backs and submitted to hours of interrogation by their trainers. In short, they as officers were being made aware of what would probably happen to them if taken prisoner. This training went on for 48 hours.

Jim volunteered to go to Vietnam. In the summer of 1965, he went to San Francisco and boarded an aircraft to fly to 'Nam. When he landed and got off of the plane, the first thing that greeted him was 13 body bags lined up on the airstrip with a memorial service being conducted prior to them being flown to Hawaii.

His first assignment in Vietnam was as Naval Advisory Officer to the Vietnamese Navy utilizing some three patrol boats about 20 feet long with a four-man crew in each boat. Their duty was to patrol the various inlets and streams of water running inland to see that arms, ammo, etc. were not being moved by boat. With the exception of Jim, all of the crew members were Vietnamese under the directions of a Vietnamese Officer. These patrols would go out from 26 to 36 days.

After a couple of tours, Jim was reassigned to a larger boat as part of a mine-sweeping unit. The Viet Cong and North Vietnamese would use submergible mines placed in the water in an attempt to stop the allied shipping going into the small unloading points. Their job was to keep the channel open for these smaller supply vessels. These boats, not much larger than a PT boat, about 80-feet long, were armed with 20 MM cannons, and the crew consisted of two officers plus 20 enlisted men. Occasionally, these river patrols would lose some of their boats and men as a result of fire fights both on water and from the river banks.

While on these advisory assignments, Jim was promoted to the rank of lieutenant, resulting in his receiving a bigger job aboard a much heavier and more well-armed vessel, a U.S. Navy landing craft. They journeyed up the Mekong River to the Cambodian border, always receiving hostile fire from the banks of the rivers. Their job was to make sure no mines were anywhere in the river channel, knowing that if one ship was sunk, the entire river would be blocked for any traffic.

Occasionally, they would put into bank and go ashore to check out villages. Jim stated, "You can not believe the poverty those people were enduring." Once, they had a Chinese ship they were tracking out of the South China Sea off the southeast coast of the entrance into the Mekong River when it got stuck on an island sand bar. Needless to say, the vessel was grounded and when the ship was boarded, they found that it was loaded with arms and ammo.

When asked about his food aboard these patrol boats, Jim said at first he took c-rations but started eating Vietnamese rice and fish using chopsticks with the best of them. He said that one village made a banquet for them with all of the eats being very pretty until he found out what looked like strawberry Jell-O was actually congealed pig's blood. One of their soups was made from fish eyeballs, so he passed on some of their goodies.

He would remain an advisor to this landing craft during the balance of his time in Vietnam. Jim had conversations with some of the English-speaking officers to discover they were upset with some of the decisions of running the war. The South Vietnamese wanted to mine Haipong Harbor, so no shipping could leave North Vietnam. They also wanted to make some amphibious landings with their own army. These request were turned down, making them feel like they were playing second fiddle in their own country.

Jim and I talked at length about the fiasco of this war, and we pretty much agreed that this became a political war that we had no intention of winning. We agreed that the TET Offense was won by the Allies, but our Washington politicians lost the war.

Jim came home in October, 1967 and was assigned to train speed boat teams at Mare Island, California. For his efforts in Vietnam, Jim was awarded the American Bronze Star for Valor and the Vietnamese Cross of Gallantry with a Gold Star. He was discharged and did not stay in the reserves.

This young man had a very unusual job to perform and did it well as the Mekong and other rivers were never blocked from making their port calls available. Little did he know what danger lurked around each and every bend of those waterways. Jim Goodson is a patriot without question, and I consider it an honor to be able to call him a very good friend.

CHAPTER 25

He Saw Action Aboard the U.S.S. Mississippi

I would like to give you a portrait of someone most of you know and yet you with all probability know very little about him. I've had the pleasure of having known him for 60 years but really had no idea what a patriot he was until we did some research on his life. Our portrait this week is of a man who felt the call to duty of his country because of the Naval battle at Midway in the South Pacific. This young sailor's name is Gilbert Baker, Jr., who held the rank of Water Tender First Class, part of the crew of the Battleship U.S.S. Mississippi.

The year is 1942, and our country was in an all-out war with the Axis powers. Gilbert was working as a carpenter at Paris, Texas, and newspapers announced the first American naval victory at sea after the surprise attack at Pearl Harbor. The Midway victory took a heavy toll on our navy, yet it inspired young men from everywhere to join the service of their country. Gilbert was never anyone to run from a fight, so he packed his tools, came home to Atoka to see his folks and to join the service.

Gilbert, Oscar Folsum, Jr. and Bill Clifford went to the old Jefferson Hotel on North Ohio Street in Atoka to volunteer for the military. They were sent to Oklahoma City to complete their enlistment papers; however, they were all three small in stature, and they understood their weight not to be sufficient to meet the requirement for enlistment in the army but the navy might be interested. The three of them spent the rest of the day eating bananas to gain weight, and they all made the grade. Gilbert managed to get his weight up to 127 pounds, and that evening he was sworn in as a member of the U.S. Navy. On August 14, 1942, he was shipped out for a three-week boot camp to San Diego Naval Base, California.

By the middle of September, 1942, he was on his way to Pearl Harbor for sea duty assignment. When he arrived at Pearl, one of the first people he saw was Tommy Lowe of Atoka. Gilbert was assigned to the battleship U.S.S. Mississippi to be a part of the 4th Division, Port Side, #4 turret, #4 gun crew. Even though he had no training as a gunner, they said, "We will show you." He was later assigned a different job, becoming a member of damage control and in charge of fueling and refueling other ships. He was there when the #2 gun turret blew up, killing all of its crew. (A flare back resulted in 42 men dying.)

The month of November found the Mississippi standing by an uncommitted reserve in the Central Pacific, in Hawaiian waters, supporting the forces and carriers who had borne the brunt of Japanese aggression since the beginning of the war. The Mississippi would sail up to the Aleutian water in June, 1943 and was engaged in the bombardment of Kiska, Alaska.

In November, 1943, they sailed down to the Gilbert Islands to become a part of the amphibious landing of the Marshall Islands. It was here that the ship came within 1,800 yards of the beach and did so much heavy bombardment damage that the Japanese resistance to the landing was very minimal. From there they went to the New Herbides and supported the Emirau landings. In October, 1944, they became a part of the Battle of Leyte Gulf in the Philippines in what became known as Surigan Strait. They followed a mine sweeper into the Strait. In 29 days they operated in the Gulf, they underwent 38 aerial attacks.

December, 1944, found the Mississippi underway for

Lingayen, Luzon, and it was there on January 9, 1945, that a Kamikaze suicide plane came low over the water and out of the sun, hitting the port side of the foremast structure and crashing on the boat deck. Considerable damage was done and 27 more men were killed, but they continued to carry out all of their assignment before being ordered back to dry dock in Pearl Harbor. At Luzon, Gilbert witnessed Gen. Douglas MacArthur wade ashore to say, "I have returned."

In June, 1945, they received orders to steam to Okinawa and become part of the Shuri Castle battle. They were firing three gun salvos scoring 56 direct hits from 69 salvos. In June they also took another Kamikaze hit and steamed towards dry dock in Leyte.

On August 21, 1945, the Mississippi became a part of the task force which entered Sagami Wan, Honshu, Japan and on September 1, 1945 they moored in Tokyo Bay and were present during the signing of the surrender terms the following day.

Let us give you a few statistics concerning the action of the U.S.S. Mississippi; they had 677 days in combat zone, journeyed 165,231 miles, used 24,838,600 gallons of fuel, firing 12,592,495 pounds of powder at the enemy while firing 9,995,605 rounds, shot down nine enemy aircraft that were destroyed, sunk two enemy battleships, of the some 1,400 crew members, 71 were killed, 100 wounded in action and three missing in action.

Baker would also get to see some of our fellow Atokans when he met with Sgt. Archie O'Quinn in Hawaii, Walter Durbin in Hawaii, Mark McCasland at Bogenville Island and David Chappel boarded the ship in the Philippines for the last trip to Pearl Harbor. It has always amazed me at how many people that you run across in service that you know.

Because of his time with the U.S.S. Mississippi, Gilbert was

awarded the following medals:
  Asia-Pacific Ribbon with nine battle stars;
  Navy Unit Citation Ribbon;
  American Defense Ribbon;
  Good Conduct Ribbon;
  Philippine Defense Ribbon with two battle stars;
  Philippine Presidential Citation;
  Philippine Liberation Ribbon;
  Philippine Occupation Ribbon;
  Victory Medal.

He participated in the following battles:
  Aleutian Campaign;
  Gilbert Campaign;
  Marshall Campaign;
  Bismark Archipago Campaign;
  Palan Island Campaign;
  Philippine Campaign;
  Okinawa Campaign.

Gilbert came home and was discharged November 26, 1945, then spent seven years in the Naval Reserve. In case some of you may have forgotten, he carried the U.S. Mail on Route 4, Atoka for some time or maybe you worked with him at the Savanna Naval Depot.

In interviewing him for this story, he swore to me that he learned to like the little white navy bean and cornbread for breakfast. Needless to say, I told him he must still be having a problem with the South Pacific heat hitting his head.
The ol' boy went through a lot and to me he is a patriot. Gib, good to call you my friend.

CHAPTER 26

Bessie Was Surrounded by Patriots

I would like to do something a little different as once again there will be a co-author for this portrait. I have asked my granddaughter, Miss Melissa Ann Bledsoe, to help put our story together and hopefully by the end of the article you will understand why she is a participant.

We all know of the Pioneer Woman Statue that helps make a name for the State of Oklahoma, but we would like to tell you about another pioneering woman of Texas that some of you have met. She was born Bessie Thelma Custer on September 10, 1903 on a stormy night in a tent on the banks of the Nueces River at Camp Wood, Texas. She was one of five children born to Effie Annie Connell and William C. Custer. Mr. Custer was the great nephew of General George Custer of the famed 7th Cavalry killed at the Battle of Little Big Horn in South Dakota.

The purpose of this story is to tell you about the patriotism of the men related to Bessie.

Bessie's father worked for the railroad, and when she was 11 years old, her father was killed in an accident. Widow Custer moved to the Cisco-Eastland, Texas, area to marry a man known as Pap Bisbee, and together they had several children. For the purpose of this article we will only mention Bessie's half brothers Walter Bisbee and Louis Bisbee. Bessie also had a full brother by the name of Steve Custer.

When Bessie was a relative young woman she met and married a man by the name of Henry Hector Lamb. They had a son by the name of Bennett Graham "Barney" Lamb then later they would have another son called Henry Allen Lamb and in 1935 the Lambs had a daughter, and we'll give you her name later.

Bessie was known throughout the Cisco-Eastland oil patch as a woman who was always caring for others. She was constantly helping her neighbors in various ways and people called on her in helping with the sick, teaching women how to cook, sew and on more than one occasion she found someone to watch over her own children while she would do the customary thing of sitting up with the body of a neighbor who had passed on. Regardless of where she and her family lived, people learned to love her and depend on her. I can testify that she made the best homemade hot rolls and strawberry fig preserves that you ever "sunk a tooth in."

World War II began, and Bessie found herself in an unusual situation in which her son, Barney, had just graduated from Holdings Institute School at Laredo, Texas, and at the age of barely 18 years had enlisted in the Army to become a fighter pilot. He was sent to Foster Field at Victoria, Texas, then to Aleo Field for cadet training. Her husband, Henry, feels that he must do his part in defending his country so on June 6, 1942, he was accepted as a Naval Seabee and was sent to Camp Allen, Virginia for training then was shipped to the Pacific area, Guadalcanal.

Earlier we had mentioned a Steve Custer, a full brother of Bessie. During the early 1930's, he joined the Marine Corps and in the mid 1930's he was part of the Marine Detachment that had a part in the Chinese Boxer Rebellion. He had spent so much time in the Orient that when the war came, he was assigned as the first sergeant of the 5th Marine Intelligence Section, 1st Marine Division and made the landing at Guadalcanal. After the beachhead was established, Custer led a patrol to go from Kukum to Lunga on a recon mission. (This account is documented in the book "Guadalcanal Starvation Island" by Eric Hammel.) The plans were drawn up and just as the patrol was to leave a new officer by the name of Lt. Col. Frank Goettge changed the plan and stated he would lead what would become known as "The Goettge Patrol." They moved out at 1800 hours on August 12, 1942 using a ramp boat to move up the Matanikau River, when the craft got stuck on a sand bar. The men got out of the boat to push it off the bar when the Japanese began to shoot them. Steve Custer was one of the first ones killed. A young man from Mississippi volunteered to try to go back to camp for help; he went into the water for a six hour swim and when he returned with help not one member of the patrol could be found. Even to this day they do not know what the Japs did with the bodies. There is an empty burial plot in Cisco, Texas for 1/Sgt. Stephen Custer.

We told you that Bessie had two half-brothers. They both served in the U.S. Army. Walter Bisbee served with the 101st Airborne Division and made the parachute jump on D-Day, June 6, 1944, and was killed in the air by the Germans. Bess's brother, Louis Bisbee, became a member of Patton's 3rd Army in France and was killed while driving a tank. Both of these brothers are now buried at Cisco, Texas.

At the time her brother, Steve, was killed on Guadalcanal, her husband, Henry, was on Guadalcanal and was hurt during a Japanese raid on an air field that he was working on. Henry's injuries were severe enough that he was sent to several naval hospitals in the states for treatment.

During 1944, her son, Barney, had become a fighter pilot and was sent to England to fly P-47 Thunderbolts as cover for returning bombers. He named his fighter planes "Lambsy Divey."

He would fly cover for ground troops during the D-Day landings and the march to Berlin. At one time he was considered an ace due to the number of enemy tanks and trains that he had destroyed while working to the call of support from infantry units. He had four of the fighters shot out from under him due to the enemy fire received in low strafing attacks. Barney brought two of the planes back to England, rode one down in the English Channel and crashed one just inside the American lines in Germany. The last time I saw him, he had small lumps on the thighs and on his forearms caused from the strain of pulling his planes out of various maneuvers. He left the Army in 1946 but returned in 1947 to become a multi-engine pilot and fly the Berlin Airlift. He retired as a lieutenant colonel and a command pilot.

 The son, Allen, would be called into the Korean War as a member of the Texas National Guard. Upon discharge, he went to college, received a commission in the Air Force ROTC program at North Texas State College and re-entered the service in 1955. He was sent to Kinston, North Carolina for pilot training then to Goodfellow at San Angelo, Texas for multi-engine training. He flew C-47's and T-29's in England, the RC-45 in Spain, from 1963 to 1967; he was an underground Missile Captain; in 1970 he flew out of Okinawa; he was to be the officer in charge of the ROTC program at the University of Mississippi. In 1973, Allen flew C-130's out of Clark AFB in the Philippines, and then out of Thailand. While flying in Vietnam, he was awarded the Distinguished Flying Cross due to a hit to his aircraft by the Viet Cong. While taking off from Camran Bay, his load of 105mm ammo caught on fire, along with the hydraulic system that controls the plane. Even though on fire, Lamb made the assigned cargo drop and brought the aircraft in for a crash landing at Bien Hou airstrip with his full crew on board. When the North

Vietnamese began to negotiate for the return of American bodies, he was the pilot that flew in the team and the bodies were returned by the enemy. He was a lieutenant colonel and a command pilot now retired.

Bessie never served in the military, but I think you would agree with me that this pioneering stout-hearted woman has given so much of herself and her family, we could call her a patriot. Rest in peace, Bess; you have earned it.

Oh, by the way, you may have never met Bessie Custer Lamb, but you can see the spitting image of her in her daughter, my wife, Thelma Lamb Bledsoe.

CHAPTER 27

The Saga of the Boggy Bottom Boys

This time we are going to do a different kind of portrait in order to answer one of your most frequently asked questions. At the same time tell you a true story about three Atoka classmates and their 45th Division National Guard experience.

In several articles, we have mentioned about 14, 15 and 16-year-old boys joining the guard. You have to remember that after the end of World War II, young men came home from the service and tried to put their lives back together, but jobs here were few and far between. With these scarce jobs going to veterans, high school students were extremely lucky to even find a part time job. So when the National Guard offered openings for enlistments for men who were 18 or older, a bunch of us lied about our ages and offered our services.

The guard paid $2.50 per one night of weekly drill, which was a lot of money for me. I was working on Saturdays from 6:30 a.m. until 10 p.m. for Clyde Cooper Grocery and Feed Store for the same amount of money. When the opportunity came for me to join Headquarters Special Troops, I jumped at the chance.

I was not quite 15 years old, but Col. Hicky McCasland assured "Ol' Doc Cotton" that anyone as big as me had to be of age. About the same time Jesse Wayne Phillips and Tinker Ray, both looking at their 16th birthday approaching, became members of Co. H, 180th Infantry under the leadership of Captain Willie Bowman. My commander was Captain "Barney" McCall, and I was assigned to T/5 Scott Wells for him to whip me in line and make me a soldier. McCall's exact words to Wells were, "See what you can do." Then he walked off leaving me at the mercy of "Ol' Scott." Tinker and Jesse were put to the test under the direction of a new second lieutenant by the name of Lon Robert Fink. Both Fink and Bowman were seasoned veteran infantrymen of World War II.

In August, 1948, we made our first two-week summer encampment plus got our first train ride, a taste of Ft. Sill and its heat. What we really were looking for was that $37.50 cash payment we would receive when the encampment had come to a close.

When we arrived back at Atoka, we found out that Col. Hicky McCasland, Division Provost Marshall, had managed to politic the 45th Military Police Company from Marlow, Oklahoma to Atoka. It was then that both Atoka guard units would become one. When the transfer of units became final, they immediately asked for volunteers to go to Camp Gordon, Georgia for training at the Army MP School.

With spring upon us, "Ol' Jesse" knew that when school was out, he could look forward to being on the end of a cross-cut saw in the logging woods; Tinker would be a part of a haying crew and working of cattle and I could look forward to a 30-acre corn patch. We decided to solve our summer employment and signed up to go to Georgia.

Lt. Fink had heard that three men had volunteered to go to school and asked Scott Wells, now a new second lieutenant, if he knew who was going to which. Wells answered "Winkim, Blinkim and Knod." The puzzled Fink asked, "Who?!" and Wells replied again "Winkim, Blinkim and Knod—Phillips, Ray and Bledsoe." It was very evident what he thought about the three of us and just what kind of mischief would fall upon us.

All haste was made to get us ready for travel, so we couldn't back out. Sgt. Fred McCaskle got us extra uniforms, another pair of combat boots and 1st/Sgt. Sidney Camp applied to the division for our train tickets and our meal allowances. The time came for us to begin our journey, so we boarded the Katy Flyer headed for Georgia. We certainly had some surprises in store for us when we found out that our rail passes called for three days and two nights in a chair car and the meals were limited to what you got to eat and the amount. We should have realized that this was only the beginning of our new adventure.

Boy, were we surprised when we arrived at Camp Gordon and were greeted by the meanest man I've ever met, SFC Felica Schmidt. He was a barrel-chested, weight-lifting paratrooper, veteran of three combat jumps in Europe, twice wounded. He had a crew cut, and his voice was very authoritative, using about all of the cuss words that we had ever heard. The first thing he did was to line us up in three squads of eleven men each, then we heard for the first time that "our behinds were grass and he was the lawn mower." He flat dab read us the riot act, and we believed him. It was then that he told us to hit the barracks, find us a bunk and be prepared to fall out in 15 minutes. We ran into the barracks and the three of us selected our bunks on the first floor. It was then that we were to receive the first test of regular army that Wells, McCasland and Sid Camp had warned us about in that we being from the National Guard would be tested by the regulars. (They each told us to stand together no matter what it took.)

"Ol' Tinker" had no more than put his duffel bag on the bunk beside me, when a soldier from New Jersey by the name of Baker told him that was his bunk, so move out. Tinker said that Sgt. Schmidt told us to get a bunk, and he was staying right there.

Baker immediately proceeded to tell him what he was going to do to him, to which Tinker doubled up his fist and told him, "Come on if you want a piece of me." Tinker didn't weigh 135 pounds with both boots full of water.

About that time Ol' Jess walked up and asked Baker if he had packed a lunch. Baker was told if one lick was struck on Tinker, he'd better eat up in a hurry as he had all three of us to whip and it would be an all-day affair. We stood there for a moment, then I told Baker that his wagon was loaded and to move on. He did.

Jess, seizing the moment, jumped on his foot-locker and announced, "We have this prayer meeting called and let's get a few things straight." He told them our outfit was called the "Boggy Bottom Boys, the Fighting Thunderbirds;" this patch on our left shoulder was to be called a Thunderbird or a T-Bird; we did not want to hear any remarks about buzzards, chicken, etc. and furthermore there would not be any running of hand down our left shirt to wipe off the bird manure. Jess then asked "any questions?" Then he dismissed the "prayer meeting" about the same time as Sgt. Schmidt came in and wanted to know what was going on. No one said a word. Incidentally, the guy Baker who was going to tear Ol' Tinker apart turned out to be one of our best friends.

Sgt. Schmidt knew that something was amiss involving those three National Guard week-end warriors so when the duty roster came out, you would never guess the three men assigned to latrine duty. However, this would all change at a later date.

We were told to stand by for inspection and the sergeant came through viewing how each man had his bunk area arranged. When he got to me, I had a pair of the most beautiful paratrooper jump boots, shining like a new moon, displayed under the side of my bunk. The sergeant asked who those boots belonged to, and I very proudly declared my ownership. He then asked if I was a trooper, did I have jump wings and if not that I had better put them in my duffel bag, that he never wanted to see them displayed again. He would later have an opportunity to see those jump boots.

Every morning before marching off to classes, Winkim, Blinkim and Knod would go in to clean the latrine while the rest of the men lay in their bunks. They would tell us how nice and soft our hands were getting to be and that once we left the service, they were sure we could get jobs with some hotel or motel. Again, we would have the last laugh at a later time.

The first week of training as a member of 86 TMPS, we were subjected daily for two hours on map reading and how to use a compass. Map reading was very familiar to the three of us; a great deal of time on our Monday night drills was spent teaching us to "read right and up." On the first Monday after a week of classes, we were told that a night problem would be held, and it would be necessary for us to find our way out of a river bottom. We were not the only ones doing this exercise as the entire training school was to be on the same operation finding their way out of the river area. All of the top brass of the school would be awaiting our successfully completing the venture.

We went into the bottom area just before dark, all 33 of us, being led by Sgt. Schmidt. The sergeant had the compass, map and an OD green colored crooked neck flashlight and occasionally he halted the platoon and let us have a go of finding out where our position was on the map. We had been walking for a while when the three of us noticed we had been in this area about 30 minutes earlier and watched while the sergeant used the flashlight to look at his wrist compass. Shortly, we started to walk again, and it just so happened that we came back to the same spot. The sergeant was again looking at his compass, then Jess, Tinker and I decided we were lost.

The three of us talked about our situation and I told them I would talk to the sergeant, to which they both said that we were on his bad list already so leave him alone. I just had to say something and in my own diplomatic way, I said, "Sergeant, are we lost?"

Sgt. Schmidt gave me a cussing then said, "You weekend warriors are so smart; you probably think you can get us to our objective." The three of us held a very quick conference; we surveyed the night, which was almost like day, found the big dipper and north star (We had learned how to get around at night from hunting.) and decided we would make the attempt of finding our way. So I told the sergeant that we could do it.

Jess seized the moment, stood up and spread his arms out, started to turn in a circle, and blurted out a few words in unknown tongues. The sergeant wanted to know what was going on, and I told him Jess was the son of an Indian witch doctor and medicine man and that strange powers had been passed on to him.

Tinker jumped in and said that when Jess came to a stop we would know exactly which way was north.

Sgt. Schmidt said, "You illegals stop the crap and get on point!"

Jess took the point with me right behind him with the map and Tinker had the flashlight. Every once in awhile Jess would stop, and we would look at the map. In about 30 minutes, we had found a two-lane dirt road then we turned north and after another 30-minute walk, we could see these vehicles.

Sgt. Schmidt immediately came to the front column and led us up to the command post. He proudly proclaimed to all of the school's brass and commandant, "Sergeant Schmidt, 86 TMPS platoon, reporting and our mission has been completed." We just happened to be the first unit in, and boy did the brass commend our sergeant for a job well done.

The next morning when we looked at the bulletin board, we found that we no longer had the latrine duty and had been assigned to the Butt Can Brigade. For those of you who have never served in the army, let me explain. On each barracks floor you will find between six and eight one-gallon cans. Obtained from the mess hall, they are to be filled one half full of water so that the cigarette butts and ashes may be disposed of, thereby keeping the floor and area clean. In our case, we had 12 cans to look after, six on each floor.

Our job was to see that those 12 cans were full of clean water each morning before class. It was the best job in the army. The three of us pulled no other details for the rest of the summer. This was Sgt. Schmidt's way of saying thanks for getting us out of that river bottom. All of the rest of the platoon would tell us how flat our noses were getting and how full our lips were from "kissing up."

Pay day came around, and we all went to the PX to buy our toilet supplies and cigarettes as we knew by the next pay day we would be "skully punta;" that is Choctaw for money all gone or I am flat dab broke. Some of the guys went to the beer garden for a few cold ones and when they got back to the barracks, they found the three of us playing cards. It was decided to play a little poker and with Winkim, Blinkim and Knod playing together, we managed to split a nice night's work. In fact, one of the "sore losers" had the nerve to indicate that we might be cheating. Tinker told him, "Where we come from, a man could put himself in a heap of trouble accusing someone of being dishonest." We split some pretty good money that summer because "we were lucky".

When the guys ran out of money, we devised another game

of chance whereby you would follow the leader and discard your cards by suit and when the last card was played, the man with the most cards left would pay a penalty. If you were the loser, you were required to make a fist, the dealer would take the deck of cards, slant them at a slight angle, cup the cards and proceed to raise his hand about 12 inches while coming down on your knuckles, taking away a little of the skin on the fist. The most anyone was allowed to be hit in any one hand was five times.

If you did a good job, you could really roll up the skin and in some cases a little drizzle of blood. One day three of the boys had been to the beer garden and came in wanting to play that card game called "Knucks," except they wanted to play it with the loser getting scraped one time on the nose. We agreed to the venture and before you knew it, they each had blood running down the bridge of their nose. Sgt. Schmidt just happened to come in, saw what was happening and said there would be no more "Knucks." For some reason the three of us never lost, again, just pure luck I guess.

On the Thursday before our graduation, Sgt. Schmidt called me into his room, and I had no idea what I had done. He told me to sit down and said, "I want to thank the three of you for that night in the river bottom. You all made me look good in front of the school brass and effective the first of the month, I have been promoted to master sergeant and will move to TMPS training headquarters. Previously, I had been passed over twice but I can't help but think that night helped me get the new stripes."

It came time for our Saturday morning graduation, and we all fell out for inspection. The sergeant trooped each of the three squads of men, and he would say "Looking good, soldier." When he got to me, he looked me up and down then he spotted me wearing my paratrooper jump boots with spider laces like his. He stood there for a moment and then said, "Looking damn sharp, trooper," gave me a wink and finished the inspection. These were the same boots he made me put in my barracks bag telling me on the first day "that he never wanted to see them again."

After graduation, we went to company headquarters to get our rail passes and meal tickets to begin our trip home. Tinker's tickets were not there, mine and Jess's were all messed up as it showed us stopping in Atlanta. They tried to contact the post transportation office, but it was closed until Monday. They put the two of us on the train and had someone meet us in Atlanta and take us to the Ft. McPhearson Casual and Convey Company until they could get the mess straightened out. They took us to a barracks where five other soldiers headed to Fort Knox, Kentucky had incomplete travel tickets. On Sunday night, a sergeant first class came to the barracks and lined us up saying they had no idea how long it would take for post transportation to get us to the right place. Meanwhile, he continued, the army could ill afford for us to lie around. He looked at me and said, "You look like a truck driver." I answered, "I could drive anything in this man's army." He said, "Good, someone will pick you up at the orderly room at 07:00 hours and take you to the motor pool, and you other six will be woke up at 04:00 hours for KP."

I went down to the chow hall for breakfast, and there was "Ol' Jess" all decked out in a white jacket serving food. When I came by, he said, "You had better not say one word." Needless to say, I had to snigger.

On Monday morning they drove me to the motor pool where a trip ticket had already been made out for a KB7 long-wheel-base school bus that was so long it looked like it should have hinges in the middle to make a turn. A buck sergeant and I got on the bus, and I finally figured out how to start it, managed to get it

SHERMAN AVNER
"SHUG" BLEDSOE, JR.

(R) SHERMAN "SHUG" BLEDSOE, JR. RECEIVING AWARD
FROM (L) SAM HAMM, COMMANDER OF THE V.F.W.
"IN GRATEFUL APPRECIATION FOR 'PORTRAITS OF PATRIOTS'
BY THE ATOKA COUNTY VETERANS COUNCIL, 1999"

ORVILLE M. BONHAM

LEVI ROBERTS

OLIE BONHAM AND DAMMIE D. MORRIS

LOUIS MILLICAN

PAUL E. MILLICAN

OLIE & MARVIN BONHAM

EDDIE VANDENBURG

CHESTER BONHAM AND EDDIE VANDENBURG

EDDIE VANDENBURG

ROBERT (BOB) CHRISTIE

KOREA

ZACHARY TAYLOR
CARTWRIGHT

KNOLLY ANN "SHANKS"
CARTWRIGHT HOFFELT

JESSE BILLY "SLICK"
CARTWRIGHT

SAMUEL FULTON
CARTWRIGHT

CLYDE ANDREW COATS

ODIS PAUL BURLESON

AUDIE & ODIS BURLESON

BOBBY SWINDELL

MART RECTOR & EDDIE VANDENBURG

BILL & LEE RECTOR

WILLIE MOORE

DOYCE STANFORD BURKE

CLAUD D. TIDWELL

(L TO R) SHERMAN "SHUG" BLEDSOE, JR., ELBERT BRENHAM, "BUD" MOFFATT, & BOB PRAYTOR IN CHORWON, NORTH KOREA, SPRING, 1952

MEDICS, ATOKA, 1938: LEFT TO RIGHT, TOP ROW: O.H. CHATMAN, L.A. RAINS, A.W. SALMON, W.L. W.L. EMBREY, H. JONES, L.D. BLACKBURN, T.M. STARK, 2ND ROW: C.B. MCKEE, C.C. ROLLINS, L.W. UBER, C.P. TARRON, THOMAS LOWE JR, W.F. WILLIAMS, BOTTOM ROW: W.M. BETTS, J.L. MUSLER, L.F. MILLICAN, A.J. SALMON, L.D. SHOREMAKE, J.C. BUTTS, J.H. MCCASLAND

INFANTRY, ATOKA, 1938: LEFT TO RIGHT, TOP ROW: J.S. JACKSON, A.E. MOORE, A. DOWNS, E. CURTIS, A. RIGSBY, S. DOWNS, W. MOORE, J. CLARK, 2ND ROW: W.L. JONES, JR., G.C. JONES, E. EVANS, C.C. MOORE, TOM ROUNSAVILLE, W.S. BEARD, C.N. GREEN, J.T. MCLEROY, BOTTOM ROW: H.S. WILLIAMS, C.E. DUNN, R.E. DUNN, V.I. HOWARD, J.B. CARTWRIGHT, J.A. CHITWOOD

INFANTRY, ATOKA, 1938: LEFT TO RIGHT, TOP ROW: J. COLLIER, D. WARREN, H. JOYCE, SAM CARTWRIGHT, O.L. WHITTINGTON, R. CHITWOOD, R. NUTTALL, R. TURNER, 2ND ROW: C.E. RAINS, E.V. JOYCE, W. MOFFATT, J. DANEY, E.J. HENDRIX, R. CLARK, BOTTOM ROW: C.E. LEONARD, L.V. RUSSELL, E.D. STALLINGS, T. WEAVER, W. BOWMAN, L.A. BRADSHAW

KOREA AIR BASE ENTRANCE

"SHUG" BLEDSOE AND FRIEND,
HOKAIDO, JAPAN, AUGUST 1951

in low gear and started out of the motor pool gate where I made a right turn (no power steering in that day and time) when all at once I had the left front tire upon the opposite curb and the right duals were about to take down the corner post holding the motor pool gate. I finally got the bus straightened out and went to change to second gear, and you have never heard such gear grinding and jamming in your life. The sergeant asked, "Are you sure you know how to drive?" Little did he know that they had just given me a license at Camp Gordon to drive a Jeep, but I assured him that "if it had wheels, I could drive it." Got the bus in high gear, and we went leap-frogging down the street.

I was directed to an area where a whole load of WACs were waiting to go to the firing range. These ladies boarded my bus and immediately I started having trouble shifting gears and "announced that the bus had a new transmission that had not yet been broken in." All that morning, while the ladies were learning how to fire a .45-caliber pistol, I sat in the driver's seat and learned how to shift gears. I drove that bus for three days and was told if I was needed anymore, they would let me know.

Meanwhile, Jess was being awakened very gently every morning at 04:00 hours for KP and did not get off until 7:00 pm or so, and he was beat. I upset his apple cart when I presented him with a small bottle of Jergen's lotion so he could continue to keep his hands nice and soft. For some reason he was not very appreciative of my gesture, started using obscene words and threw the bottle at me.

Jess and I both got Thursday off, so we asked some of the men stationed there where we could go for some entertainment. They suggested the Blue Shield Night Club on Peach Street. We caught a bus and finally managed to find this joint. When we arrived, this "hawker" was standing outside the door with a scantily attired woman telling us what a fine lady she was and about all of the gyrations she could do with her body. We had never seen a strip-tease show before, so we thought that we would take it in for the afternoon. When we went to get our ticket for admission, they made us show our IDs. They would not let us in saying we were too young and that was after we had lied about our ages by three years.

We left the Blue Shield and proceeded down the street when we heard this haunting music with a heavy beat of a drum. Curiosity got the best of us, so we returned to the Blue Shield. It got its name from a shield of blue paper on the glass that was high enough that I could stand flatfooted and see the dancers runway, but Jess could not see in so I got to describing to him what was going on. I would tell him, "Boy, wish you could see this." and just kept on antagonizing him about this dancer. Jess could not take any more, so he started jumping up like a beagle pup in tall grass after a rabbit. It was so funny that I had to leave and as we were walking away, he had the nerve to tell me that I was lying to him, just stringing him along. As a result, he wouldn't walk with me.

We went back to camp, and they had been trying to find us to put us on a train for Chattanooga, Tennessee. We boarded late that evening and reached the station in Chattanooga, where we would have to change trains. We got off and found out that we came in on a lower level, and the train we were to catch was on an upper level. We started to find our way around when this familiar voice was hollering at us; it was Tinker. He had finally gotten out of Augusta, Georgia.

We found our way to where you went up to the upper level but to our surprise, we saw something like we had never seen before. There in front was a machine that had steps that folded down and noticed there was a sign pointing to the escalator. For some time the three of us just watched that contraption work and were google-eyed how the people were getting on and off. Finally, Jess said "I'm gonna give it a try." He got on and looked back as if to say "Haw, I've mastered it. " However, when he got to the top to get off, he jumped and Jess and his duffel bag went all over the lobby. Tinker was the first one to Jess, picked up his head and asked "Jess, are you hurt? Jess, are you hurt?" To which Jess said, "You know the ride is not bad but that getting off could kill you." Tinker dropped Jess's head on the floor and began to tell him how sorry he was. If I had some tickets to sell, we would have done real well that day and made a killing as we gathered a crowd.

We left Chattanooga late Thursday evening for a long ride all the way across Tennessee, then Arkansas, on to Indian Territory with supposed arrival in Atoka on Saturday afternoon. The first night we lumbered up to the dining car, and boy did we put on the feedbag. There was a lot of difference with the regular army handling our transportation than it was with the National Guard as even our seats were upholstered and quite comfortable.

Before we left Arkansas to cross into Oklahoma, one of us had asked the train conductor if there was a place where we could change our uniforms. He saw to it that we were taken care of and provided us with a private berth.

As we went in one-by-one to change our uniforms, it took a little more time to dress than normally as we wanted to look sharp for the home folks, especially for those sweet young things we were sure had missed us terribly. Our khakis were so stiffly starched that you could hardly put your leg in the pants, our collar brass was really glistening and our boots had a mirror shine that you could see yourself. We decided that it was not necessary to wear a tie, being the weather was rather hot.

We got off of the Katy in Atoka and, boy, were we looking sharp; that overseas cap with the green braid was cocked on our heads just right. The general public had no idea that soldiers could look that good. After unloading from the train, we took our duffel bags to Coopers Store to leave, said hi to my father, then we headed for Court Street. Look out, girls, here we come. As we made the corner on Court in front of Cates Drugstore, we met several of the girls coming out of Cates. I remember that Chris Heck was one of the girls and believe another was Elma Lou Byrum. I can't recall who else was there, but anyway, we talked for a little bit when Tinker asked the girls if they had missed us. Chris immediately said, "No, have you all been somewhere?" Boy, she had really let the wind out of our sails.

The three of us sashayed on up the street and crossed over to the pool hall for one of Gus Miller's hamburgers. In fact, we ate two each. After completing our meal, we walked down to the Thompson Theater where Joy May Sprouse and Gloria Darken were working. I tried to talk Joy May into letting us in the movie free, and she asked, "Why should I?" Tinker told her that we had been on alert all summer protecting her. Joy May said, "And I thought the heat was the reason I couldn't sleep." Now that was the final straw. All of the wind had been let out of our sails, so we went home. The question has been asked, "What did your parents say when they saw you?" The answer was "Oh no; he's back."

The following Monday was drill night, and we reported in. First Sgt. Sid Camp said, "We didn't think we would see you boys for a couple of years."

"What made you say that Sgt. Camp?" I asked.

"We thought you would be in the post stockade that long."

Then he told us we had each been promoted to corporals.

Shortly, we went up to the high school and enrolled for our senior year. Tinker and I began working out with the football team, and Jess started getting in shape for boxing. Incidentally, Atoka's Wampus Cat football team had a record of 8 wins, 1 tie and 1 loss under new head coach Jack Murray.

Before we knew it, graduation arrived, and on May 25, 1950, we walked across the stage to receive our diplomas from Atoka High School. We knew that our summer employment would be Jess back on the cross-cut saw, Tinker to the hay field and myself back to the corn field. The summer was looking rather bleak until July, 1950, when the North Koreans attacked South Korea, causing the U.S. to be in all-out war. President Harry S. Truman proceeded to call up four National Guard divisions for mobilization into federal service, and the 45th was one of them.

The following are those men called up with our unit who had just graduated with us from Atoka High: Harold Bussey, Bob Decker, Ted Connelly, Frank Bryant, John Glover, Eugene Swindell, Bud Moffatt, Elbert Benham, Doyle Yates and Hagan Folsom. Also called were several guys who would have been seniors that fall: Alfred "Hoss" Fitzgerald, Hershel Eastridge, Bob Praytor, Don "Fuzzy" Foster, Tommy Williams and Shirley Allen. (These guys would come back and finish school after completing the service.) The following are the men who were 15 and 16 years old and would have been sophomores who were willing to go: Glo Rounsaville, Jimmy Poole, Jimmy "Guts" Walker, Robert Harris, Ferman Mayo, William Bussey, Bob DeGrazia, Hub Arrington and Alonzo Shoemake Jr.; however, it was decided they were too young. (Rounsaville, Poole, Mayo and Bussey would later enlist in the service and each is now retired from the military.) I think that you will have to admit that was a lot of 15 to 18 year-olds to come out of a rural school to be willing to serve their country. This does not include men from Caney, Tushka and Stringtown. Quite a group of young patriots.

In August we started reporting to the armory in Atoka to get ready for our movement to Camp Polk, Louisiana. We left by motor convoy and spent our first night in tents sleeping on the ground at Perrin Air Force Base, the second night at the airport in Marshall, Texas, and on the third day we arrived at Camp Polk. It should be noted for the record that when we left Atoka for Polk that Cpl. Jesse Wayne Phillips was Lt. Scott Wells' Jeep driver and once we arrived at our destination, Jess lost his job and Wells got himself another driver. Scott should have known that Jess could only drive a team of mules and a logging truck.

We trained at Camp Polk until March, 1951, then the entire division moved to a port of embarkation at Camp LeRoy Johnson. We boarded the U.S.S. Gaffey, sailed down the Mississippi to the Gulf of Mexico through the Panama Canal, finally to Otahu, Hokkiado, Japan.

We lived in squad tents on the old Chitose Air Base where the Japanese kamikaze pilots were trained. Some of our unit went to Camp Crawford at Sapparo to live in barracks that formerly housed the Imperial Japanese Marines. Finally, some of us were assigned to regimental combat teams at Einiwa and Shimamutisu for another tent city. We trained in Japan until November, 1951 and were notified that we would replace the 1st Cavalry Division in Korea. The 1st Cal had taken an extremely large number of casualties. On December 5, 1951, we made an amphibious move landing at Inchon. The next day we moved to the Jamestown Line on the Yonchon-Chrowon sector in North Korea.

As our outfit arrived in the area where we were assigned, we found our new homes to be tents dug back into the side of a hill and 105 MM ammo boxes full of dirt being used as sidewalls for protection. It was cold, and we had not been equipped with cold weather gear, so we wore just about every piece of clothing we had when we went on assignments. The freeze line was 36 inches in the ground, so you could not dig. Now that's cold!

We all spent a rather cold winter together, with the entire front line staying just about where it was when we arrived. This group of men Col. Hickey McCasland had put together was probably one of the best and sharpest units in the 8th Army; he was extremely proud of his outfit and its ability.

In the late spring, some of the Atoka men started rotating home. Tinker and Jess were sent to Ft. Sill, Oklahoma, and when my time came, they sent me to Ft. Hood, Texas. The three of us were coming home to be discharged after four plus years of National Guard and mobilization. They had both turned 19 years of age, and I sailed under the Golden Gate Bridge on my 19th birthday. We had paid our dues and were proud to have done so.

Our second return to Indian Territory has now been completed. The three of us are over 66 years of age, and we all live here in Atoka County. Ol' Jess is known as "The High Potentate of Crystal," raising emus and cattle; Tinker is the Vice Commander for Standing Rock and raising cattle, and me, well I'm just living at Lane, loving it and trying to keep Thelma busy.

In closing, Winkim, Blinkim and Knod all agree that the best thing we ever did was to join the National Guard. We are extremely proud to be called "Thunderbirds" and "Boggy Bottom Boys."

CHAPTER 28

A Special Soldier in a Special Unit

Let's look at a local hero who fought in World War II, the "Korean Police Action," Vietnam, and led a daring rescue mission in the Belgium Congo. This soldier was buried on April 19, 1999 at the Ft. Benning Main Post Cemetery, Georgia, with full military honors. I was told that there were so many generals and colonels in attendance to honor their comrade and friend that all of the medals these men were wearing would be a double armload. This man was Col. Tom J. Rounsaville, retired, United States Army.

Tom was born at Midway, Bryan County, Oklahoma to Delbert and Mittie Garner Rounsaville on July 23, 1919 and grew up in Atoka County. He lived with his nine brothers and sisters at 215 North Delaware across from what is called Mamie Johnson Elementary School. His father, D.H., was a school teacher, at one time the county superintendent, and later the postmaster for Atoka.

Those who attended school with Tom said, "If there was ever a fierce competitor, it was Tom." Anything he went after he gave it everything he had, then some. Tom has always been like the little boy says, "He'll hit you, scratch you and throw sand in your eyes; he'll do anything to you." Tom was always very personable and drew a crowd of friends around him. He was a natural born leader and one who thrived on being able to have others willing to go the last mile and give the final "grunt and groan."

After graduating from Atoka High, he enrolled in Oklahoma

A&M College at Stillwater and in his junior year was called to service, as he had enlisted in Co. B, 180th Infantry, 45th Division, Oklahoma National Guard and was a part of the Atoka Unit.

The 45th went to Louisiana for maneuvers. Tom was there as a part of the outfit that received praise from Gen. Patton and Gen. Krueger. In 1940, he mobilized with the 45th and went to Ft. Sill, Oklahoma, later on to Camp Barkley, Texas.

It was while at Camp Barkley that he was promoted to first sergeant of B Co. As usual, Tom immediately proceeded to give his new job his all. Col. Scott Wells, then Corporal Wells, tells the story, "While at Barkley, Tom and Slick Cartwright (one of my uncles) got a 3/4 ton truck, stole and hauled gravel from the Texas Highway Department over at Buffalo Gap, Texas, to line our company streets to get us out of knee deep mud; however, Doc Dean, our C.O., nearly fainted when he found out where they had gotten the gravel. Needless to say, the Texas Highway Department raised holy hell and so did the battalion commander. Tom and Slick just looked innocent."

While at Barkley, Tom had quite a group of men he was associated with and two of those were my uncles, Sam and Slick Cartwright. There was also Bill Soules (who would end up being kin by marriage), "Cactus Jack" Garner (his first cousin), and an 18-year-old corporal by the name of Scott Wells. Back in their earlier days of service, while on pass, they had more fun and got into more trouble than a cage full of monkeys trying to figure what to do with a football. Evidently, nothing was sacred when they hit town; everything was full speed ahead.

In 1942, the army came through asking men who wanted to be officers to take a test. All of the above except Garner and Wells took the test, and the next thing they knew Sam, Slick, Bill and Tom were off to Fort Benning, Georgia for Officers

Candidate School. They each made the grade and graduated in the last part of 1942 as brand new second lieutenants (shave tails). Each of them were then sent a different direction and never returned to the 45th Division.

Forgive me, but I must insert a little personal thing about Tom Rounsaville. Since I was just a small lad, I had flat dab worshiped the ground that my uncle Sam Cartwright walked on; and the same was true for his best friend, Tom. The two of them use to heckle and kid me, which I loved.

In the late summer of 1942, Tom and Sam made a fast weekend pass trip to Atoka and upon leaving on a Sunday, after partying all weekend, they started driving towards Abilene, Texas and Camp Barkley. Sam was driving just south of Tushka at the old railroad underpass the road makes a curve, and there was a deep slough. Well, Sam tried to straighten out the curve and wrecked the car upside down in the water. Somehow Tom managed to get out, then he pulled Sam out of the car and held his head up to keep him from drowning. Sam had a broken neck, but thanks to Tom he survived until help arrived. This was when he became my hero.

After receiving his commission, he started training as a paratrooper at Ft. Benning, receiving his jump wings in November, 1943. He also completed ranger training there, then was assigned to the 11th Airborne Division located in the South Pacific.

Shortly after graduation, Tom learned that Gen. Krueger was needing men to volunteer for special mission training and only the fittest and strongest men would be retained for an organization to be called the "Alamo Scouts." Needless to say, Tom asked to receive a tryout and on July 31, 1944 reported as a part of the fourth class at the Alamo Scout Training Center located at Cape

Kasso, New Guinea. It was here that he was schooled in pre-assault reconnaissance, how to collect information on terrain, beach conditions, estimation of enemy troops strength, locations and morale, reporting of enemy coastal shipping, to serve as advance teams, safely guiding a host of hydrographic and topographical experts through the dense jungles and back out again, locating and rescuing downed pilots, displaced civilians and allied prisoners of war. The training was some of the toughest ever undertaken by any American service men. However, out of the 98 men of that class, only Rounsaville and Nellist teams were retained. Within two weeks both teams would be operating on Roemberpon Island off the eastern coast of the Vogelkop.

Within one month, near Cape Orangbari, Dutch New Guinea, he truly proved himself an Alamo Scout and won the Bronze Star. The citation read, "Landing by PT boat, Lt. Rounsaville with a small number of officers and enlisted men, proceeded inland to effect the rescue of 14 Dutch and 52 Javanese being held prisoners of war by the Japanese. Rounsaville within 12 hours had effected the rescue without loss to the party."

Within one month, Rounsaville earned his second bronze star. "As it was nearing Christmas Eve, he commanded a five-man reconnaissance patrol, landed by night on jungle islands near Luzon and reported an estimated 6,000 Japanese troops, provided daily enemy strength information and reported activities on Masbatae Island. This information was boldly obtained often dangerously close to the enemy garrison and under the ever-present danger of capture and inevitable death. With the mission successfully complete, Rounsaville took his men from the island in a sail boat during daylight hours within full view of the enemy."

Tom would win his first silver star as a result of an operation beginning January 27, 1945. There were only 13 men chosen, all Alamo Scouts who were to play a vital part in the rescue of 511 men held prisoner at Cabanatuan Prison, Philippines. They were accompanied by a force of rangers. They arrived at the prison by 10:00 hours on January 30, 1945 and were within 500 yards of the camp. The scouts began to observe the positions of the guard towers, etc., until dark and at 7:45 p.m. they began firing at a shack in the back of the compound. A ranger shot off the lock of the front gate, and the men went pouring in.

Suddenly, a Japanese mortar shell exploded wounding Rounsaville, Alfonso and four Rangers. Rounsaville had gotten a piece of shrapnel in his rear and later Lt. Nellist pulled it out with a pair of pliers. The prisoners started running wild all over the place, but within 30 minutes the evacuation was complete. The scouts withdrew and formed a firing line on the northern bank of the Pampanga River. The Alamo Scouts were to fight a delaying action until all of the prisoners and Rangers had reached safe lines. This surprise action resulted in over 500 Japanese soldiers being killed and no Americans killed and 6 wounded. Tom would write his parents, "We stayed behind to delay Japanese pursuit. We made one hell of a nuisance to the Japanese forces throughout the problem." One of those liberated was Pvt. J.M. Lillard of Caddo, Oklahoma, the uncle of Atoka County Treasurer Richard Lillard.

In a letter home, Tom wrote "Dad, the training you gave me in the woods as a boy is paying off... I carry your name on the field of battle with honest pride."

On May 2, 1945, a combat jump was made into Luzon trying to locate Japanese Gen. Yamashita, but it was to no avail. They found out that he had left earlier by a private car to a plane that took him to Japan. They found out and reported 9,000 Japs still in the area.

Japan signed an unconditional surrender on September 2, 1945, at the time of the signing the Alamo Scouts were making preparations and training for the invasion of Kyushu. On August 6, 1945 the Enola Gay dropped the first atomic bomb on Hiroshima, which was located on Honshu; on August 9 the second bomb was dropped on Nagaski in western Kyushu. On August 13th, the Sixth Army directed all Alamo Scouts teams in the field to cease operations and to return to their training center. Incidentally, the code name for the invasion was "Operation Olympic."

Rounsaville would accompany General Walter Krueger to Kyotoa where Sixth Army Headquarters was located in the Daiken Building. The Alamo Scouts were attached to the 6th Ranger Battalion for quarters and rations, but had few or no occupational duties. The Scouts were formally de-activated on October 10, 1945, and Tom chose to make a visit home. A total of 21 officers and 117 enlisted men were allowed to wear the Alamo Scout patch. There were only some 600 hundred of the patches made and issued; in 1994 one patch was worth over $500. My researcher for several of my articles, Ditters Cole, has one patch that was in his father's possession, and we have no idea how he acquired it.

Tom came home to visit his parents and friends; one of the first people he got with was his old friend Sam Cartwright. They had not seen each other in over three and a half years, so they decided to celebrate by buying a box of cigars, driving to Leighi, Oklahoma and purchasing several quarts of their famous "Chock Beer." It was then that they proceeded to try and find some of their old friends from high school and B Co. comrades.

Rounsaville decided to stay in the army and was assigned to a couple bases here in the states. He went to one of the airborne camps and was promoted to the rank of captain. While he was stationed there, he received a personal letter of gratitude and thanks for a job well done from President Harry S. Truman.

During the time the Alamo Scouts were in existence, they performed 106 known reconnaissance-intelligence missions without a single Scout being killed or captured. Their contribution can still be seen today as military textbooks and lessons have been devised on amphibious warfare, scouting, patrolling, intelligence collection, raiding and guerrilla operations. In 1988 the Alamo Scouts were finally awarded the Special Forces Tab and recognized by the JFK Special Warfare Center and School as a forerunner of The Special Forces. At Fort Bragg, N.C. is located the John F. Kennedy Special Warfare Center and School. They have a Hall of Fame, and one of those enshrined is Col. Tom Rounsaville.

When the Korean War broke out, Rounsaville was sent to Japan, supposedly to rejoin the 187 Airborne RCT; however, by the time he arrived, he was assigned as a company commander in the 1st Cavalry Division in Korea. The cavalry needed experienced combat officers as they had taken quite a beating. Tom arrived in Korea in November, 1950 and shortly was promoted to major.

Col. Lon Robert Fink, a long-time friend of Tom's from high school, tells about Rounsaville's Korean experience:

"I feel at a loss trying to add to all the known information about Col. Tom Rounsaville. There are so many incidents of his service from his enlistment in the Oklahoma Army National Guard-Co. B 180 Inf. 45 Inf. Division through WWII, Korea and Vietnam to include many responsible assignments in tactical units, service schools, training commands plus many more. Col. Rounsaville's WWII feats as a part of the Alamo Scouts is a classic within itself!

"From the day of mobilization (of the Oklahoma Army National Guard) until recent years, I was well aware of Col. Tom's achievements both militarily and "off duty." Never have I known an individual whose activities were so closely monitored. Through my close and frequent association with brothers Speck and Glo Rounsaville, his uncles Big Tom and Carl, and our friend Hoyle Strickland, I learned that to these five there was no soldier like Tom Rounsaville. (Note: the Rounsaville family always referred to Uncle Tom as "Big Tom" and Col. Tom as "Little Tom.") As Glo remarked during the gathering of "the Rounsaville clan" earlier this year, "Big Tom" weighed about 130 lbs. while "Little Tom" weighed about 230 lbs.

"Personally I kept track of Col. Tom for better than 30 years. I never had the pleasure of serving with him, but had many close friends that knew him well.

"I had the pleasure this spring of talking to Col. Tom for many hours, reliving and sharing military experiences to include training, combat and some "off-duty" escapades. Our conversation centered on Tom's experiences during WWII and Korea. Since his days with "the Alamo Scouts" has been covered in print, I would like to write of Col. Tom's Korean experience with the 1st Cavalry Division (while he served as an executive officer, battalion commander and G3 operations and training as Division level). I guess what I would like to cover is his role in the retrograde movement from the Chinese border to position, quite a distance south in South Korea.

"The 1st Cavalry Division along with other organizations were in the path of the Chinese hordes bent on pushing the allies out of

Korea. Tom was the executive officer of an infantry battalion taking the brunt of the attack. The allies were forced to withdraw.

"As is a well known fact, some troops were in a "bug-out" situation. Included in these troops was the battalion commander of Tom's battalion. Seems as though he found a tank that was operative minus a crew. The battalion commander drove that tank south, not stopping for "wood, water or coal." This left Tom "holding the bag" all alone. He organized his troops and started fighting a delaying action. He was sure all of his men were fighting as they should. Tom made a point to tell me his unit took all their crew-served weapons and utilized them. Each time they fell back to another delaying position, all of the machine guns, mortars, anti-tank guns, bazookas, etc. were taken with them.

"When a line of consolidation was established, Tom had 300 men (fighting men) and all their crew-served weapons. Other organizations left their crew-served weapons in place and "bugged out" without them. Also during the retrograde movement Tom's units crossed the airport in North Korea where war supplies had been stockpiled. There had been no attempt to remove or destroy supplies, i.e. weapons, ammunition, fuel, food and other supplies that would be required. Tom said they had a deuce and half truck that they kept throughout the engagement. He told his men to take any food they wanted and load it on the truck. He said evidently one man liked olives, since he selected a five-gallon bucket of black olives.

"Tom said all the weapons, vehicles and ammunition were left behind for the Chinese to use on them later. He reported that there were a large number of tanks parked there, and he personally dropped a thermos grenade down the muzzle of each gun which destroyed the firing mechanism of each tank. Tom said, 'They may be able to run over us with those tanks, but they sure could not fire the guns.' When the battalion commander arrived back at the 1st Cav. Division C.P., he reported to the commanding general that he was the only one left of the battalion. The commanding general replied, 'That's odd, Rounsaville is up there with 300 Indians.'

"Tom Rounsaville was the greatest soldier I've known. Here was a man who liked war, born to be a military leader and lived 100 years too late . . . had Tom Rounsaville lived in the 19th Century, he would have been a great "soldier of fortune" and involved in every war occurring in the world."

This action Fink told of was in the Sinmarc Area, near the Yalu River, near the end of November, 1950. Tom was wounded and decorated for bravery while serving in Korea. Once recovered from his wounds in Japan, he was assigned duty in the states.

In 1953 Rounsaville was assigned as Commandant of Cadets of the ROTC program at his old alma mater, Oklahoma A&M College in Stillwater. He served in this capacity as commandant until 1956. It just so happened that his younger brother, Glo Rounsaville, was a member of the Cadet Corps. On one of the first VIP inspections, Tom gave his brother 25 demerits for the soles of his shoes not shining. This meant that Glo had to go to the Armory and clean 25 rifles. Tom kept trying to get his brother to take his commission in the army. However, when Glo graduated, he took his commission as a second lieutenant in the US Air Force. Glo, himself, made a career in the military and is now retired as a lieutenant colonel.

Tom was assigned to the War College at Carlisle Barracks, Pennsylvania. Somewhere during this time he was promoted to lieutenant colonel and assigned to the Command General Staff School in Ft. Leavenworth, Kansas.

In May, 1963 he became J-3 at MacDill Air Force Base in

Florida and was shortly promoted to full colonel. He became the chief of staff of Joint Task Force Eleven - U.S. Army, a position he held until May 1966. It was during this time he went to Vietnam for a short period, and we have no idea for what reason.

In May, 1966 he was assigned as chief of staff at Fort Gordon Georgia. It was here that Lt. Col. Scott Wells was sent to a MP Officer Advance School, and he called his old friend Tom. Scott said that Tom "would send a sedan over to pick me up to take me to his home." My fellow officer would say, "You must know somebody." Wells went on to say, "He should have been a general and the commander of Desert Storm." Scott added, "To soldier with guys like Tom, Slick, Sam, John Henry Turner, Doc Dean and others has been a high water mark for me."

Something else unusual happened in Tom's military career while he was in command of the strike force. He had part in planning a surprise raid deep into the Belgium Congo to rescue some white missionaries. Tom took a C-119 or C-130 and a few Special Forces men, flew into the area unannounced, landed and took control of the airport, loaded the hostages and was airborne again in something like 30 minutes. He never lost a man or had anyone wounded during this raid. Incidentally, some years later the Israel commandos pulled the same type of raid in Uganda. They apparently patterned themselves after the Rounsaville raiding party.

After the assignment with the Strike Force, Tom was sent as chief of staff of the Command General School at Ft. Leavenworth, Kansas. He retired there in 1972 after almost 32 years of service, having been awarded the following decorations:
- 2 Purple Hearts for wounds in World War II and Korea
- 2 Combat Infantrymen badges
- 5 Bronze Stars
- 2 Silver Stars
- 3 Legion of Merits
- Bravery Gold Medal of Greece
- Asiatic-Pacific Ribbon

- Army Commendation Medal
- Army of Occupation Medal
- Philippine Liberation Ribbon
- Joint Service Commend. Medal
- United Nations Medal
- The Norwegian Cross
- Korean Service Medal
- Distinguished Unit Citation
- 4 Overseas Bars
- Expert Carbine Medal
- Republic of Korea Presidential Medal
- Master Parachutist Badge with over 500 jumps

During his military tenure, he completed his degrees from Oklahoma State University and a masters in international law from George Washington University.

Sgt. Perry Ray and I were talking when he said, "You know, it would have been something to serve with a unit that Tom commanded. He was unusual in that he helped plan missions, led men to the mission, accomplished the mission and brought his men back safely. He was truly a leader ahead of his time."

Tom is now gone on to his reward but he has left something for each of his countrymen plus a bundle of good thoughts for those who knew him. He was laid to rest with full military honors; the Honor Guard has ceased firing and they have played Taps for my boyhood hero. Rest well, Colonel, from a grateful nation.

Writers note: If you wish to know more about Col. Tom Rounsaville, may we suggest books entitled Hour of Redemption, Raid on Cabanatuian and Silent Warriors of World War II and newspapers and periodicals *Indian Citizen Democrat* 5-31-45, *Atoka County Times* 8-1988 (courtesy of the *Daily Oklahoman*), *Dallas Times Herald* 12-1-1967, *Saturday Evening Post* 6-30-1945, and the *Jeffersonian* 11-9-1950.

I would like to thank Col. Lon Robert Fink, Lt. Col. Scott Wells, Sgt. Perry Ray, Lt. Col. Glo Rounsaville and my associates Ditters Cole and Connie Johnston Zalenski who together made this story possible. Thanks gang.

CHAPTER 29

He Disappeared at the Battle of the Bulge

This patriot was involved in one of the major battles of World War II, a conflict that very few know anything about, yet had the allies not won this dramatic battle, the war in Europe would have been in grave danger of being lost. This engagement happened in December, 1944 and January, 1945 in the Ardennes Forest of Belgium and Luxembourg. It is now known as "The Battle of the Bulge." A great sacrifice was made here by both the German Army and the Allied Forces.

One of the participants in this famous battle was a 22-year-old corporal, acting squad leader, Albert L.C. Yandell of Bentley, Oklahoma. L.C. was born in Roaring Springs, Texas, in 1922 to Jack and Rosie Yandell, one of 13 children. In the middle 1930s, his family settled on an 80-acre tract of land in rural Atoka County in the Black Jack, Bentley area. The family managed to weather the great depression and during the first part of World War II, L.C. moved to Holdenville, Oklahoma to learn the trade of auto body work from his brother-in-law, John Dossett.

It was while living in Holdenville that he met his bride-to-be, Miss Edna McGee. The two of them were married in 1942 and shortly thereafter, L.C. enlisted in the U.S. Army. He would be trained at Camp Gordon, Georgia and Ft. Benning, Georgia as a combat infantryman, learning all of the skills of ground warfare and the firing of various weapons. He was assigned to a newly created 10th Armored Division, known as "The Tiger Division," as a member of Co. J, 55th Armored Engineer Battalion.

In November, 1943, L.C.'s wife, Edna, made him the proud father of a baby girl, Linda Carol. He saw his new daughter only a couple of times before he was shipped overseas to the European Theater of Operation. His unit landed in England in September, 1944, then his division was transported across the English Channel to France. They joined Patton's 3rd Army for the drive across Northern France towards Germany. They were a part of the breakout, and no unit could move fast enough for Patton. His division saw combat in France, Belgium, Luxembourg and Germany in 1944 and 1945.

Let's go to the Ardennes Forest where the Allied Forces had a MLR (Main Line Resistance) or a front line that was some 242 miles in length, reaching from the English Channel-North Sea in Holland to the Black Forest in Germany. Hitler knew that unless something drastic was done, the Nazis would lose the war and everything they had conquered since the beginning of their invasion of Poland in 1939.

Hitler decided on a last-minute gamble, feeling that the Americans were over confident and perhaps overextended. His generals devised an offensive plan called "Wacht An Rein," meaning Watch on the Rhine. It was a well-planned offensive move that caught the Allies flat-footed. The Germans had called in 24 of their most experienced battle-hardened divisions for this assault. They even had their men in white camouflage clothing and some English-speaking SS Troopers who infiltrated the American lines as U.S. soldiers.

Adolph Hitler had decided that the weakest point in the line was the American 1st Army under Lt. Gen. Courtney Hodges and that the U.S. 99th Infantry Division would be the initial target as they were spread from Monsehau to Loshein. They were right and where they struck was called Colmar Pocket.

Hitler's plans were to launch his offensive, hoping to reach the Meuse River by the third day of the drive. The Germans had massed 38 divisions for this assault, and they were to pursue a two-pronged attack along a 50 mile battle line with one attack springing from near Dusseldorf, Germany toward Antwerp, Belgium and the other to Dijon, thus encircling the Allied Armies West of the Mesuse River.

Ironically, American reconnaissance units by photo reported in early November, 1944, showing heavy rail activity both east and west of the Rhine River, detecting railroad flat cars crammed with trucks, tanks and ambulances. Marshaling yards were crowded west of the Rhine, piles of supplies and lumber stacks were spotted, a column of infantry moving near Monshau, over 120 vehicles moving from Heimbach, yet nothing aroused G-3 or G-2 interest. It was intelligence at Frastructer and the Allied High Command failing to communicate with each other that started this disaster.

At 5:30 a.m. December 16, 1944, at the snow covered village of Hosingen, along what was known as Skyline Drive, the darkness suddenly became alive with a maelstrom of bursting shells. (This is also known as front of St. Vith.) The Germans struck primarily at an area of the Losheim Gap that was defended by the 14th Cavalry Group consisting of some 800 men. The commander had no experience, and shortly the group was destroyed. The 106th Division consisting of green troops with no combat experience had just arrived from England and replaced the 2nd Division with some 16,000 men. The 106th engaged the Germans in combat the first day with the 422nd, 423rd and 424th Infantry Regiments and due to the lack of leadership, they had over 6,500 men captured on their first day of combat, thus the initial bulge in the line moving backwards into Belgium.

The commander of the VIII Corps, General Troy Middleton, once the commander of the 45th Division, was running distressingly low on troops and on the morning of December 17 started moving his men to try and stop the bulge the Germans had made in the line. With precious little time to delay, two German Divisions long enough to move L.C.'s outfit, the 10th Armored and the 101st Airborne Division, moved to Bastonge, hoping to get there by December 18. That night the 10th Armored reached a town by the name of Longvilly on the Belgium-Luxembourg border and was welcomed by the Germans dropping mortar shells most of the evening. The 10th Armored Unit that was sent out for roadblocks from Longvilly was evidently L.C.'s with a code name Team Cherry, consisting of one medium tank company, two light tank platoons, the 20th Armored Infantry Battalion with recon troops, engineers and medics.

Gen. Morris, commander of the 10th Armored, was now to be committed to Luxembourg to work with the 4th Division and recover the territory lost in the last three days. The morning of the 19th a major battle brewed with the smaller, light-weight American tanks and infantry plus engineers becoming the victims of the dreaded "Screaming Memmie" German 88MM artillery pieces. All tankers and infantrymen hated to see this weapon as it was the German's most accurate and powerful artillery piece, and these weapons were firing directly at the tanks. L.C.'s column was under heavy shell-fire, and the men left their vehicles to take up defensive positions. After the artillery barrage was lifted, a search was made for L.C., but he could not be found.

An eyewitness to this tragedy, Sgt. Jack Sanborn, would write a letter to the Yandells from Parnissh-Pasternkirehen, Germany stating, "The Germans counter-attacked, and they were throwing 88 and mortar fire at us. They came too close to the squad L.C.

was in, and he ran to an American tank that was close by. We didn't see L.C. come out and afterwards, when we were able, we went to look for him. The only thing we found were the badly broken bones of three men. So the army classified him as missing in action."

By the middle of January, 1945, the Allies had recovered all of the territory that had been lost, and once again the drive was made towards Berlin. Bastogne was encircled by the Germans, but never fell into their hands. By the middle of January, 1945, the trap was broken. The cost of the battle was high in lives as the Germans had lost over 100,000 killed and wounded and some 110,000 had been taken prisoner, while Allied losses were 19,000 men. Some months later, L.C. was declared by the Department as having been killed in action.

L.C.'s widow married Bill Huff, and they would have five children of their own. Bill was asked one time by Linda, L.C.'s daughter, as to why she never adopted the Huff name. Bill answered, "The Yandell family has always been there for you. Your dad fought honorably in war. You should keep his name."

L.C.'s body was never found, not even his dog tags; however, at the request of the family, the Department of Defense sent a grave marker, and it is placed along side the gravestone for Bill and Edna Huff. This marks the place where he would have been buried.

We owe a great deal of gratitude to our patriot willing to give his life at the age of 22 years, leaving a young wife and his 13-month-old daughter. This young family sacrificed everything for us. In case you are wondering, this daughter of Albert L.C. Yandell still lives in Atoka; Miss Linda Yandell is Mrs. Maurice Jackson, one of our dedicated school teachers.

Even though L.C. didn't get to come home, no flag ever

draped a coffin for him, no firing squad was ever heard and no taps ever blown. He is a patriot of the highest order. We all owe him!

Writer's Notes: The following are some of the outfits that fought in the Battle of the Bulge, and you can identify that some of your kinfolks were there: 3rd Armored Division, 4th Armored Division, 6th Armored Division, 7th Armored Division, 9th Armored Division, 10th Armored Division, 11th Armored Division, 1st Infantry Division, 2nd Infantry Division, 4th Infantry Division, 5th Infantry Division, 8th Infantry Division, 9th Infantry Division, 26th Infantry Division, 28th Infantry Division, 30th Infantry Division, 35th Infantry Division, 66th Infantry Division, 75th Infantry Division, 78th Infantry Division, 80th Infantry Division, 83rd Infantry Division, 84th Infantry Division, 87th Infantry Division, 90th Infantry Division, 106th Infantry Division and the 101st Airborne (which became known as "The Battling Bastards of Bastongne").

Here are some of the men I knew who were involved with the The Battle of the Bulge: John Cole of Bentley, Dale "CID" Wilson, Lon Robert Fink, Leo K. Williams all of Atoka, Slick White, Buck Coates, John David Whitten and Samp Nichols of Lane. There were several others whose names I can't remember.

If you wish to know more about this battle, may we suggest the following reading: A Time for Trumpets by Charles B. McDonald; Nuts, The Battle of the Bulge by Donald Goldstein; The Battle Story of the 10th Armored Division by Lester M. Nichols; Company Commander by Charles McDonald and Battle of the Bulge by John Tolar.

CHAPTER 30

"Groucho Marx" Wins the Navy Cross for Heroism in Vietnam

Most people have heard of the Congressional Medal of Honor, our nation's highest medal that can be awarded for bravery in the face of the enemy, but very few know that if you are a member of the Navy or Marines that the second highest honor to be awarded is the Navy Cross. Our portrait this week is of a local man who won the Navy Cross for his bravery in Vietnam.

In addition to having received this distinction, he is one of the few men to ever have a battle named for him. This portrait is of First Sgt. Billy Marvin Donaldson, United States Marine, retired, a resident of Atoka, Oklahoma.

Let us look at a short period of time in this man's life. He was born March 6, 1936, at Valliant, Oklahoma. When he was very young, his family moved to the small community of Carter, in Beckham County, Oklahoma, where he would attend and receive a GED from Ocina High School. He answered the Marine recruiting ad of "needing a few good men" and enlisted on March 23, 1954 at the age of 18.

Bill was thought to have leadership potential and graduated from the NCO Leadership School in 1958. In 1960 he reported to the Army Paratrooper Training School at Ft. Benning, Georgia and received his Jump Wings. In 1961 he completed Patrolling School and in 1962 became an instructor in the school that he had just completed. The year of 1965 found Bill going through Scuba Diving and Demolition Training; later, he was an instructor in this school.

Bill was assigned to Vietnam, where he became a member of Team 61, 6th Platoon, 1st Force Recon. based out of Dong Ha. On an earlier mission, Bill had been decorated with a Bronze Star for valor in combat with the North Vietnamese Army (NVA).

The mission that we wish to tell you about began on August 6, 1966 at 19:00 hours as a four-man team led by then S/Sgt. Bill Donaldson left base Dong Ha in a Huey VMO-2 helicopter for a 12-mile trip to an area known as Razorback Valley. Bill's group answered to the call of "Groucho Marx" for all contact. They departed from the chopper and proceeded into the dense jungle with enough rations and water to sustain them for three days. The mission assigned was to observe and maintain surveillance of the main valley running east-west through the area of operation; capture one prisoner, and be prepared to call supporting arms on enemy targets of opportunity.

They proceeded towards their harbor site and at some 23:00 hours they heard voices in the valley and movement in the undergrowth. At 11:00 hours on the next day, Bill could hear voices and smell camp fires, so he called in artillery then departed the immediate area. The second night out they could smell the odor of livestock (water buffalo) and could feel the NVA soldiers within 100-150 feet of them throughout the night.

On the morning of August 7, the team heard voices in the valley below them, so they again called in artillery. The NVA immediately dispatched patrols to search for them, and at times the enemy came within 50 feet. The patrol passed by and the team called for more artillery and fired WP rifle grenades to mark the NVA position so the helicopter gun ships could come and strafe.

    Quietly speaking into his radio mike the morning of the 7th, Bill "Groucho Marx" continued to call the NVA position to Cam Lo for artillery fire and reported back, "Coverage good." The helicopter gun ships then came in for several strafing passes over the area then turned east headed back to Dong Ha. Bill's team congratulated themselves but knew they would have to leave the area swiftly as the NVA now knew spotters were in the area. As they had determined, the enemy was battalion size of some 400-500 NVA soldiers.

    At 09:00 hours on August 8, daylight prompted an increased effort by the NVA to locate the recons. The valley was huge and till this time, they were well hidden by thick vegetation. The enemy patrols came within 50 meters of "Groucho Marx," so Donaldson called in the artillery once again. The recon team could hear the screams of the NVA, indicating that the high explosive rounds had impacted right on target. Bill knew now that the enemy would really intensify their search so he radioed for help from the helicopter gun ships.

    At 10:00 hours a pair of Huey copters made contact but could not locate the recon team in the tall grass, and Donaldson was afraid that if they fired "pop smoke," it would give their position away; so he fired white phosphorus grenades towards the enemy.

    Meanwhile, back at Dong Ha, it was decided to extract the patrol, but the only suitable landing spot was 150 meters away from where "Groucho Marx" was located. It was decided to send in a reaction force of 40 men to help get them out. Bill advised against this, but they sent in the force anyway.

    At 12:15 hours the reaction force was on the ground and made contact with Bill. This force was under the command of a new second lieutenant. Immediately, Bill told him to set up a defense perimeter and dig in fighting holes with their backs towards a rather large rocky hill that they called the "Rockpile". For some time that afternoon, it was thought that the NVA had vanished as the marine "Grunts" poked and probed through the thick up-growth within 200 meters of the "Rockpile."

By the middle of the afternoon, a command decision was made that the four men of the recon team and the 40 members of reaction force would be extracted from the valley. They went about securing a small landing zone for the helicopters to land, but just as the first chopper began to settle down they received heavy automatic weapons fire. Then four H-34 choppers came in to lay down fire in order to help get the one aircraft off the ground that had taken on board twenty of the marine "Grunts."

On the ground the rate of fire became more intensified. The young second lieutenant waved off the second chopper that was going to try to come in and get the other 24 men in the area. The remaining marines moved, making a hasty withdrawal back towards the knoll where they had freshly dug holes. They had some two hours of daylight left, plenty of ammo and felt they could defend the knoll. They didn't have long to wait when a company of NVA tried to assault the marines' position. Almost 200 enemy soldiers charged the 24 marines, as they poured out of the jungle and began to run up the side of the knoll, shooting and throwing hand grenades. Everyone was firing, yelling, screaming; the overwhelming noise of the battle rose to a deafening fiasco. The NVA attacked, so they fell back to regroup, waited for reinforcement and then to charge the knoll again.

The enemy attacked again, and the small number of marines were successful in their defense for the second time; however, the young second lieutenant had been killed, and Bill was now in command. The NVA rushed the sides of the "Rockpile" knoll for the third time and again were unsuccessful. During the engagement, Sgt. Pace had been shot in the head so the command of the "Grunts" and recons fell to Bill, the "Groucho Marx" patrol leader.

Daylight and their ammo were both running out, and the desperate garrison radioed Dong Ha, "You had better hurry." Just before dark, the front part of the marine perimeter was hit hard by a constant hand grenade attack, and one of the grenades fell among Bill and some of his men. Bill, without thought of himself, picked up the grenade and threw it, but it exploded just as it left his hand. The shrapnel from the explosion went to Bill's right arm and shoulder, wounding him in his right arm and the right side of his head. His wound was so severe that he could not use his right arm nor his left hand.

They knew with darkness coming that they had to move further back up on the "Rockpile." Somehow, Bill managed to crawl back up towards the top of the knoll and fell in a hole with a young marine. They could see this one NVA soldier crawling towards them with a sack of grenades and Bill, unable to hold a weapon, told the young marine to throw a grenade at the attacker but the "Grunt" shot him instead when he was some 12 to 15 feet from their hole.

The battle ensued throughout the night into the next morning. The next morning, August 9, at 07:10 hours, a silver-gray marine A-4 Skyhawk came out of the dawn, headed down the valley and laid down a phosphorus smoke screen between the marines and the enemy on the north ridgeline. Then a flight of H-34 choppers began to come in with relief troops. The "Groucho Marx Battle" was now over and a part of history. This small handful of marines had a body count of 37 dead NVA soldiers inside their perimeter, and it was estimated that the enemy had pulled 100 plus men back into the jungle. The marine losses of the 44 men involved in the battle were 5 dead, 35 wounded and four who managed to make it through the fight unscratched.

Donaldson was air-lifted to Dong Ha then to Da Nang then to Clark Air Force Base in the Philippines and finally flown to a hospital in California.

The Marine Corps would honor Sgt. Bill Donaldson in two ways. First, he was one of a very few marines to have a battle named after him. History now knows of "The Groucho Marx Battle" named after Bill's radio call name. Bill was also awarded the Navy Cross for risking his life to save his men by being willing to give up his own life when he got rid of that hand grenade.

Bill stayed in the Marines and retired as a first sergeant on September 3, 1973. He, his wife Shuzie and three children moved to the Atoka area to pursue his interest and love of horses. If you don't know Bill Donaldson, you should, as this is truly a great man and is definitely a patriot.

CHAPTER 31

He Helped Secure the Victory at Iwo Jima

Most of us have heard about the Pacific Battle of the Japanese-held island of Iwo Jima and the raising of the American flag on Mount Suribachi, a 550-foot extinct volcano that dominates the topography of the little island. The island is just a little over four and one-half miles long and some two and one-half miles wide, yet this tiny dot in the Pacific was of great importance to the Allied forces that it must be taken regardless of the cost. This portrait is of a 19-year-old marine from Atoka who was a part of the force assigned to take the island, PFC Morris Carr, the son of Mack and Celia Roach Carr.

Morris answered his country's call "for a few good men" in Dallas, Texas, on December 9, 1943, becoming a member of the United States Marine Corps. I have always kidded Morris that the reason he joined the Marines was because the women thought that to be the prettiest service uniform. He was immediately sent to basic training at San Diego, California, then shipped to Camp Pendleton, California for seven months of advanced training. It was here he became a member of a new outfit the Marines were forming called the 5th Marine Division. Carr became a member of I Co., 3rd Battalion, 26th Marine Regiment, 5th Division.

About September, 1944, they were shipped out supposedly to meet with a task force to go to Saipan then on to Guam; however, when they had been at sea for some two weeks, their orders were changed. They were sent to Hilo, Hawaii, to train for some four to five months on what was called the Parker Ranch.

One day they received orders again to board transports and were told this time it was the real thing. They finally learned that their destination was the island of Iwo Jima containing two full airfields and another almost completed. Intelligence had said that Iwo was well fortified and defended. Little did they know that the Japanese had some 22,000 soldiers stationed there and were committed to fight to death for their Emperor. Our intelligence did not know the extent to which the enemy had prepared themselves with tunnels and deep shelters. The Japanese had some 20,000 light guns and machine guns, over 22,000,000 rounds of ammo and 22 tanks, all on this relatively little strip. The enemy also had fire markers covering the entire island, so they could rapidly know the exact point to call for fire. They understood that this piece of rock in the Pacific was only 800 miles from Japan and was very vital to the defense of their homeland. Our troops were told that the island was vital to us, because we needed those airfields for our B-29 bombers to fly off of to strike anywhere in the group of Japanese Islands.

The decision was made that the first part of the amphibious landing would be made on February 19, 1945 at 0900 hours, and the first units to go ashore were elements of the 4th and 5th Marine Divisions under the command of General Holland Smith. Before the assault began, for several days the navy had bombarded the island to soften up the defense. Because of all the tunnels and bunkers that had been built by the Japanese, all of the firing had done very little to destroy the enemy defenses.

Meanwhile, the Marine landing party was getting ready to go over the sides of their transports, down the cargo nets and into the Higgins boats to one of the worst experiences of their lives. Once in the Higgins landing craft, they began to go in a circle with the rough seas picking up and slapping the flat bottom plywood boats roughly on the high swells. Men were getting sea-sick, then the boat coxmen told them they were going in and when they felt him hit the shallow beach to get out as soon as possible.

Some of the men making this landing had fought at Guam, Saipan and Guadalcanal, so they had an idea of what was to come. The landing craft headed towards Green Beach, and Morris said that he had never been so scared in his life. But it got worse when the Higgins boat ramp went down, and they were greeted by enemy mortars and machine gun fire. They lost several men of the platoon just as they left the boat and those who successfully got ashore were over-laden by all of the equipment they were carrying. Morris said with his pack and weapon, he had about 100 extra pounds, not to mention the fact that he was the one designated in the platoon to carry a 15-pound explosive satchel; however, the man that was overloaded was the one assigned to the flame-thrower.

They got out of the water and on to the beach but could hardly move as they were lying in the sand while trying to get out of that burdensome equipment they had strapped on their bodies—and all this while under enemy fire. The first day they got inland from the waters edge about 200 yards and spent the night digging in the sand on the beach to get some protection from the fire they were receiving from the Japs. Morris said it was the loneliest feeling, lying in the dark with the ocean behind you and the enemy in front of you with a decision which way to go. Keep in mind they could not get up and move.

The second day of the invasion, the Navy big guns off shore and our fighter planes were trying to help them get off of the beach, so finally they were able to start moving inland. They had taken so many casualties that they now sent the 3rd Marine Division to help the assault up towards the airstrips. Tanks were brought in on Green Beach to give the infantrymen something to shield themselves while they tried going up the hills; however, the tanks became bogged down in the volcanic ash.

It took three days of determined fighting before they captured a plateau on the northern part of the island and made a small dent in the enemy fortifications. They finally got some tanks with flame-throwers to stand up on ground to incinerate the Japanese in their caves and bunkers. Some of the men became deathly sick from smelling the badly burned enemy bodies.

On February 26, 1945, Morris was advancing up a hill with his fellow Marines when they had to hit the dirt from a grenade attack, and he was wounded in both legs. He managed to crawl some 50 yards to the Company CP where they got a Navy Corpsman to help him with his wounds. They put him in a Higgins boat with other wounded and ferried them to a transport named the U.S.S. Dark.

The hospital ship was full so they had to use what medical facilities that were available on the transport. They brought Morris aboard the ship on a stretcher and placed him on the deck. Shortly, he watched them bring in his company commander, Capt. Charles Eusey, and placed his stretcher along side of Morris. The Captain had been wounded in the throat right after they had evacuated Morris. Capt. Eusey died there right beside Morris; he watched as they wrapped his captain's body in sail cloth and placed two empty shell casings inside the cloth. He heard them say a few words over the body and saw them place the body on a board and gently slide it into the waters of the Pacific.

They would take this load of wounded to Guam where they were housed in hospital tents. A little later, Morris was taken aboard a C-54 aircraft and flown to Hawaii. He was transferred to a liberty ship at Pearl Harbor, headed immediately for the San

Francisco-Oakland Hospital, then finally to Portsmouth, Virginia for additional medical treatment.

The open resistance on Iwo Jima was finished by March 10, 1945; however, it was not until March 25, 1945 that the battle was finally over. The Marines had lost 6,000 killed and 17,000 wounded, while the Japanese lost over 21,000 killed and only 216 captured.

Morris was discharged from the Marines on July 24, 1945 and immediately was considered disabled due to his wounds. He returned to his home on the Mack Carr Ranch in the Wards Chapel area just west of Atoka and has spent the biggest part of his time here ever since.

Morris was a young man who was willing to give his life for his country and is definitely a patriot.

Writer's Note: I know of two other young Marines from Atoka who were wounded severely in the Battle of Iwo Jima: Hoyt Lee and Doyce Burke, both now deceased. Capt. Eusey we mentioned as buried at sea was awarded the Navy Cross for his bravery on Green Beach. Incidentally, Capt. Eusey's son who was born after his father was killed, came to see Morris this past spring to get to know the man who served with his dad.

CHAPTER 32

A Wide Array of Area Patriots

This time let's do something a little different in this column and talk about this and that. Come on in, sit down and let's eyeball each other while discussing some things that you may not know about the patriots from the Atoka area.

Now while we are talking about those individuals that are part of our lives, I want you to understand that to the best of my knowledge and ability, we have vigorously endeavored to obtain the names and events mentioned. If we have excluded anyone, we deeply regret as we just simply did not have any other information at this time.

Did you know? . . .

The first man called by the Atoka County Draft Board for service in the U.S. Army at the beginning of the Korean War was W.J. Mulkey who received his greetings on July 27, 1950.

The first area man involved in fighting in Korea was PFC William Mead of Lane, a member of Co. B, 21st Infantry Regiment, 24th Division, who was there when the war broke out. Mead was wounded in October, 1950 and rotated back to the states in February, 1951.

The first area man taken prisoner during the "Korean Police Action" was SFC Walton "Bunt" Wilson of Crystal. A member of the 24th Infantry Division, Wilson was taken prisoner by the North Koreans in July, 1950 and about six hours after his capture, while being marched north by the Koreans with some 40 other men, an American plane began strafing the road they were on, so they all dove for the bar ditches along each side of the road. Walton and two other men rolled down a hill and escaped. The next day, while trying to find their way back to the American lines, they came upon the men they had been captured with and each one of them had been shot.

While we are talking about "Ole Bunt," here is a little thumbnail sketch of his military life. He was in World War II, Korea and in Vietnam also served as the Protocol NCO at the American Embassies in Iran and Formosa. He retired as a sergeant major from the army and received the Purple Heart twice, Silver Star, Bronze Star, Combat Infantry Badge twice and numerous campaign ribbons. He was wounded in World War II and Korea.

The first area man killed in Korea was 17-year-old PFC Joe Charles Hamlin. He was captured August 2, 1950 and found shot to death with his hands tied behind his back.

PFC William S. Muncy was reported as killed in action but was found some time later in a military hospital in Hot Springs, Ark. very much alive.

P.C. "Preacher" York was reported missing in action in Korea as of July 27, 1950 from his unit, the 24th Infantry Division. York, a member of the World War II famous "Battling Bastards of Bastgone," was cut off behind enemy lines but managed to find the American lines on October 5, 1950.

Cpl. Dean Armstrong, USMC, though wounded, walked out of the Chinese trap at Changjin Reservoir to the port of Hungnam, where he was taken aboard ship and sent to Japan. Dean became a "Gunny" sergeant and made the marines his career. He had 17 years in the corps and was on his third tour in Vietnam when he was killed; he is buried in Denver, Colorado.

PFC Tommy Jeff Williams was the first member of the 45th

MP Company decorated with the Soldiers Medal for bravery in Korea. Jeff rescued two members of the 45th Signal Company who had walked through a marked mine field, opened a door to a hut and both were wounded by a booby trap. Tommy ran into the mine field and brought both men out. Tommy was 18 years old and would have been a senior in high school.

Lt. Laverne Collins was the first area man killed in World War II as he was shot down over the English Channel on September 19, 1942.

PFC John J. "Cue-Ball" Bennett was the first man from Atoka's Company B, 180th Inf., 45th Division killed July 10, 1943 in Sicily. "Cue-Ball" died trying to knock off a German tank that was coming towards his fellow soldiers of B Company.

T/Sgt. Henry Turner was one of the first men of Co. B, 180th Infantry wounded during the landing on Sicily July 10, 1943.

Capt. Paul York, Company Commander of A Co., formerly a platoon leader of Co. B, 180th Infantry, was the first area man to become a German POW. He was taken prisoner on July 10, 1943 in Sicily.

First Sgt. James "Jabo" McLeroy was the first B Co., 180th Infantry man decorated for bravery having been presented the Silver Star for action during the Battle of Biscari Airport, Sicily on July 11, 1943.

PFC Roy Mead was one of the first soldiers to enter the Dachau Prison Camp at Munich, Germany. Roy was formerly a member of Co. B, 180th, however, he had been transferred to the 157th Infantry. Mead would be with the 45th Division for the entire 511 days of combat, serving with two different infantry companies and received only a small cut from a piece of glass. He was extremely lucky when you consider that the casualty rate of the 45th was 127 percent.

T/5 Scott Wells was the only man from this area who became a famous "Mule Skinner" of the mountainous Italian Campaign. Wells led pack mules up the narrow mountain trails at night in order to supply the men of Co. B with ammo, food, and water. His return trips down the mountains, he transported on the backs of his mules the bodies of the dead and those wounded.

Let me tell you a story about three Atoka High School students who were very good friends, played football together and in 1943 decided to join the U.S. Navy. These three new sailors were James Arthur Sutherland, Hal Gene McAnulty and Zachary Taylor Cartwright. Sutherland became a member of the submarine crew U.S.S. Herring based out of Pearl Harbor; McAnulty became a medical corpsman aboard a ship out of England and Cartwright became a member of the flight crew of Utility Squadron 7 flying PBY-2 patrol recon and photography assignments out of Pearl Harbor. Here is what is unusual about these three buddies when S/3 James Sutherland's submarine left Pearl, the sub never returned from James first mission; PHM/3 Hal Gene McAnulty was aboard naval vessel LST-133 in the English Channel helping with the wounded coming off of the beaches of the D-Day landings of June 6, 1944 when a German plane hit his ship and Hal was killed on his first mission. AMM/3C Cartwright's patrol bomber left Pearl Harbor for his first recon mission when the aircraft was forced to make an emergency landing in the Pacific Ocean. Three men, buddies, all had misfortune on their first missions with two of them meeting death. Cartwright served out the war, returning to Oklahoma to enter the University of Oklahoma. To earn a little extra money, Zack took a commission as a second lieutenant with the 160 F.A. Co., 45th Division. Cartwright's guard enlistment was to expire in 1950, just when the "Korea Conflict" happened, so he joined the U.S. Air Force and eventually was sent to Korea. Zack once again served out his enlistment and joined the Air Force Reserve. He has now retired as a full colonel. He was in the primary zone for promotion as a one-star General when he decided that he was tired of the military politics. Cartwright had served his country as a sailor, a soldier, and an airman -- very unusual.

Let's talk about Atoka men who have been prisoners of war.

Japanese POWs:
    Coats, Clyde, 4-9-1942
        - survived the Bataan Death March
        - was in prison camps in the Philippines and Japan

    Ewing, Richard D., 4-9-1942
        - survived the Bataan Death March
        - was in prison camps in the Philippines and Manchuria

    McFarland, Edward, 4-9-1942
        - survived the Bataan Death March
        - prison camps in Philippines

    Bohannon, Edward, 4-9-1942
        - survived the Bataan Death March
        - prison camps in Philippines

    Lillard, J.M., 4-9-1942
        - survived the Bataan Death March
        - was at Prison Cabanatuan, Philippines when liberated by Lt. Tom Rounsaville's team of "Alamo Scouts" and a force of Rangers on 1-30-1945 - he was one of 511 prisoners liberated and brought through the Japanese lines

German POWs:

Heard, T.J.,
- Wounded 1-22-1945 prisoner in Germany

Dunn, Paul
- Taken in Sicily 7-10-1943

Linton, John
- Wounded and captured by the Germans at Cassino, Italy 12-30-1943 and died in POW camp 1-29-1944

Soules, Bill, Lt.
- Shot down over Metz, France - 4-25-1944

Turner, Alfred, "Cotton,"
- Italy 7-1943 - Co. B, 180th Inf.

Dunn, Charles
- Italy 7-1943 - Co. B, 180th Inf.

Franklin, Jess
- Italy 7-1943 - Co. B, 180th Inf.

Morrow, Bernard G., Lt.

Goss, Herbert

Dodson, Jess

Williams, James I.

White, Claude, Lt.

Maloy, Floyd E.

North Korean POWs

    Smith, Roy, Tushka
    - taken prisoner by the North Koreans, Spring, 1952

    Wilson, Walton "Bunt"
    - Taken prisoner by North Koreans in August, 1950 and "Bunt" managed to escape within six hours after his capture

    Shingleton, John R., Seaman
    - U.S. Navy aboard the U.S.S. Pueblo AKL 44 when it was captured by the North Koreans on 1-23-1968 and declared a "spy ship." His ship was an Oceanographic and Research Vessel that was fired upon in International Waters outside the 12 miles Territorial Limit and boarded by the members of the North Korean Navy. The crew of the Pueblo numbered 83 men and four of those died at the hands of their captors. He was cruelly beaten many times and was told that he was a CIA spy. He was finally released December 20, 1968.

CHAPTER 33

More Area Patriots

Sidney A. Camp was the first and only first sergeant the Atoka original 45th MP Company ever had. He was mobilized in 1940 as a member of Co. F, 120th Medical Regiment, 45th Division in the Capacity of a medical corpsman. In 1942 his company was split off from the 120th Regiment and sent to Panama.

In 1943 his platoon transported to the European Theater of Operation serving in Sicily, Italy, France and Germany. In 1945 Sid came home and when the National Guard started organizing again in Atoka, he was one of the first members to sign up.

In 1950 he was again mobilized with his beloved 45th Thunderbird Division as a part of the 45th Military Police Co. serving Japan and Korea. When he came home in 1952 and the guard was again reinstated in Atoka, one of the first members to enlist was 1/Sgt. Sid Camp. He eventually earned the rating as command sergeant major of the Army National Guard and was named Mr. National Guard of Oklahoma.

There are a bunch of us men from this area who owe a great deal to our sergeant, including helping us to grow up. Quite a man.

Col. Rowe Cook, formerly of Atoka, was the Beachmaster in charge of the 45th Division in Sicily landing of July, 1943.

Col. John "Hicky" McCasland gave the Atoka men the name that became famous world wide when he called us "The Boggy Bottom Boys." In Italy, Hicky got tired of telling outsiders where the men from Atoka called home so he coined this term that has stuck all of these years.

SFC Dale Wilson became a member of the U.S. Army in January, 1943 and received his training at Ft. Belvoir, Virginia, becoming a member of the 346th Engineer Battalion. His unit was a part of the June 6, 1944 D-Day invasion in France, landing with the third wave on the fourth day at Utah Beach. Little did Dale know that one of his high school buddies enlisted in the navy when he went into the army. PHM/3C Hal Gene McAnulty was in the waters of the English Channel aboard LST 133 at the same time and was killed during the landing. Wilson's company was assigned the duties of clearing land mines, removing the thick hedge rows, building bridges and clearing the battle field for movement of both men and equipment.

Most of you have heard of the famous bridge at Remagen on the Rhine River in Germany. Let us look at this bridge as Dale Wilson had a very large part of this successful battle victory. On March 7, 1945, it was reported to Allied Headquarters that the Ludendorff Bridge across the Rhine was still standing and recognizing the enormous opportunity they would have by capturing this bridge, ordered a unit to try and take the Ludendorff. The Germans had attempted to blowup the bridge; however, Lt. John Brentwood crawled under the structure of the bridge and disarmed the explosives that had been placed by the German engineers. The U.S. Army managed to get some 8,000 men across the bridge before Hitler vented his wrath by launching air attacks on the bridge and sent in a Panzer Division of 11,000 men and 60 tanks from Bonn to plug the entry. By March 17, 1945, the Germans had managed to destroy the bridge with the American troops that had crossed trapped on the German side of the Rhine.

The battle was fierce for control and command knew that

they must get some relief for our forces that had their backs to the river and the Rhine must have a crossing. It was then that Wilson's company began to build Bailey Bridges to be pontooned down the river by using small outboard motors. All the time the engineers were putting together these bridges, they were under constant fire of the Germans. Each time they got a bridge in water and started down stream, the Germans would manage to blow it out of the water. After three tries, Dale's company was successful in getting a Bailey in position, anchored ready for use. Immediately four army divisions with tanks managed to get across the newly built crossing thus the route to Central Germany was opened. Many of those brave engineers in Wilson's company died or were wounded in making this crossing possible. If you will pardon the phrase, "these boys went through hell to cross the Rhine."

Wilson came home to Atoka after seeing combat action in France, Battle of the Bulge in Belgium, Luxembourgh and Germany. He was very fortunate as he made it through without being wounded. He was discharged in November 1945.

In September 1950, Dale was mobilized as a part of the 45th MP Company, 45th Infantry Division becoming the head of the Criminal Investigation Department, so naturally we all gave him the nickname of "CID". Wilson would serve in Japan and combat in Korea with the 45th and would return home in the summer of 1952. This is quite a courageous man; "he has been there."

People from outside our beloved Southeastern Oklahoma area have a tendency to "poke fun" due to the way we talk among other things, and laughingly refer to us as hillbillies, whiskey makers, country bumpkins, etc. But let me tell you something, when it comes to defending this country and leading men into battle, we take a back seat to no one. One that shows is our capability in the number of military leaders that "we have grown" by giving you examples of what I mean by just listing some of the officers that the Atoka area has produced:

Generals
JASPER N. BAKER
- Commanding General of the 45th Infantry Division from November 1964 to January 1968, Atoka High graduate also became President of Eastern Oklahoma A&M College.

JAMES C. STYRON
- Commanding General of the 45th Infantry Division from September 1946 to May 1952. He was our commander in Japan and Korea. He was co-owner of Boone-Styron Department Store in Atoka and Caddo.

Colonels
VANCE RICH
JOHN "HICKY" McCASLAND
LON ROBERT FINK
ZACHARY TAYLOR "ZACK" CARTWRIGHT
ROBERT RANDOLPH
ROWE COOK
TOM ROUNSAVILLE
CHARLIE WEAVER
WYLIE CLYDE TURNER
VERNON REEVES
JOHN W. MOORE

Lt. Colonels
SCOTT WELLS
JESSE "ED" GRIST
MARION "CHUCK" HAGGARD
TOMMY JOHNSON
GLO ROUNSAVILLE
JIM POOLE
VINCENT HOWARD

Majors
ROBERT "DOC" DEAN, D.O.
CALVIN MEAD, JR.
TIM COOK
ROYCE BLAKER
LEO K. WILLIAMS
WILLIE BOWMAN
WILBURN CARTWRIGHT
ROBERT G. "BOB" CATES

Captains
HAROLD HEDGES
ERNEST COLE
PAUL HAYES
CHARLES DUNN
WENDELL CATES
STANDFORD DOWNS
DR. W.W. COTTON
CONNER MONTGOMERY
VERNON SEWELL

Lieutenants
BILL PINGLETON
DOMINIC VIETTA
FOREST "SPECK" ROUNSAVILLE
BILL SOULES
RED TURNER
SAMUEL FULTON CARTWRIGHT
JESSE BILLY "SLICK" CARTWRIGHT
BILL PHARR
CLYDE HALL
WILFORD HORN
FLOYD LACK
LEE McKINNEY
OPAL "SHUG" DeARMON
RALPH DUNN
HOWARD ARRINGTON, JR.
MAXINE CHAFFIN
LEWIS C. COOKSEY - USMC
B.R. "RED" COOK, JR.
GEORGE MOFFATT
WALTER PENNINGTON, JR.
DELBERT ROUNSAVILLE
JIMMY PRAYTOR
JOE D. FUGATE
LARRY KENNEDY

Warrant Officers
EDDIE MARK WINTERS
WESLEY SHERRARD

Naval Officers

C.A. "BARNEY" McCALL - LT. COMMANDER

BILL L. BLEDSOE - LT. COMMANDER

JIMMY GOODSON - LT.

MARCELLA FAUDREE - LT.

HENRY COOPER - LT.

Following is a list of some of the area men who went through airborne training and received the "jump wings" of a Paratrooper.

MICKEY JACKSON - 82nd Airborne

RUSSELL MAINE - 82nd Airborne

R.C. BURNS - 82nd Airborne

WESLEY SHERRARD - 187 RCT

RAYMOND DAVIS - 187 RCT, 11th, 101st

TOM ROUNSAVILLE - CO B, 180th Inf. 45th Div.

"ALAMO SCOUT", 1st Cal. Div.

FOREST "SPECK" ROUNSAVILLE - 45th MP Co., 10th Ranger

OVERTON SULLINGER - 45th PM Co., 10th Ranger

OSCAR FOOTE - 45 MP Co., 10th Ranger

OLIVER FOOTE - 11th Airborne

BURRIS "BUCK" BICKLE - 11th Airborne

ARNOLD HOPSON - Co. B, 180th Inf., 45th Div., 11th Airborne

WILBUR WILLIAMS - 187 RCT

RAN HAGGARD - Special Forces

CLEM TRENT - Special Forces

BILL DONALDSON - USMC Special Recon.

The first man wounded from Lane in Vietnam was Specialist Jim White, a member of the Big Red One, 1st Division, 1st Engineer Company. Jim was driving a tank on February 8, 1967, during the Tet Offensive, when his track vehicle hit a land mine right under his driving position sending shrapnel through the floor pan of the tank and wounding him in the foot.

The first officer in the 45th Division from Atoka wounded in Korea was Lt. Bill Pharr who was one of our division chaplains. He was hit by shrapnel when a mine exploded while up on the line with the 120th Engineers. Bill had been the preacher of the First Christian Church in Atoka. His wife, Janet, taught Speech and 9th grade English at Atoka High School.

CHAPTER 34

Men Who Served at Sea and Men Who Gave It All

When we hear about naval warfare, generally speaking, we don't think about submarines as part of our battle plans. You are probably not aware that two men from this area served aboard submarines during World War II. Sl/C Thomas White served aboard the U.S.S. Argonant and was lost at sea on January 10, 1943 off the coast of Rabaul, New Britain (Pacific), and Sl/C James A. Sutherland served on the U.S.S. Herring (Pacific) and was lost on his very first mission. Statistics show that for every nine men that served on submarines, one never returned.

September 2, 1945 was quite an occasion for all of the Allied Forces as this was the date of the signing of the Japanese surrender ending World War II. A young Atoka sailor, Water Tender 1/C Gilbert Baker Jr., had a front row seat watching the officials of the Japanese government sign the document giving up their forces "with no holds barred." The Japanese agreed to surrender terms on August 14, 1945 and Baker's ship, the U.S.S. Mississippi, was at Leyete when they got word to journey to Tokyo harbor.

When they arrived, the Mississippi tied up just behind the U.S.S. Missouri, the ship on which the surrender signing was to take place. Gilbert sat on the #2 gun turret and was able to see Gen. Douglas "Dug-out Doug" MacArthur, Admiral Chester Nimitz, Admiral Bull Halsey, Tojo, General Yoshijiro Umezu, and Foreign Minister Mamoru Shigemitsu as the surrender document was signed. Baker said it was something to see our men all dressed in white and khaki and to see the proud look on the men of all allied forces faces; they each seem to say "you didn't think anyone could beat you."

In addition to the regular days to fly flags, Baker flies his American flag on August 14 and September 2, remembering the men on his ship who lost their lives.

PCR/2C Leo K. "Bobby" Camp enlisted in the U.S. Navy in 1943 and after boot camp was assigned to a PBY Squadron as a sea plane tender. He served in New Guinea, Australia, Saipan, Guam, and New Calonadra. When he arrived at Bea Act Island, it was learned that he had just missed his brother, T/5 Bill Camp, and T. Greathouse by one day.

Bob returned home and was discharged in 1945. In 1946 he became a member of Co. H, 180th Infantry, 45th Division, Oklahoma National Guard and was promoted to the rank of SFC serving in the capacity of mess sergeant. In 1949 he became a member of the 45th MP Company mobilized with the unit in 1950 and saw duty in Japan and Korea. Camp retired from the guard in 1982.

S/1C Loyd F. Edge Jr. enlisted in the U.S. Navy on March 22, 1944 and completed boot camp at San Diego, California. He was trained as a member of an amphibious landing crew on LVCP Higgins boats. Later, he was assigned to APA 190, U.S.S. Pickens, a new ship that made its shakedown cruise in August, 1944, for Pearl Harbor then on to Saipan. The Pickens would steam to a small island called Iwo Jima and would become a part of a marine landing on February 19, 1945.

The navy big guns bombarded the Iwo beaches for several hours then at 09:00 hours the fire was lifted and at 11:00 hours the first of the Higgins boats, his was boat #25, began to make their runs to deliver their load of thirty six (36) marines to the beach head. Edge's part of the landing beach was very difficult as where they were assigned, the Japanese had sunk four of their ships and used that part of the vessels sticking out of the water as pill boxes. The troops they took in for the landing was the 5th Marine Division. (This was the unit that Morris Carr landed with.)

After making their first deposit of men on the beach, Edge's landing craft went back to the transport ships to bring in more troops and on their return they transported wounded to the hospital ships, U.S.S. Soltis and the U.S.S. Hope. The hospital ships became so full of wounded and dead that they began to take the wounded to the LSTs. On some of his return trips to the beaches, he was transporting the dead marines back to the island for later burial.

Edge would also make the landing at Okinawa and after the Japanese surrendered he was shipped back to the states and was discharged December 19, 1945.

Following is a list of some of the men from the area who were killed in action:

Blackburn, Houston	McKinney, Alex
Lyles, Dubley	Sutton, Clouser
McAnulty, Hal Gene	Walker, LeRoy
McLeroy, James	White, Thomas
Maxey, Curtis	Beard, Wilbern
Merrit, Ray	Cole, Ernest
Moffatt, William	Shields, George
New, Eldred	Linton, John
Yandell, Albert L.C.	Edge, Lawrence
Collins, Laverne	Bennett, John J.
Cox, R.E., Jr.	Bloyd, William L.

Bryant, Andrew R.	Ramsey, Herschel
Burrows, John	Shannon, Leonard
Crites, John	Shields, George
Brawner, Lesly	Smith, L.G.
Davis, Otis O.	Standifer, Frank
Davis, Charles E.	Strain, Dan J.
Sutherland, James A.	Tedford, Charlie
Eaves, Otis	Tom, Benjamin
Franklin, William D.	Wolfe, Garvie, Jr.
Garner, Curtis "Cactus Jack"	Wood, Lige P.
Hinkle, Clarence	Hamlin, Joe Charles
Howard, Earl L.	Moore, Carl
Hunt, Charlie C.	Thompson, Jackie
Jarvis, Walter J.	Armstrong, Fletcher
Jim, Anderson	Arrington, Donnie
Locke, Charles W., Sr.	Arrington, Howard, Jr.
Lovinggood, Carl V.	Taylor, Jim
Maxey, Curtis R.	Moore, Eugene
Maxey, Walter L.	Daily, Sam
McDougal, Dood	Armstrong, Dean
McGue, Jason H.	Culverson, Larry
Melton, Edward	Deaton, John C.
Moore, Amous E.	Durant, Forbes P., Jr.
Overstreet, Harding	Evans, Benny L.
Praytor, B.E.	Lewis, Benny
Ragsdale, Burnis	McBride, Virgil
Rains, Warren E.	Shields, James C.
Self, Billy H.	Swindell, Bobby D.

KILLED IN ACTION:

We have just been notified by Lt. Col. Scott Wells, former member of Co. B, 180th Infantry Regiment in World War II and a platoon leader of the 45th MP Company during the Korean "Police Action," both units of Oklahoma's 45th Infantry Division, that a memorial to the 180th Regiment will be placed at the entrance of the Sicily-Rome American Cemetery honoring the regiment's men who died during the Nettuno-Anzio engagements from January 22, 1944 to June 4, 1944. The 45th lost 858 men killed in action during this period with 378 from the 180th Infantry Regiment and 14 of those men from Atoka County. Dedication to be May 30, 2000. You will hear more concerning this memorial.

CHAPTER 35

An Eyewitness At Iwo Jima and Other Area Patriots

On September 22, 1999, we buried a Marine, Cpl. Herbert Grist, who was a wounded combat veteran of three amphibious landings in the World War II Pacific Theater of operations.

Herb joined the Marines when he was 19 years old, in January, 1944, and after basic training was assigned as a BAR man in the Fleet Marine Force. Within six months after joining the corps, on June 15, 1944, he made the amphibious landing at Saipan along with 20,000 other American servicemen. Their Japanese enemy had some 32,000 men on the island dug in and waiting for the invaders.

The Marines fought a grueling campaign across rocky and mountainous terrain in which small pockets of Japanese soldiers were able to dig themselves in using caves and rocky defiles for cover. The enemy made several desperate "Banzai" suicidal attacks, but the Marines made a wearying and grisly defense taking the island inch by inch. The American command thought that they had entered the final stages on July 1; however, on July 7 the last of some 2,500 or so Japanese soldiers swept down on the Marines in a final suicide attack and were annihilated.

Herb's unit, 2nd Battalion, 3rd Marines, 3rd Marine Division, Fleet Marine Force, on July 21, 1944 made a landing on Guam Island, some 30 miles long and 4 to 10 miles wide, about 1,500 miles from the Philippines, containing one large airbase at Orote. Guam was inhabited by some 18,500 Japanese army and navy personnel who vowed to die for their Emperor.

On July 2, 1944 the Navy began a bombardment of Guam, preceding the landing of July 21. The landing took place south of an area known as Agana, and at first, all went well with the Marine forces advancing rapidly, despite fierce fighting, towards the airfield and high ground. On July 25 the Japanese launched a counter-attack, and there was a furious battle that all but overwhelmed the U.S. headquarters, inflicting appalling losses of our troops. It was during this battle that Herb was wounded severely in the left leg and 10 members of his platoon were killed.

Herb evacuated to a medical unit for treatment then on to a hospital ship to remove some of the shrapnel in his leg. By the next day, the Marines had retaken the lost ground and by August 10, 1944, Guam had been taken. The Marines had lost 2,000 men killed, and the Japanese had lost 17,300 killed in action. (If memory serves me correctly, Hoyt Lee and Leo Evans were in this battle.)

Herb's wound healed, and he later rejoined his outfit for the Iwo Jima landing on February 19, 1945. Herb's unit was in floating reserve and went on the beach at Iwo as a replacement for some of the companies that had taken heavy casualties. His platoon had just started the incline up a 550-foot extinct volcano, called Mt. Suribachi, and they were some 300 feet from the top when he looked up and saw the men of Lt. Harold Shrier's platoon raising the American flag; the photo of this occasion has become famous. Herb was an eyewitness to this great moment in American history. If you ever visited his home, he would probably show you a copy of this famous event.

Herb has suffered with his wounded leg for the past 56 years; in fact, every once in a while a small piece or pieces of shrapnel would work itself out of his old war wound.

The last time I saw Herb was in the lobby of the Atoka State Bank, and I noticed he was using a walking cane for support on his left side. We greeted each other and I asked, "How are you doing?" He answered, "Mighty slow, Shug, mighty slow." If there was to be such a thing as calling the patriots to order, Herb Grist would be found standing in the front row. Semper Fi, Herb, Semper Fi.

Not many of us give any thought as to anyone from this area serving in the Spanish-American War of 1889. We know of two men who had part in this war. One was Matt Stowers of the Standing Rock community, and the other was John Chitwood of Atoka. I was fortunate enough to have known John and got to see the campaign hat he wore as an Oklahoma Volunteer upon becoming a part of Colonel Teddy Roosevelt's Rough Riders. Our home place here at Lane was purchased by my parents from John in 1943. Some of you may remember that Chitwood operated a pine shingle mill northeast of Lane in the McGee Creek area.

World War I would find several men from our area who served in the military. The ones that can be recalled are Joe Ralls, Offie Muncy, Audie Phelps, Ray McDonald, Allen Dodson and Mart Rector. There were others but I am not aware of their names.

Most of you will probably recall knowing my uncle, "Slick" Cartwright. His name was Jesse Billy Cartwright; he enlisted in the Army as a 16-year-old right after the end of World War I. Slick served some six months in the horse cavalry and was sent home. He managed to finish school and started working towards a teacher's certificate from East Central College at Ada; he earned the right to teach the first eight grades. Slick became a teacher of all grades in a one-teacher school at Dok Ranch.

In the mid 1930's he joined the Oklahoma National Guard as

a member of Co. B, 180th Infantry Regiment, 45th Division and within 3 years was promoted to the rank of sergeant. Slick was mobilized into federal service in September, 1940. Along with other members of the 45th Division he would eventually be stationed at Camp Barkley at Abilene, Texas.

In 1942, Slick went to Ft. Benning, Georgia to Officers Candidate School and received a commission as a second lieutenant. In 1943, he was assigned as second in command of a German Prisoner of War Camp at Huntsville, Texas, where he had the responsibility of overseeing some of the hard-core soldiers of Hitler's African Corp.

At the end of the war in 1945, he was sent to Germany to handle thousands of German prisoners. It was here that he was given an unusual job as Slick became the captain of Hitler's personal yacht. Let me explain about this boat called Das Spiegel.

The people of the city of Frankfort, Germany were so proud of Hitler's conquests of various countries in Europe that they took up a collection and had a yacht built to cruise the Rhine River for German dignity. The Americans captured this boat and decided to use it for excursion tours up and down the Rhine.

Slick was made the Army's transportation corp officer in charge. He had this job until 1946 when he brought his family home and resigned his commission only to re-enlist as a non-commissioned master sergeant. Slick would be sent back to Europe and in 1952 was assigned to Korea. He stayed in the Army until he had enough time for retirement. He is now deceased and buried at Fort Gibson National Cemetery here in Oklahoma.

Some of you have asked "if ole so and so served with the 45th Division during the Korean War." The following is a list of those that I can recall that were THUNDERBIRDS and the units they served with beginning August 1950 thru the summer 1952:

<u>120th ENGINEER COMBAT HQS & SERVICE CO.</u>
PHARR, BILL, LT.

<u>45th DIVISION HQS.</u>
BURKHALTER, EARON
CRITES, CYPUS
LANOY, FRANK
LANOY, HENRY
LEMONS, JOHN
MOSES, MARION
NOWLIN, FRANK
OLSEN, TOMMY

<u>145th AAA</u>
<u>BATTERY B</u>
BARTON, CLYDE
HALL, HAROLD
KEETON, CLAUDE
LAWRENCE, JULIUS
MORRIS, DAMMIE
NIX, BOWDEN
NORTHCUTT, WALTER
PETERS, HARLON
PIEARCY, BILL
TURNBULL, JAMES

<u>279th INFANTRY</u>
<u>COMPANY B</u>
HOMER, JOSEPH
ROBERTS, STEVE

<u>COMPANY C</u>
ALLEN, DAVID
ALLEN, JOEPHENE

<u>179th INFANTRY</u>
<u>COMPANY B</u>
BONHAM, MARVIN
NICHOLS, BUCK
RECTOR, BILLY
RECTOR, MART
VANDENBURG, EDDIE

<u>COMPANY E</u>
NANNEY, BOB
PAYNE, ONUL "COTTON"
SMITH, ROY

<u>COMPANY F</u>
UMSTED, CHARLES

180th INFANTRY
HQS. COMPANY
VIETTA, DOMINIC

SERVICE COMPANY
HARAWAY, JACK

2ND BATTALION HQS.
RICH, JOHN, COL.
HAGGARD, MARION "CHUNK", MAJOR

COMPANY E
SHEFFIELD, LEONARD, JR.

3RD BATTALION HQS.
BOWMAN, WILLIE, CAPT.
JONES, DONALD

K COMPANY
BONHAM, OLIE
NEWSON, FRANK
PIERSON, SAMMY
TRULOCK, GRADY
WILLEBY, LEROY

45th MILITARY POLICE COMPANY
ALFORD, TRAVIS
ALLEN, SHIRLEY
ARMSTRONG, ALVIN
BARDWELL, ODIS
BARNHILL, JIMMY
BENHAM, ELBERT
BENHAM, GLENN
BLEDSOE, SHERMAN "SHUG"
BONIFIELD, WALLACE
BRYANT, FRANK, JR.
BUSSEY, HAROLD
CAMP, SIDNEY, 1ST SGT.
CAMP, LEO "BOBBY"
CHITWOOD, JACK
CONNELLY, TED
COOK, HOLLAND
COOK, JAMES
COOK, ROBERT
DASHNER, BRICK
DECKER, BOBBY
EASTRIDGE, HERSHEL
FITZGERALD, ALFRED "HOSS"
FLOWERS, BILL
FOLSOM, CHARLES "HAGAN"
FOLSOM, BILL
FOOTE, OSCAR
FOSTER, DON "FUZZY"

FRYER, BOB
GLASGOW, BOB
GLASS, LESLIE
GLOVER, JOHN
GREATHOUSE, CECIL "BUD"
GRIFFIN, WILLIAM
GRIST, JESSE "ED"
HARAWAY, ROBERT "PEPPER"
HENDERSON, RILEY
HERROD, BILLY
HODGES, ELDON
JOHNSON, CLIFFORD
JOHNSON, WINDELL
KEITH, LEONARD
LOVE, HARLAN
LOWE, NORVELL "TOOPIE"
MANSELL, HERBERT
McANULTY, JACK
McANULTY, OREN "SMUT"
McGEE, JAMES
McKASKLE, PAUL
MILLICAN, HERBERT
MILLS, EUAL
MITCHELL, BOBBY
MOFFATT, HAMILTON "BEANS"
MOFFATT, WALLACE "BUD"
MOORE, DWIGHT "RUSSELL"
MOORE, LUTHER "SWEETIE PIE"
NELSON, JOSEPH "SHORTY"

NORTHCUTT, CLARENCE
PHILLIPS, JESSE WAYNE
PINGLETON, BILL
PRAYTOR, BOB
RAY, O.P. "PERRY"
RAY, THOMAS R, "TINKER"
RICHARDSON, BILL
RIDGEWAY, W.R.
ROBERTS, LEVI
ROGERS, PAUL
ROGERS, WILLIAM III
SMITHART, DONALD "DOE"
SMITHART, WILLARD "WES"
STEELE, HAROLD
STRICKLAND, JAMES
STRICKLAND, HOYLE
SULLINGER, OVERTON
SWINDELL, EUGENE
TIDWELL, CLAUD
TRAIL, KENNETH
VIETTA, ALBERT
WALLACE, JESSE "POT"
WATSON, DOYLE
WATSON, HARLEY
WILLIAMS, CHARLES
WILLIAMS, JOE
WILLIAMS, TOMMY JEFF
WILSON, CLARENCE "CID"
WINTERS, EDDIE

<u>45th MP CO, continued...</u>
WINTERS, IRVING
WINTERS, THOMAS "HOGJAW"
WOMBLE, LARRY
WYATT, BILLY BURR
YATES, DOYLE
WILLIAMS, LEO. K., CAPT.
FINK, LON ROBERT, LT.
McCASLAND, JOHN "HICKY", LT. COL.
MEAD, CALVIN, LT.
RANDOLPH, ROBERT, LT.
WELLS, WALTER "SCOTT", LT.
DOWNS, STANDFORD, LT.

The above are all the names that I had a list for knowing that with all probability someone has been missed; however, I assure you that it was not intentional; after all, it has been 49 years.

<u>The following is a list of the sets of brothers from this area who served with the 45th during the "Korean Police Action":</u>
BENHAM, ELBERT & GLENN
CAMP, SIDNEY & LEO "BOBBY"
COOK, HOLLAND & JAMES
HARAWAY, JACK & ROBERT "PEPPER"
FOLSOM, CHARLES "HAGAN" & BILL
JOHNSON, CLIFFORD & WINDELL
McANULTY, JACK & OREN "SMUT"
MOFFATT, HAMILTON "BEANS" & WALLACE "BUD"
RAY, O.P. "PERRY" & THOMAS "TINKER"
SMITHART, DONALD "DOE" & WILLARD "WES"
WATSON, DOYLE & HARLEY
WINTERS, EDDIE & THOMAS "HOGJAW"
BONHAM, OLIE & MARVIN
RECTOR, LEE & MART
VIETTA, ALBERT & DOMINIC

CHAPTER 36

Another Guard Company, More Patriots, and an Intelligence Officer

You have noticed that a lot has been written about Co. B, 180th Infantry but you probably are not aware that Atoka had another National Guard Company that drilled in the south side of the old armory building, and it was called Company F, 120th Medical Regiment. (At one time it was a horse drawn ambulance company.)

In 1940 when the 45th was mobilized, part of F Co. was sent to Panama where Sgt. Houston Blackburn and others were assigned to the 158th Infantry Regiment and were sent to the Pacific. Sgt. Sid Camp's platoon was sent to the European theater of operations. The remainder of F Co. stayed with the 45th and was renamed Co. A, 120th Medical, and they did the entire 511 days of combat with the Thunderbirds.

Some of those who became a part of A Co. were Roy Mead, Pat Sullivan, Herman Barton, James Jackson, James Thompson and a soldier by the last name of Dale. These six Atoka boys came through alive, and Sullivan was the only one wounded. They were medics and litter bearers. Thompson and Mead were assigned to the 157th Infantry and were two of the first people to enter the famous Dachau Prison Camp.

Thompson and Mead could tell you about the things they saw and how unbelievable it was to see first-hand what cruel and horrible things the Germans had done to their captives. Mead is now gone to meet his maker, while James Thompson lives at

Wardville enjoying his ranching operation. If you don't know James, you have missed getting to meet one of the nicest persons you would ever get to know.

Sgt. Houston Blackburn's platoon was assigned to the 158th Infantry Regiment that was transferred from the 45th and eventually saw a lot of combat action in the Pacific. It was in the Philippines, on Luzon, where Houston and an ambulance driver went to the front lines to bring back some wounded for treatment at a regimental hospital. The date was January 23, 1945, and Blackburn, his driver and some Filipinos were loading the wounded when a Japanese mortar round got a direct hit on their location, killing Houston, the Filipinos and wounding the driver. At the same time Houston was killed, his brother, Leroy Blackburn, was aboard ship in the gulf just off of Luzon laying down supporting fire for those involved in the land battle.

We have not mentioned much about those that were crew members of aircraft involved in World War II. Lt. Laverne Collins was shot down over the English Channel on September 19, 1942 and died in the crash. T/Sgt. R.E. Cox, Jr. was shot down over Germany on February 20, 1944 and was listed as killed in action. S/Sgt. Alex McKinney was shot down over France in May, 1943 and killed. Lt. Veron Reeves, now a retired full colonel, had landed his B-17 bomber at Hickman Field, Hawaii, but could not get to his plane to get it off of the ground when the Japanese bombed Pearl Harbor. Lt. B.R. "Red" Cook, Jr. was a crew member of a bomber that had to ditch in the Pacific; Zack Cartwright floated on the Pacific for a while when his navy patrol bomber went in the drink. There are others, but these are the ones I can think of right off the top of my head.

S2/C Herman Bledsoe was at Pearl Harbor on December 7, 1941 aboard the U.S.S. Arizona. He became one of the 2,403 men who died that day during the Japanese attack. Herman is entombed in the hull of his ship sunk in the dark waters of Pearl Harbor.

The next portrait we would like to give a glimpse at is my brother, Commander Bill L. Bledsoe, U.S.N. Reserve, Retired. Bill finished his first eight years of schooling at Lane and his freshman year at Atoka High School. During his sophomore year, our folks moved to Texas, and he graduated from Forest Avenue High School in Dallas, Texas in 1953. He enrolled at North Texas State College at Denton, Texas, where he earned a B.S. in the School of Education with his major in the field of English; however, all at once he decided not to teach but enlisted in the military to learn to fly.

After receiving his degree in the spring of 1957, Bill contacted a U.S. Navy recruiter and a deal was made whereby he would immediately become an officer, Ensign, and a Naval Aviation Cadet. Bill was sent to Pensacola Naval Air Station, Florida, where he was subjected to boot camp and then started receiving instructions in basic flying.

The new officer was having the time of his life and shortly he had soloed. The training was stepped up, and there were many touch-and-go landings when all at once Bill had a problem. It seems that on a couple of his landings, there were pieces of pine tree tops in his landing gear followed by a piece of telephone wire. The school immediately gave Bill an eye examination and found that he had lost his depth perception so that he could not judge his distance coming down for landings. Once this eye problem was determined, they met with Bledsoe to give him the news that he would not be able to fly for the navy, that he would be sent to Air Intelligence School at NAS Alameda, California.

Bill completed the intelligence school at Alameda and was

promoted to lieutenant junior grade and assigned to a P2V Neptune Patrol Squadron Two based out of Whidbey Island, Washington. His unit went to TDY to Kodiak, Alaska, and later to Adak, Alaska. In 1959, his unit was assigned to a six-month tour of duty to Iwakuni Marine Air Station in Japan. This base was located about 50 miles from Hiroshima where the U.S. had dropped an atomic bomb in August, 1945.

As squadron intelligence officer, his primary responsibility was to keep the Pacific Naval Command advised of all the submarine activity and Russian shipping leaving various ports, what was their cargo and what was their destination. Bill had no more than gotten to Japan when they were notified that the navy could not locate the Russian ship Petrograd. The navy had already spent a small fortune in search time and man hours but to no avail. Bill's unit immediately joined the search for this ship and upon returning from one of their recon flights off the coast of China, he passed by a Japanese newsstand and noticed a picture of a ship on the front page. Bill bought the paper and got an interpreter and made an appointment to see the Admiral in charge of all of the Pacific area. He walked into the Admiral's office and stated "Sir, we have found the Petrograd." then he asked the interpreter to read the paper. The article disclosed from what port the ship had sailed, its cargo, how long it would be docked and what its next port would be. "Ol' Bill" received another promotion to full lieutenant.

After six months of flying off the coast of Communist China, Siberia and North Korea, his unit was sent back to Whidbey Island. Bill remained stationed at Whidbey until his enlistment was completed.

Once Bill had been discharged from the Navy, he made the decision to join the reserve intelligence unit based at Grand

Prairie, Texas, NAS. He went to a two-day drill once a month and two weeks of encampment per year. Much to Bill's surprise, one day in August, 1962 he was called and told to report to NAS immediately for a special assignment. Bill reported to NAS Dallas and shortly was aboard an aircraft headed for Guantanamo Bay, Cuba. It seems that U2 photos and other pieces of intelligence information showed some very unusual Russian shipping into Cuba. In working with other intelligence officers, it was determined that the Russian ships were loaded with military equipment and technicians, and that they were in the process of installing missile bases 90 miles from the U.S. coast.

On October 22, 1962, President Kennedy announced to the world what was going on; six days later the President confronted Russian Premier Khrushchev and told him to get his military hardware out of Cuba and ordered a naval blockade of the island.

By the first week of November, Khrushchev started the removal of the Soviet equipment from Cuba, and Bill and other alerted personnel were returned home.

Bill stayed in the Naval Reserve and retired after 20 years in 1977. He and I have always had fun out of the fact that I served some 80 days aboard ship while being a member of the Army; however, in 20 years of navy life, and having his trouble with carrier landings, Bill was aboard a ship only one time, and that was just taking a tour with the average civilians aboard an aircraft carrier on Navy Day. He always comes back "They still deposit a check every month in my bank."

I'm proud of my brother; he's a patriot for his country.

CHAPTER 37

1949-52 with the 45th MP Company

With your permission I would like to digress for a while and respond with a few happenings concerning the 45th MP Co. from 1949 through 1952. I have been asked by several members of the families of those who served to give them some insight of what went on during this tour of duty.

When we were mobilized for federal duty to report to Camp Polk, Louisiana the first week in September, 1950, the members went through the county trying to get young men to go into the service with us. The slogan was "Go with the men you know," and this Atoka unit reported with the largest number of men in any company in the entire 45th Division. We left here with 168 enlisted men and seven officers as members of the 45th MP Company. We were unusual in that all of our officers, our first sergeant with all but one of our platoon sergeants being combat veterans of World War II. They were very insistent that we each receive an intensive training background. Most of us reported to the Atoka armory two weeks before we were to convoy to Louisiana for advanced military training.

We reported to Camp Polk after three days and two nights of convoying on September 3, 1950. Upon arrival, we found a base that had been closed for nearly five years with bad or no plumbing; some of the barracks floors had rotted; grass, bushes and weeds had grown up; snakes and spiders were everywhere, plus the civilians the army hired to get the post in shape were way behind on their job.

Our company not only had to train our new recruits and do our routine police work but also help get our area livable. It was not an easy chore but through the efforts of all working together, our mission was accomplished.

Let's go back to the spring of 1949 when Lt. Col. John "Hicky" McCasland was the provost marshal of the division; he was the one who always bragged about Boggy Bottom folks and how well some of our local boys were at using their fists and boxing. You see in that day and time, many of the schools in the state had boxing teams and there was always a few matches going on. We were fortunate in Atoka that we did have a great many exceptional fighters in Brick Dashner, Jack Chitwood, Bob Chitwood, Jesse Wayne Phillips, Hershel Eastridge, Leonard Sheffield, Jr., W.R. Ridgeway, Dean Armstrong, Billy Bob Hacker, Tommy Jeff Williams, Joe Weston, Billy Armstrong and others that I cannot recall at this time, but we did have a bunch that were good with "der mitts."

Several of these boxers belonged to the National Guard and during our annual summer encampment at Ft. Sill, the division would always hold a boxing tournament championship. Hicky was quite a fight fan and was always getting his men well up in the winning bracket but was unable to produce a weight champion. It seemed when his men would get to the finals, they would be beaten by men from Chilocco Indian School, Bacone Indian School, Goodland Indian School or Minco.

McCasland wanted a championship fighter; he kept watching Dashner win bout after bout and decided that even though Dashner was small in size, he would recruit him as a member of the 45th MP Co. Hicky was successful in getting Brick to join in the late spring of 1949; Brick was primed and ready to go to summer camp that August.

McCasland was grinning and spitting snuff in a Dixie cup saying, "Come on and meet my new boy." Dashner crawled into the ring at 107 pounds and nearly killed his first opponent. The corner man was none other than Bud Greathouse, who at the end of each round would comment, "Boy, you hammered his head." Dashner fought seven times in three days and won the championship in addition to receiving the nickname of "Hammerhead." During the summer of 1950, Brick won the 112-pound division championship and he was "Hicky's boy."

In the summer of 1948 encampment, Hicky encouraged some of us Atoka boys to play baseball for special troops (consisted of 45th Recon Company, 45th Signal Co., 700 Ordnance Co., Hq. Spe-Medical, Division Hqs, and 45th MP Co.). We just happened to win the 4th Army championship there at Ft. Sill. If my memory serves me correctly, playing on that team from Atoka was Johnny Surrell, Don Parham, Mark Winters and myself. McCasland got to stick his chest out and brag about his "Boggy Bottom Boys."

During the 1950 recruiting campaign, two of those men decided to join the 45th at the Boys Training School at Stringtown; they were Privates Bill Pingleton and Harold Steele. Shortly after our arrival at Camp Polk in September, 1950, Lt. Lon Robert Fink had Steele go to the motor pool and check out a Jeep. Steele was to be the driver, and Pingleton was to be part of their mission. It seems that as they journeyed through the back country of Louisiana, the Jeep developed a flat tire on the right rear. As was the case on many occasions, they went to change the tire, but the jack did not work properly. Here the three are out there in the boonies with no way to raise up the vehicle in order to put on the spare. It was decided that Harold would loosen the lug nuts, Pingleton would try to lift the corner of the Jeep off of the ground, while Steele would take off the tire and put on the spare. Well, "ol'" Bill grunted, groaned and strained and finally got the Jeep high enough to change the tire. Fink's part of this operation was that he stood on the shoulder of the road and laughed at Steele and Pingleton.

On more than one occasion I have asked Lt. Fink, "Why did you not help them instead of standing there laughing?" Finally one day he told me, "They said that when I got my commission as a lieutenant that I was now an officer and gentleman, and officers and gentlemen did not do certain things in public such as push baby buggies, carry grocery sacks and change flat tires when there were two privates around."

It was said that when Fink first told this actual story concerning the changing of the flat that Pingleton replied, "That was an easy one as where I was raised at Haileyville, sometimes it took two or maybe three of us to change a truck tire, depending if the truck was loaded with logs or not." I don't know if that statement was made or not but knowing Bill Pingleton, I would not doubt that it came out of his mouth.

In October, 1950, we began to get the first draftees called into the "Korean Police Action" (this was what President Harry Truman labeled it and not a "war"). Col. McCasland and Capt. Leo Williams would meet the incoming troop trains loaded with new draftees, and their mission was to select men for replacements in the 45th MP Company. To become a part of our company, the new men had certain specifications to meet. Those requirements were at least 21 years of age, 6 foot and 2 inches in height, 180 pounds of weight and a I.Q. of 110 or above. Some of these new men selected were former merchant marine sailors during World War II (most of them were just under 26 years of age), professional football players, professional baseball players, college basketball players, college football players, law enforcement officers and pro motorcycle riders. They selected quite a conglomerate of men who would be assigned to our company for their introduction from civilian life to the military way of doing things.

When you get this many men together, you are bound to have some very unusual characters. One of the men from an adjoining county joined our unit in Atoka at the last minute. It was not his idea to join the service but a matter of one of two choices that he was given by District Judge Laveren Fishel. This new recruit had been caught by a county sheriff making illegal booze. It was the first time that he had been caught and he was required to appear before the judge as to his plea of guilty or not guilty. Judge Fishel talked at length to this man and finally the judge said "I'm gonna offer you a deal, if you plead guilty and agree to join the army, we will drop the charges. If you plead not guilty, we will hold a trial, and if you are convicted then you will be sentenced a maximum term in the state pen." Well, needless to say, the ol' boy decided to join the army and became a part of the 45th MP Company. He reported to Camp Polk with the rest of us.

In about 60 days, Judge Fishel was on the street of the county seat from which he had given this man the choice - the army or the pen. The judge greeted the man and asked how things were going with his military career. The man replied, "Judge, I'm no longer in the army; they gave me a medical discharge and kicked me out of the service." Now I don't know if he went back to his old trade or not; however, the judge would tell the story and get a big laugh about the man who beat his decision.

One of the draftees selected by Col. McCasland and Capt. Williams was an Englishman who had just become a citizen of this country. During World War II he was a merchant seamen in the service of England's Queen Royal Merchant Marines. He was an 18-year-old seaman, Eddie Evans; the first time his ship was sunk by a German submarine torpedo, causing he and his fellow crew members to float around the Atlantic Ocean on a raft for a few days.

Evans would have the misfortune of once again having a ship torpedoed out from under him in the Gulf of Mexico. It was back aboard a life raft for Eddie and his shipmates until they were picked up by an American vessel.

After the war, Evans moved to New Orleans, became a U.S. citizen, but he had to register for the draft. He was just under 26 years of age when Uncle Sam sent him the "greetings" letter - he had been drafted. When he arrived at our unit, we noticed that he had the prettiest white teeth and was the bitchiest man we had ever met. We immediately gave him the name of "Lymie," because of his nationality and his manner of speaking. Evans was a very likeable guy but he never quit griping about the military or those young NCOs from Oklahoma. Would you believe that after he was released from the army he joined an army reserve unit, became a sergeant major in rank and retired after more than 30 years of service from the military?

We also had another soldier who was almost as good of a bitcher as Evans; his name was Joe. He was a dead ringer for the Cpl. Clinger from the Mash TV series in that he was constantly trying to figure some way of getting out of the army; anything he was required to do would set him off griping. He thoroughly disliked the National Guard with its young corporals and sergeants.

Joe loved to play poker, so the men would get him in a game and team up on him to watch him get mad for losing. Joe was a laugh a minute even when he was giving us the "ol' Billy." He staggered all over Japan and Korea trying to get some sort of minor injury that would get him back to the states and out of the army. I understand that about two weeks before he was to leave Korea, he was involved in a Jeep accident that caused him to break some bones and required him to be hospitalized in the far east for a period of time. When we all get together, we always talk about Joe and what a character he was.

We had another unforgettable character who we will call "Josh" who was drafted from the state of Minnesota. He stood about six feet, five inches, weighed about 250 pounds, was blond headed and would remind you of someone of the Germanic blood line. This guy was one more weird duck but probably the most remembered was his failure to take a bath. Josh had a skin condition on his face, his shoulders and his back that made little pimples, causing his body to give off a sickening odor, plus he was very uncooperative in doing what he was told to do. His bunk was at the door of the first floor of the barracks and when you came in, you could immediately smell the odor that his body gave off.

Josh was in Sgt. Bud Greathouse's squad, and Bud had told him that he needed to take a bath on several occasions, but his warning fell on deaf ears. Greathouse talked to the platoon leader, Lt. Lon Robert Fink, about this problem child and Fink told him, "I believe you know how to handle this problem but be discreet." That was all Bud needed to hear, so he enlisted some of the men in his squad and suggested that they help their fellow barrack mate take a bath. There were several of the rather large in size draftees who had served in the Merchant Marines, so they took it upon themselves to tell Josh to take a bath or they would give him one. Evidently, the soldier did not believe them, so several of the men took him to the shower, pulled off his clothes and spread eagled him on the floor, took GI brushes, GI soap and began to scrub him. He fought them but to no avail as the more he fought the harder the scrubbing got. Josh was given clean sheets and told to change his bed.

The soldier had not learned his lesson, and in a couple of days they suggested to him to bathe. He did not heed their call, so the men took him back to the latrine for another scrubbing procedure. Meanwhile, Lt. Fink had been telling Capt. Leo Williams and Col. Hicky McCasland about his problem child as Josh had done some other things that were contrary to the way of military life. They had charges brought and Josh was given a Section Eight—Undesirable Discharge from the service and that very afternoon was removed from the Company. After he left, the Supply Sgt., Paul McKaskle, had us to roll up his mattress and all of his other belongings so they could be taken to division quartermaster and be issued new bedding. I must say that we never were sorry to see the guy leave.

We would now get back to our job of putting our new recruits and draftees through basic training. Various non-coms were given the assignment in teaching these new men how to soldier. Some were assigned to the firing range, some how to throw hand grenades, firing of a bazooka at a moving target, crawling the infiltration course under live machine gun fire, but the one that took time was the teaching of close order drill. Now please keep in mind that most of us sergeants and corporals were 18, 19 and 20 year olds that were teaching older men how to be soldiers, and they thoroughly resented us. Later, that problem would work itself out.

In the military first judgment often is made of how good or what kind of a unit it is by watching the men doing close order drill and how they relate to the drill instructor. Col. "Hicky"

McCasland was one who believed that way and all of the officers serving in his command were taught the same thing; therefore, one of our company's strongest requirements was always time to be spent drilling. Our officers picked sergeants and corporals who were excellent drill instructors to see that we were the sharpest and best trained soldiers at Camp Polk.

Let me give you an example in the way this drill task operated by telling you about 33 new men, both Atoka National Guardsmen and draftees who spent at least two hours and some days as much as four hours in learning to march. They were assigned drill instructors Sgt. Elzie Hale, Cpl. Leonard Keith and Cpl. Oscar Foote, all who had previously served in the U.S. Army. Each had a great voice for counting cadence, a natural marching rhythm, the ability to have men willing to listen and obey their commands. Both Hale and Foote had served in Honor Guard units and loved the job they had been assigned. These trainees got the message in a hurry that these three drill instructors were not out there for their health or a bunch of foolishness, but this matter of learning to drill was serious business to them.

The first thing these DIs did was assign 11 men to each of three squads; they would line up the men according to height with the tallest in front and graduating down the line with the shortest at the back of each squad column. They found an old parking lot about three-quarters of a mile from the special troop barracks and chose to use this as a drill field. These DIs would divide up their time in instructing these new men to understand the drilling terms and how each command was to be interpreted. It took a little doing but before long the men began to whip into shape and to make their learning period a little more enjoyable; they were gradually taught some fancy marching movements along with singing strange sounding verses of cadence. Foote had the best voice for calling swinging cadence and got the men making up little "ditties" or verses for them to march to in order to show "their stuff." You could hear Foote a half a mile away saying, "I can't hear you, ladies." which meant he wanted them to sound off with more volume.

One afternoon, when it was time to knock off for the day and report back to the company area, it was decided to march this platoon down the entire special troops street and show off a little bit. It got to the point that every afternoon they would march this street just as the other troops were getting in for the day. The DIs would get that platoon singing and counting cadence from the drill area down the entire street; the other companies stood with their mouths ajar to see what these 36 men with their MP helmet liners glistening in the afternoon sun, singing cadence that could be heard a half of a mile away, would do today. Then to top it off, as the platoon got in front of each company's headquarters, they would do a little fancy "non" GI foot stepping, shuffling and movements topped off by the famous Queen Anne rifle salute without the rifle.

The other Special Troops officers got to telling Col. Hicky how much they enjoyed his men's afternoon showmanship, so the Colonel decided to come see what they were talking about. One afternoon Col. McCasland showed up at our company headquarters just in time to hear "Ol' Foote" sing them down the street putting on a show. "Hicky" couldn't believe what he was seeing; he liked it, but later turned to Capt. Williams and First Sgt. Sid Camp saying, "The boys are good, but we had best have the circus leave town." Needless to say, that stopped the fancy drilling and from then on, it was the same old style of drilling. The Colonel spit his snuff in his cup and left with a smile on his face; even though he had stopped the special drilling, his men had made him proud in front of his peers.

As each of these new men were on the verge of finishing up their basic training, First Sgt. Camp and Cpl. Eddie Mark Winters would be getting them accepted into six weeks of Military Police School training at Camp Gordon, Georgia. The balance of us would continue our regular work of town patrolling in Leesville, DeRidder, Alexandria, Baton Rouge, Shreveport, Lake Charles and Beaumont, Texas. The reason we patrolled out so far on the weekends was that Col. "Hicky" did not want any other law enforcement personnel handling the men of the 45th as they had some problems in times past with the civilian authorities handling service personnel. McCasland was right in his thinking, and we were always there "Johnny on the spot" to help our fellow Thunderbirds.

After most of our men had finished the MP school and returned to the company, we enlarged our patrol force to work also with the Vernon Parish Sheriff's Department and the Louisiana State Police. Boy, did we ever get some experience, especially in the handling of the average civilian lawbreaker. One of the worst and toughest places we worked was West Lake on the west side of the Sabine River just across from Lake Charles. This was an inland seaport with merchant vessels coming from all over the world to unload their cargo, and as soon as they could they would head for West Lake as it was wide open for just about everything known to man. Lt. Scott Wells used to just love being the duty officer for the weekend patrolling Lake Charles and West Lake. When someone got to thinking he was tough, he just needed a little journey to the girls and bars at West Lake.

The last part of the year of 1950, we got word that we were going overseas and got three-day passes for us to come home to

Atoka. We thought that they were sending us to Germany, but much to our surprise, when we arrived back in camp we found out that our destination was to be the Far East.

In order to kind of boost up the morale, the post commander had made arrangements with a nurses training school in Lake Charles to have some two or three GI bus loads of nurses per Saturday night volunteer to come up to Camp Polk for a big dance. It was decided by our MP officers, rightfully so, that some of the MPs should provide security for these students to and from school. It was really tough duty to have to chaperon these young ladies every weekend; to put it mildly, "it was kind of like putting the fox in the hen house and closing the doors." After one trip, all of the single men volunteered for this hazardous duty.

In March of 1951, our division moved to the Port of Embarkation of Camp Leroy Johnson at New Orleans. There were five troop transports and the ship that Special Troops boarded was the U.S.S. Gaffey. It had the division commander and some 1,800 other men on board. We moved down the Mississippi, into the Gulf of Mexico, on to the Caribbean to the Panama Canal. Most of us were seeing sights like we had never seen before and a few of our men were initiated into sea sickness and spent some time at the ship's rail throwing up.

As the U.S.S. Gaffey and our four sister ships, loaded with some 14,000 Thunderbirds, approached the entrance of the Panama Canal Zone crossing, little did we have any idea what we were about to see. Once we got into the straits of the canal, we would meet some ships going in the opposite direction when all at once we approached a place in the canal that narrowed and we could see these massive gates on the approach end of the canal. We were directed into locks in which gates would open and close with our ship inside of each lock pocket; all at once you could see and feel the ship rise or fall as the canal master would use the compartment control levers to fill the pockets with water. We had no idea that the height of the water from the Pacific Ocean to the Gulf of Mexico was so different, nor that this series of locks that we were entering was necessary to control the water level in order for us to cross the canal, one ocean to the other.

It was really something to watch as lock people used massive pumps to bring in the water to raise the water lever or lower the water, depending on which way you were traveling in the canal. We were heading west and lumbering through just ahead of us was an American aircraft carrier that was so wide that part of the wooden planking on the sides of the locks had been splintered off and laborers were in the process of repairing the sides.

Late that evening, we tied all of the ships up along docks at a U.S. Army base at Balboa City, Panama. It was decided to let the entire division of some 16,000-plus men off for the night so they could move around for a while on ground. Needless to say, the first place these troops found was the base beer garden and the beer mugs were few and far between, so the Thunderbirds improvised by drinking from any type of a container, including helmet liners and lamp globes. We found out the next day that our division drank every drop of beer they had on the base; however, it was reported that all had a great time—no fights and fond remembrances of their visit to Balboa City.

The next morning our ship prepared to get underway. As they went to untie the bow lines of the Gaffey from the dock in order for us to cast off and continue our trip through the canal, we were unexpectedly detained as we had a major problem. It seems the dockmaster in charge of all shipping through the canal was missing his small Crosley automobile that he had parked on the dock the night before. Shortly, someone noticed a car located on the bow of our ship. Needless to say, we were amazed and had no idea of how that car had gotten on the bow of our transport. It became necessary to undo a bow wench line to hoist the car from its resting place and back on to the dock. It seems that during the night on the return from the beer garden, several men had apparently lifted up the small car and carried it up a double gangplank and deposited it on the bow of the Gaffey. Some remarked that "it kinda looked like a radiator cap or some sort of a hood ornament." You would probably not believe me if I were to reveal some of the names that just happened to be in on the "car napping." Don't worry, comrades, my lips are sealed. But it was funny, wasn't it?

We exited the canal on the west side into the waters of the Pacific Ocean and after about one-half day of sailing, we turned north towards the Golden Gate Bridge and San Francisco to pickup more troops and supplies.

We headed from the states again and sailed off the north coast of Hawaii on a line through the Japanese straits to a seaport on the northwest side of the coast of Hokkaido to Otaru, Japan; our trip over to Japan took 28 days aboard ship. We debarked and loaded onto a narrow gage railroad that would take us to two different locations. One was Camp Crawford in Sapparo, which was formerly an army base that had housed the Japanese Imperial Marines. Lt. Fink's and Lt. Wells' platoons were sent to a newly made tent city located on the Chitose Air Field where the Japs had trained their Kamikazi pilots.

As we rode those little trains to our new homes, we discovered some rather unusual things about the Japanese way of life. First, even though these were passenger trains we were riding, they were not made for large people, and the only rest room available was a hole cut in the floor of the car on one of the coaches. Secondly, as we rode the rails, we saw radishes over three foot in length along with fish, squid, etc. lying on tin roof tops to dry in the sun.

The two platoons of us that were assigned to Chitose's tent city thought that we had received the kiss of death as this was a new camp being set up by hired Japanese laborers, but little did we have any idea that for the time being we had been blessed. The three platoons and headquarters that had been assigned the brick barracks at Camp Crawford was almost the downfall of that part of our company. It seems that the barracks were infested with body lice, body crabs and spiders. The men had to go through a series of spraying of their bodies; their clothes, bedding and even the walls of the buildings were infested with the varmints. Needless to say, they received a great deal of kidding from us at Chitose. We even suggested that maybe they had brought those "little critters" with them. They did finally manage to get this problem under control after several sprayings. I think that some of the guys were sprayed so much that it just became a part of their routine.

All haste was made both at Chitose and Camp Crawford for our town patrols and road patrols to begin to operate. At first we worked the towns only on weekends as the entire division was busy the rest of the week getting everything in order.

The first part of the summer of 1951, it was decided to break the infantry regiments up and with elements from other service companies to form Regimental Combat Teams (RCTs). Part of us were assigned to Lt. Robert Randolph's platoon to become a part of the 279th RCT, and we were to move into another tent city on top of a hill. They named this Camp Shimamatsu; it had been a sheep farm. From this new camp we were responsible for the Town of Eniwa, plus we trained with the 279th.

One of our responsibilities was acting as bodyguards for Regimental Commander, Col. Frank Meridian, a regular army West Point officer who only knew one way - his. Whenever the Colonel left the camp, he always had one of us with him, not only to protect him but to carry all of his crap that he felt necessary to carry to the field. Part of the time we felt like we were one of "ole Scott Wells' " pack mules. Depending on where he was going, there could be anywhere from one to four of us accompanying him. Sgt. W.R. Ridgeway was in charge of these ventures, and boy did he always catch old billy from the Colonel as nothing, according to him, was done right. The Colonel was finally sent home and none of us in the RCT hated to see him leave.

In addition to our regular police work, six of us were assigned as part of the amphibious landing unit and in October, 1951, we made a landing on the beach of Tomakomi; the first of November, 1951, we landed at Urakawa. Both of the landings were on extremely rough seas.

The first morning of the Tomakomai landing as the navy put the Higgins landing craft in the water, the waves overturned our small plywood boats. Incidentally, each morning before the landings, the navy got us up at three o'clock in the morning and fed us a breakfast of white navy beans, cornbread and pork chops. We finally made the first landing after three days of rough water before we could get a boat to stay afloat. I have always thought they made us get off because they had run out of pork chops and navy beans.

The last of November, 1951 we boarded APA 272, the U.S.S. Bexar, that took us into the harbor of Inchon, landing on the 5th of December, 1951. We moved out to a place called Pong Yong Ni and spent our first night in South Korea. The next day we boarded open railroad cattle cars for a nice cold scary ride up to the Yonchon-Chorwon front to our position along the Jamestown Line.

After a very scary dark night, we were trucked towards Seoul, the capital of South Korea, across a recently engineer-made bridge over the Han River (all of the other bridges had been destroyed by previous advances and retreats by both sides) for military traffic. As our truck crossed, we could see the bridges destroyed, some were practically submerged in the river; all around us were blown up tanks and other equipment, homes, trains, etc., but the one thing that remains very vivid in my memory was seeing the South Korean Capital Building. This was the only thing left standing in this one area, as everything else had been flattened by artillery fire or bombs. The capital building was just a skeleton hull left standing with visible pock marks from being shelled and all of the glass had been blown out.

We rode in open two and one-half ton trucks to a railroad track just south of a place called Oijongbu; then we boarded open cattle cars, a little narrow gage rocking train, for a trip towards the Iron Triangle to an area called Chorwon. The little engine pulling our cars went very slowly, and we could see through the cracks in the car walls that on both sides of the track was mass devastation and incredible damage caused by war. There were groups of children running after our train with their hands out begging for food.

The night came and we were just rocking along in the cold air not being sure just what we were going to have to contend with when all at once, along side of the railroad track were several loud booms, and the whole night sky was lit up. Several times this happened in rapid succession and not knowing what was going on, we were all about ready to open that sliding door and jump out of that cattle car when Sgt. Bud Greathouse hollered, "It's outgoing artillery going over the top of us for a called fire mission." We all drew a deep sigh of relief being thankful that our sergeant knew what was happening as he had been a combat infantryman in World War II. Incidentally, this was the only stretch of railroad track left in this part of Korea.

Our train came to a stop just south of a town called Chorwon, North Korea, which was just about 35 miles north of the famous 38th parallel that divided the two countries. We were in the very middle of Korea in an area called Iron Triangle near the town of Chorwon, which had the corner of a bank building left standing as the rest of the town had been destroyed.

In our earlier writings, we had mentioned that Lt. Robert Fink was one of the staff officers flown in secretly from Japan to Korea to plan for the placements of our troops to relieve the 1st Cavalry Division. As we approached the area that was to be our home for the next few months, it was not a very pretty sight. Our unit was dug in on the south side of a hill with a header located to our right, behind us was another hill, to our left was the entry road leading us out of the area to the south, toward Seoul.

I mentioned the hill in front where the squad tents and bunkers were dug in, but what made this even worse was on top of this hill was a Korean graveyard. This graveyard was something else in that the Koreans buried their dead sitting up facing the east on top of the ground. They piled dirt all around the body, then placed tall stone grave markers next to the bodies. Wouldn't you know it—we inherited a machine gun nest located in the middle front of this cemetery. The gun emplacement over looked the north slope of this hill into a valley and for our defense; it had three different lines of barbed wire laid up the hill with each line having trip-flare markers attached, so that anything that touched those wires caused the whole area to light up. Down in front of the wire there was a flat valley that contained a mine field.

I mentioned the company area; well, it was a series of squad tents dug back into the side of the hill with empty wooden 105 MM artillery boxes filled with dirt to act as walls. Some of us were used to sleeping in tents as that was all we had at some locations in Japan, and we were about to spend our second winter in this type of comfort. We had no lights, each tent had one worn out diesel heating stove for us to keep warm. The stoves were something else, but SFC Herb Millican and his men from the motor pool finally salvaged enough parts from other stoves to get some working pretty good.

Our mess sergeant, Leo "Bobby Lee" Camp, had also inherited a field kitchen that was a holy nightmare. Camp's men, Brick Dashner, Freddie "Sweetie Pie" Moore, Shorty Nelson, Jesse "Pot" Wallace, Jay Cook, Benny Ray and Grady Cockrill managed to tear those field ranges apart and eventually got a couple of those pieces of junk in workable shape.

The mess kitchen tent had no lights, so Camp would have one of his men drive the front end of one of the Jeeps through the end opening, close the tent flap with the front part sticking inside the cook tent with its motor running and the lights on. Capt. Williams liked to have had nine cats when he saw what they had done for lights. He was afraid the enemy would catch a small ray of light and start dropping in artillery rounds, but thanks to our mess officer, Lt. Scott Wells, he finally soothed the captain's feathers by finding a old diesel truck motor; with the help of SFC Millican and his men, they used a little Boggy Bottom Engineering as they built a power plant for Camp's mess tent. Let's say this: It was amazing the amount of talent, with the ability of making the unusual work, that these boys from Atoka possessed; they could make almost anything worn-out workable.

At this point let me explain just where the position was that the 45th was assigned to defend and hold. If you go to the middle of Korea, about 35 miles due north of the 38th parallel you would be in a combat area known as the Iron Triangle; inside this area was the Chorwon-T' son Corridor and Hill mass 487-477 (we called this Double X Hill). Going to the right side of this area was Sniper Ridge, Triangle Mt., Osong Mt. (a.k.a. Papa San Mt.), Finger Ridge, Heartbreak Ridge, Luke's Castle, Punch Bowl on to the Sea of Japan. From the left side there was Iron Horse Mt., White Horse Ridge, Old Baldy, Pork Chop Hill, Little Nori, T-Bone Hill, Bunker Hill, then the Yellow Sea. Directly behind the Iron Triangle was Sniper Ridge.

I realize that most of you could care less about this string of mountains, but to several of us who were there at the beginning of 1951, it altogether was called the Battle of the Hills. This string of mountains wound up being the MLR (Main Line of Resistance) that was held by the U.N. after the attack by the North Koreans and Chinese beginning July, 1951 through the signing of the peace agreement on July 27, 1953 at Panmunjom. Our instructions were to hold this line at all cost, and we did. This is the present line that separates North Korea from South Korea. What the allies did was fight a stalemate war by defending and holding the territory battle won. This was not an easy task but on occasions in January, 1952, the 45th was required to make deep probes into enemy territory by using ambush patrols and raiding parties.

The enemy launched heavy attacks on the night of February 11, 1952 and a massive attack on May 25, 1952. Both battles lasted several days but finally the assaults by the Communists were called off; the 45th had held.

When we landed in Inchon the 5th of December, 1951, not all of our company was with us as Lt. Robert Randolph's platoon that was attached to the 279th RCT had been left in Camp Shimamatsu, Japan. These men were left to close out the division's operation; they departed for Japan the last of December, 1951, landing at the port of Pusan, South Korea.

Several of us had been pulled from Randolph's platoon to go into Korea with the rest of the company. This left only a few men of the original Shimamatsu bunch, as the enlistments of Ted Connelly, W.R. Ridgeway, Frank Bryant and Odis Bardwell were up, and they had left the unit for the states. Those who I can remember in the last group to come from the Atoka unit were Randolph, Sgt. Perry Ray, Doyle Yates, Bob Glasgow and Leonard Keith with the balance being new draftees.

Randolph took his men to oversee a POW camp located at Yong Dong Po, South Korea, which was just off the end of Kempo Air Strip south of Seoul. These men drew the task of guarding not only Chinese and North Korean prisoners but also those American G.I.s who had been court-martialed, waiting transfer to the military prison (Big 8) in Tokyo, Japan.

Randolph's unit also inherited several men who had formerly served with the 1st Cavalry Division who were on limited duty and did not make the trip with their units to Japan. Most of them were about to be discharged or on light duty due to wounds they had received and had not been released by the medical authorities for full duty. When I was sent down there for medical recovery the middle of February, 1952, there were two men we knew who had been with the 45th Recon Co.; they had barracks next door to us at Camp Polk. One had been hit in his right side with burp gun fire, and the other had several shell fragments from a mortar round. Both were waiting to be sent back to the states for further medical attention.

Incidentally, by the time I was sent to Yong Dong Po, Sgt. Ray had been transferred to a special 8th Army CID unit, so the boys from the Atoka unit were few and far between.

We had no idea why our Lt. Fink, Lt. Wells, Sergeants Bill Flowers, Joe Williams, Jim Barnhill, and Bob Mitchell had left us, but when we got off of the boat at Inchon, these men were there to join us. They had been secretly brought over early to survey the area of our company operation so there would not be misunderstanding as to who would go where and what they would do. Wells and Fink did an outstanding job of running this operation.

Sgt. Bill Flowers and I were talking recently at a ball game when he mentioned that he had never seen as many people "green and gray around the gills in his life." The reason most of the men looked "peaked," we had been aboard this ship for six days in the rough waters off the Japanese Strait, and a bunch of the men had been sea sick. For those of us that had been with the 279th, we made it okay as we had just spent 32 days training with the navy making landings in these same waters, so we had our "sea legs."

As previously mentioned, we boarded cattle rail cars for the trip north and, boy, was it cold. We had no winter clothing, so we just put on everything we had to try to keep warm. Lt. Fink has often said that when he met our train south of Chorwon, that he had never seen so many nearly frozen men in his life, then he had to give us a ride to our assigned area in open trucks. To top it off, we had nothing to eat except our cold c-rations. We ate those rations for four more days until the mess sergeant could get that beat-up, inherited equipment working, and Lt. Wells kept a hot trail to the quartermaster for something for our guys to cook.

At the time we were mobilized, all of our equipment was basically leftover from World War II, and some of it lacked various parts and expert craftsmanship to operate properly. Such was the case of our communication equipment and to answer that need, members of our unit contacted a navy communication technician, Jack McAnulty, and managed to convince him that he was needed to serve his country again. Jack joined up and was made the company como sergeant with the responsibility of getting our radios "up to snuff" and operating properly. With a lot of long hours and hard work, he performed the task that he was asked to accomplish.

We carried all of our equipment with us from the states to Hokkaido, Japan and through McAnulty's effort, he kept our como gear working; however, when we left Japan to go to Korea, we left all of our equipment behind. All we got to take was what few clothes we had and our weapons. When we arrived in Korea, the equipment we were expected to use had been used in combat for some 15 months, and most of it was so beat up that it didn't work; this included the radio equipment. We had to have a como net in order to do our assignments, so McAnulty was once again called upon to perform a miracle. Jack worked day and night, begged and borrowed radio parts to "get us talking." We were in such bad shape that our company headquarters could not talk to division staff. McAnulty once again proved how valuable he was and managed to get "our tails" out of a crack. Just another Boggy Bottom Boy to whom we owe a great deal due to his hard work and ability.

We had another major problem as the army had not furnished us with any cold weather gear before we went into Korea. Our unit got to Hokkiado in late winter of 1951. All we had to wear were khakis, wool dress, long underwear, and regular issue combat boots - no overcoats or parkas. We managed to survive that last of the Japanese winter in the above-mentioned clothing; however, when the sudden move to Korea happened, we had to endure the start of the North Korean winter nights that got 20 to 30 below zero.

Every day we went to our various assignments wearing nearly every stitch of clothing we had. Lt. Fink was our executive officer and he spent a great deal of his time in an almost fruitless effort trying to get the 8th Army to get us some parkas and thermo boots. He finally managed to get pile of jackets to wear under our field jackets and what we called "Russian Bear Cap" that had the fur ear flaps, but his efforts did finally get a few smaller size parkas but most of us were so large that we just had to endure the cold. When we all got together, eventually we got around to talking about how cold we got. By the way, Fink did manage to get us insulated sleeping bags.

One of the worst and coldest assignments any of us could draw was the TCP on Double X Hill. It seems that some of us, Jesse Wayne Phillips, Tinker Ray, Hershel Eastridge, Levi Roberts, Hoss Fitzgerald, Chip Johnson, Riley Henderson and myself were married to that hill. Every time a duty roster came out, some of us would be assigned this duty. We would serve two men at a time with one on the top of the hill and the other at the bottom of the hill. The only way up was by a narrow snake-steep, one-way road with no place for mistakes or areas to pass. We had to use walkie-talkies in order to control the approach and departure to the battalion of the infantry that was assigned to hold that position of the line.

Pardon me while I go into a limited description of this place we called Double X Hill, which was one of the most dreaded areas of duty that we were called on to work. Imagine, if you will, a series of very steep incline mountains located in North Korea that had been under their supervision and control since the end of the war in 1945, but was really under the rule of the Chinese Communist government with every intent of reunifying the two Korea's under their regime. They had made all kinds of defense preparations with everything in these mountains being in their favor.

When the "Korean Police Action" began, as our President Truman called it, the communists launched their attacks from this area to start the war. This region contained the main road that led to Seoul and down to the furthermost tip of South Korea. The Communist Army of North Korea crossed the 38th parallel, the line that separated North and South Korea, on June 25, 1950, and they encountered only a token resistance from unprepared South Korean army units with elements of the American 24th Division. The attack was so effective that they pushed our troops all the way down Korea to just south of a place called Taegu by August, 1950. American GHQ under Gen. MacArthur had managed to get elements of our 25th, 1st Cavalry, 2nd and 3rd Divisions from Japan into a blocking position, into an attack mode and began the allied drive north in September, 1950.

This new turn of events by these American divisions was helped by the U.S. Marines making an amphibious landing, completely unexpected, at the port of Inchon on September 15, 1950. The landing had taken everyone by surprise and the Communist soldiers began surrendering by the thousands. Meanwhile, our troops kept fighting and pushing the enemy to the north toward China and the Yalu River. They had arrived to the furthermost point north, just south of the Chinese border, by November 24, 1950. It was during this push that allied forces fought over Double X Hill for the first time. The first battle over the hill was rather light as the Communist army was retreating to the north.

On November 26, 1950 the Chinese Communist Army crossed the Yalu River by the untold thousands, entering the "police action" with a massive counter offense. Elements of the 1st Marine Division and some army units were trapped in what has become known as "The Frozen Chosen Reservoir" and had to fight their way out to the port of Hungnam by the middle of December, 1950, to be evacuated out of North Korea. Some of our tremendous number of casualties were suffered while fighting a delayed action towards this North Korean seaport.

Meanwhile, the 1st Cavalry and other units were retreating to the south and were joined by the 187th RCT from Japan to cover the retreat of these troops. This retreat brought American units over the top of Double X Hill for the second time. The U.N. forces managed to stop the retreat by July, 1951, and the 1st Cavalry Division was successful in taking Double X Hill. Though badly mauled and shot all to pieces, the cavalry made a gallant surge again taking the hill, managing to hold the line until they got new troops. In October, 1951, the communists once tried to take the hill but their assaults were fought back once again; however, the cavalry took lots of casualties, hence the call came for the 45th Division to come in from Japan to replace the 1st Cavalry Division.

By the time we replaced the First Cavalry, Double X Hill had seen four major battles and several counter-offenses, so needless to say the terrain was certainly not a pretty sight. The only way up to the top of the hill was by a single winding snake-like road, with no way to pass or turn around; so once you started up or down, you had to keep going. Our job was to control who and when the road was to be used. We kept one man on the top of the hill and one at the bottom from daylight till dark and the only contact we had with anyone was by walkie-talkie hand radio.

When the man working the top got his first view of his assignment, he would stand there in awe. If you stepped around the end of the header where you were to stay, you could see the MLR (Front Line) and across a valley looking into the communist lines. As your eyes surveyed the north side of that hill, you witnessed hills that had received so much artillery fire and bombing that hardly anything was left except charred stumps and holes in the side of the mountain. The infantry had dug trenches about waist deep parallel with the terrain of the hill, numerous points had been dug leading out from the trenches and piles of sand bags were stacked up to make for firing positions. This digging had to have been done by hand, accomplished either in spring or summer as the frost line was 36 inches, and there was no way you could dig until there was a thaw. Below the bottom of this hill was a mine field all the way across the rice paddies to the area that the communists controlled. Some of these mines were ours and part of them belonged to the enemy with most of them uncharted.

On the south side were numerous bunkers dug back into the side of the hill, sandbagged as much as possible and the men used whatever logs, boards or sheets of metal available to try to make a roof over their bunker. It was not pretty, and above all, a very uncomfortable place to live and sleep. In front of these bunkers were footpaths with a pole made handrail to hold on to in order not to lose your footing and fall off the side of the hill.

These infantrymen had not only the communists to fight but the cold and snow, horrible living conditions and rats nearly as big as house cats that got in their bunkers looking for food. Another problem was any food, water, ammo, wounded, dead, etc. had to be back or hand carried along these trails, which were not the easiest places to try to walk.

Don't hold me to this date, but the best that I recall it was the morning of December 10, 1951 that Lt. Calvin Mead, Jr. was the officer of the day and Sgt. Travis Alford was sergeant of the guard. They drove PFC Levi Roberts and myself to Double X Hill, arriving just at daylight. Mead stopped the Jeep at the bottom of the hill and explained to Roberts and myself what our assignment was to be. We left Roberts at the bottom and then in our Jeep started our climb to the top of the hill. Reaching the top, Mead gave me my instructions, verified that our walkie-talkies were working and was told that Sgt. Alford would bring someone up to relieve me after lunch.

As soon as Mead and Alford had reached the bottom, they met Co. A, 1st Battalion, 179th Infantry, starting to make its climb to positions on the hill. Shortly, what was left of the 1st Cavalry Co. they were replacing came down, then B Co., 179th started their climb to the top, then C Co. 179th came up for their new homes. D Co. was held below in reserve.

Once the last of the three companies were in position, the flow of traffic up and down Double X was in the control of Roberts and myself. The first battalion started sending ton and a half weapon carriers, one up at a time, with water, rations, ammo, etc. to the top; once there, they were rapidly unloaded. I would start the vehicle towards the bottom, and Roberts would start another towards the top. By noon all of the three companies had gotten their supplies to the top; then we had the division and regimental brass making their way up the hill. The 45th Infantrymen were about to start a series of 429 days and nights of some of the coldest weather you could imagine, and over the next few months some of the bloodiest counter offensives launched during this "Police Action."

I have been asked by some of the men of our company to tell you about what happened in Korea and especially Double X Hill because this place has untold memories in our life. Let me start by trying to describe some of us experiencing artillery fire by the Chinese and our own friendly fire. We learned quickly what it was to identify outgoing fire and "incoming mail," as anytime we cleared one of our artillery battalion's Jeeps to come up the hill, there would be a FO (Forward Observer) on board to call a fire mission over our position and into the Chinese area just across the Chorwon flat. These fire missions were called "Nuisance Rounds" as they were not usually fired on any certain target but to simply let the Chinese know we were watching them.

The Chinese would do the same type of firing; however, when we got down to serious business of firing on a particular target, you would normally see one of our L-19, a small Piper Cub type of aircraft, that would fly above ground fire to see what had been hit and the destruction. Usually our artillery was some four to five miles behind our position, and we were always relieved when we heard the whistling noise go over our heads and normally heard the explosion.

What made us get antsy was hearing the "boom" firing noise and not hearing that whistling sound go over; then we knew it was the Chinese artillery coming in and shortly, we would hear the round hit and the hill would shake. It was rare that the enemy hit anything except one time in the first part of January, 1952, one of the rifle companies about 150 yards from us had hot noon chow brought up by the KSC's (Korean Service Corp, men hired by the American army not to be drafted for service in their army) and were being served a hot meal when the Chinese managed to lob an artillery round over the top of the hill, killing three men and wounding two others.

The company called for the medics to get two ambulances to the top for the wounded. When they reached the bottom checkpoint, Pvt. Frank Anderson, one of our men from Mississippi, called saying he was sending two vehicles up two minutes apart. By the time the ambulances reached the top, we got them turned around, they were carrying the two wounded men down the foot path. We loaded them in the first vehicle and sent them on to Anderson. Then we placed the three dead GIs in the second one and sent them down.

The very next day when Cpl. Jesse Wayne Phillips was working the top, they really sent a "slavo" to the hill, but no one was hurt. A couple days later, Cpl. Tinker Ray was at the top and got the same experience. A good deal of our men got the same treatment.

This time of year people generally will ask about the Christmas that you remember the most. This is another personal experience but the one that stays in my mind was December 25, 1951. For the third time in 15 days, I had drawn duty on the top of Double X Hill. Cpl. Claud Tidwell was the acting sergeant of the guard for the day; he got me up, told me we had sprinkling snow with light winds and that I had better put on most of my clothes as they were expecting a rough day.

I got dressed, checked my little special bag that I carried anytime I left the area, went down to the mess tent for a breakfast of powdered eggs, diced luncheon meat, a piece of bread and some coffee. This day PFC Hershel Eastridge was working the bottom of the hill, while I worked the top. Tidwell gave us some c-rations to take for our noon meal, and, boy, I was not looking forward to a can of hamburger patties or a can of corn beef hash with a inch of grease on the top.

It was about 11:30 a.m. when Hershel Eastridge called up for clearance for Col. "Hicky" McCasland to come up. The colonel arrived in a regular company Jeep instead of his provost marshal vehicle; Pvt. Julis Jones was driving instead of his regular driver, Cpl. Pepper Haraway. Sitting in the back of the Jeep, surrounded by insulated hot cans, was Cpl. Freddie "Sweetie Pie" Moore.

When I saw these three, I was wondering just what was going on, what had I done to have "Hicky" come all the way up here to see me? Jones stopped the Jeep, I saluted the Colonel, and he said, "Bledsoe, we thought you would like a hot meal today." Then he told "Sweetie Pie," "Fill him up." Moore began to unload all of those cans from the back of the Jeep, brought out a mess kit for me, placed some dressing, white turkey meat, sweet potatoes, celery cheese sticks, a fruit salad, green beans, olives and two slices of fresh light bread. They gave me hot coffee to drink, followed by a piece of yellow sheet cake with white icing.

Needless to say, I was in "Hog Heaven." I placed that mess kit on the hood of the Jeep and all the time I was eating, they talked to me. "Hicky" asked a lot of questions as this was the first time he had been up there and while we were talking, it began to snow. He said that they had other stops to make and had better get on down the road. Before the colonel got into the Jeep to leave, he stuck out his hand, saluted me and said, "Shug, next year we'll be home for this holiday." This was unusual that he called me Shug, as normally he referred to most of us by our last names. When he left he was teary eyed and handed me a sack. Shortly, I looked in the sack and somewhere he had gotten me an apple, an orange, a Milky Way candy bar and two packs of Camel cigarettes. I don't think any of the others that day got a sack. I have often thought that was his way to let me know that I was special to him, as he was the who got me to enlist when I was 14 years old; plus, he and Scott Wells were kind of "My Guardian Angels." After they had gone down the hill, I threw that can of c-ration corn beef hash that I was going to have for dinner as far down the side of the hill as I could throw. The next day the weather really started getting bad and cold.

The last of December, 1951, the harshness of one of the worst Korean winters of the century began and did not let up until towards the last of March, 1952. You can not begin to believe how cold it was unless you were there. The bulk of our company was still ill equipped for cold weather not having parkas or snow pack boots. (I will mention this again later.)

Recently, while in the Atoka State Bank, Barney McCall, my company commander in 1948, came to me and told me about what our mutual friend, Col. Vance Rich of the 2nd Battalion, 180th Regt., had to say about the Korean cold. He told Barney, "It was unbelievable what the Thunderbirds had to endure." He said he had never been so cold in his life, that he had actually seen bolts freeze on rifles. He added that he was proud of the 45th to suffer the cold the way they did and not lose a foot of ground while fighting off counter-attack after counter-attack by the Chinese.

Let us go back to Double X Hill for just a little while. From December 10, 1951 to January 31, 1952, I personally worked that hill a total of 14 times at the top; in fact, even today Scott Wells laughs and calls it Bledsoe Hill. Chip Johnson, Riley Henderson, Tinker Ray and Jess Phillips had nearly as much time up there as I did. In fact, Ol' Jess said one time, "If we didn't win it, we surely had squatters rights."

The evening of January 31, 1952, Sgt. Bud Greathouse went to see 1st Sgt. Sidney Camp and told him, "Bledsoe had some trouble and we had better get him to the medics." Sid and Bud drove me to the 120th Regt. Medical Hospital, Sid got out of the Jeep and shortly, a Major, who was a doctor came out (He was a Nesi from Hawaii.) with orderlies carrying a fold-up cloth stretcher. They had me lie down on the stretcher and carried me into this medical tent where other doctors and medics were working.

They had me sit on a table, took off my gloves and started massaging my hands, while two other medics began to take off my Cochran jump boots. The Nesi doctor looked first at my hands; then he started to pull the socks off of my feet, then all at once they gave me a shot in both ankles and the pain began to go away. The doctor told them to soak my feet for awhile, then he came back and cut my socks off of my feet. I learned later that this soaking and cutting was a precautionary measure to keep from pulling off any hide from my feet that might have been stuck to my socks. Shortly, the doctor said, "Put him under." When I woke up, I was in this long tent, on that cloth stretcher, being held off of the ground by four u-posts driven in the ground, with signal wire running back and forth to hold the posts together.

My feet and hands were bandaged and under my head they had folded up my pile jacket to make me a pillow. They had covered me with two G.I. blankets. I had to rely on one of the orderlies to feed me, take me to the latrine and once in the morning and in the afternoon, they would pick me up, take me down where there was a stove, sit me on a water can to try to get warm. I laid there on that stretcher for five days. Then the morning of the sixth day the doctor said, "We are going to send you back to your company, but you are not to pull any duty and you are to report here every morning for a week." With that, they pulled off the bandages and brought me a new pair of socks.

I went back to the company, and eight days later, they said I could pull light duty but no lengthy time in the cold. It was decided to send me to Lt. Robert Randolph's POW camp located at Yong Dong Po, south of Seoul and just off of Kempo air strip. As we were riding through Seoul, you could see along both sides of the streets sidewalk vendors with GI parkas, snow pack boots and thermo-insulated "Mickey Mouse" boots for sale. These were the very items that we could not get for the men of our company; needless to say, this really hacked me.

When we arrived at the POW camp, we found the prisoners nice and warm in squad tents with new diesel stoves that worked and no doubt the most and best food that they ever had in their lives. I thought to myself that the enemy has it better than our own men at the front.

I was sent back to the company about the middle of March, 1952, and never did work Double X again. Let me mention that in December, 1951 and January 1952, that from time to time I saw some of the Atoka boys with the 179th Infantry when they would send up a truck occasionally to let them go take a shower. I saw Marvin Bonham, Buck Nichols, Bill Rector, Mart Rector, Eddie Vandenburg, Charles Umsted and Bob Nanney; all had been members of our company at one time.

Let me tell you about a couple of incidents that happened to Easy Co., 179th Infantry. James "Smitty" Smith of Tushka, Bob Nanney of Harmony and Onul "Cotton" Payne of Boehler all were a part of this unit. On May 21, 1952 they were on Hill 347 when the Chinese started an offensive but could not take the hill; however "Cotton" Payne suffered three grazing head wounds and was evacuated to the rear. Within three days Payne was back with his unit. On the night of June 21, 1952, Payne's platoon was on Hill 265 outpost and moved the next day to Hill 260. "Smitty's" platoon replaced them on Hill 265 and the rest of Easy

Co. was positioned on Hills 200, 260 and 347. On June 22, 1952, the Chinese hit Easy Company with everything they had. They managed for a short period of time to get within the defense perimeter of the platoon located on Hill 265. Though severely outnumbered, the T-birds held the outpost, but by the time help arrived, out of 33 men in the platoon, seven had been taken prisoner, 23 men killed or wounded and only three men were able to walk off of that hill.

"Smitty" was one of those taken prisoner by the Chinese and would live through hell for some 15 months before he was released and crossed over "The Freedom Bridge" at Panmunjom. "Cotton" was on Hill 260 and was severely wounded by shrapnel all up and down his side; he still has so much metal in his body that they cannot do a body MRI scan on him.

Finally, one of the duties we had as MPs was to act as honor bodyguards for any dignitaries who came into our area. While in Japan, we worked on one occasion for Gen. Matthew Ridgeway, his wife and three-year-old son. In Korea we worked with Betty Hutton, Debbie Reynolds, Monica Lewis, Edith Brown, Gen. Ridgeway and later Gen. Dwight Eisenhower and Marilyn Monroe.

The 45th had a total of 429 combat days in Korea, having been in four different battles, suffering 834 men killed in action and 3,170 wounded. In World War II, the 45th spent 511 days in combat, 3,650 killed in action, 13,729 wounded, eight battle stars and five amphibious landings.

General George S. Patton, addressing the division after the invasion of Sicily in 1943, stated, "Born at sea, baptized in blood, your fame shall never die. Your division is one of the best, if not the best division, in the history of American Armies." This statement was made August 5, 1943.

CHAPTER 38

Scott Wells Leads Delegation to Italy for Tribute

One of Atoka's retired 45th Division soldiers, LTC Scott Wells, a veteran of both World War II and Korea, led a delegation to Nettuno-Anzio, Italy, for a memorial dedication on May 29, 2000. Nettuno-Anzio is the location of an allied cemetery where some 8,000 white crosses in perfect alignment stand amidst the grave sites of fallen comrades who have been resting for some 55 years. The cemetery also has a marble wall with the names engraved of some 3,000 other U.S. veterans who were killed in action but whose bodies remain unaccounted for.

The memorial dedication is a bronze plaque placed at the entrance of the cemetery that reads "Memorial Day, May 29, 2000, 180th Infantry Regiment, 45th Infantry Division, Nettuno-Anzio (Italy), to the gallant men who fought and to those who rest in the Sicily-Rome American Cemetery, "You Will Not Be Forgotten" being engraved in both English and Italian. The memorial carries both the Thunderbird Patch and the 180th Regimental Emblem. This plaque is a reminder for years to come that this amphibious landing was one of the hardest fought battles of any war which was made at Anzio with the 180th Infantry Regiment being a major element in what has since been called "The Rock."

Some 858 soldiers of the 45th Infantry Division are buried there. The cemetery holds the remains of nine men from Company B, the Atoka Unit. Those from Atoka who are buried there are: Beard, Wilbern S.; Franklin, William D.; Moffatt,

William D.; Moore, Amous; McLeroy, James T.; Lynch, Cecil C.; Brown, Robert M.; Sico, Paul M.; Alford; and Warren. There were also two men from Atoka - Thomas Belcher and Tom Sanders - whose bodies were there but have been shipped home. Scott Wells had four members of his family from Atoka who were killed and buried here. They were his brother-in-law, William Moffatt, "Jabo" McLeroy, his uncle, and cousins Thomas Belcher and Tom Sanders.

Wells and Jessie Wall, "the last of the Choctaw code talkers" have made several trips to Italy. Once they found out that the Veterans Association does not pay for or endorse the placing of monuments or memorials outside of the United States, then these two members of the 180th decided when they came home to begin raising funds to correct this wrong concerning the men of history of "The Rock of Anzio." Thunderbirds gave willingly for this tribute and some 50 members made reservations to this dedication.

We all know and hear about D-Day landings in France on the 6th of June, 1944; however, nothing is ever mentioned that on this same day, 6th of June, 1944 that the 45th Division, along with other units of Gen. Mark Clark's 5th Army entered Rome. On that very day while entering the city area, Well's wife, the former Katie Moffatt, lost her brother, William Moffatt and as previously mentioned, he is buried in this cemetery.

At Anzio, the 45th was confronted for 125 days of furious combat under extremely adverse situations they suffered to hold and win "The Rock."

CHAPTER 39

Now a Preacher, He Led a Platoon in Korea at Age 16

This portrait is of a soldier who became a patriot at the age of 16. This individual has been a resident of Atoka for the past 23 years. His name is Glen Thomason, a replacement infantryman who became a member of Co. I, 9th RCT, 2nd Infantry Division (Indian head). Glen was originally from Shawnee, Oklahoma, and upon turning 16 years of age, decided to quit high school and join the U.S. Army, although he had to fib about his age to a recruiting officer.

I met Glen by chance several years ago when we both happened to be in Wyrick's lumber store, where he was having a few jousting words and laughs with my old friend Dick Heard. I stood there momentarily listening to their chatter, and I put out my hand to introduce myself and jokingly said, "You seem to know Dick as well as the rest of us." The three of us chatted for a little while, conducted our business and left the store.

The next week I happened to be in Wyrick's again and ran into Thomason and spoke to him by name. I could see by the expression of his face that he was doing the best to remember my name. We talked for a while, got whatever we came for and left the store.

We happened to see each other again under the same circumstances and got to know each other a little better by "swabbing" (an old oil field expression). I found out that he had been in Korea at the same time our company was there. Due to the number of times that the two of us talked and by constantly asking questions and dragging out answers, I learned a great deal about my newly made friend, so much so that when it was decided to write only about six patriots, I wanted him to be one of the stories. Glen's answer was no. After some 14 months, he has agreed to let me write briefly about him.

Upon enlisting in the army, Glen was sent to Schoofield Barracks, Hawaii, for his basic infantry training in February, 1951. Glen had the ideal assignment for any GI, having been left for duty in paradise until some time in the first part of February, 1952, when he received orders for Camp Drake, Japan then on to the Port of Pusan, South Korea.

By March, 1952 this young GI found himself on the Chorwon front on a hill referred to as "Pork Chop Hill." The third day he was on the hill, his platoon got hit by a Chinese attack, killing his squad leader and several in his company. The platoon leader told Glen that he was now the squad leader due to the fact he had a PFC stripe and the remainder of the squad were privates. So here he was, three days into combat and this 16-year-old had been made a squad leader in charge of 11 men in an infantry unit.

He had arrived in North Korea just in time to be on the tail-end of one of the most severe winters in years, plus the Chinese kept launching squad-size groups followed by platoon attacks out of the hills all along the front. It included constant fire fights and hand-to-hand combat for some time until artillery and mortar fire inflicted heavy casualties on the enemy. These types of attacks were conducted for the next few weeks all up and down the front; however, the Chinese were unsuccessful in retaking any of their lost territory.

Glen's unit was pulled off the line for a short rest only to be assigned back to the front on what was called "Heartbreak Ridge." After they had settled into their new positions, they were called upon for routine patrols that resulted in some brief skirmishes and very light contact with the enemy. All was rather quiet until June 21 and 22, 1952, when the Chinese launched very intense attacks all up and down the MLR. Each of the units were successful once again in fighting off the aggressors.

In September, 1952, Glen's company was still on "Heartbreak Ridge" when the Chinese once again hit their position. The attack began on a moonlit night about 23:00 hours when the enemy sent wave after wave up the hill to try and take "Heartbreak." It was while in hand-to-hand combat with a Chinese soldier that the enemy managed to run his bayonet into Glen's stomach. The Chinese soldier was in the process of pulling out the bayonet when a member of Glen's squad killed the enemy soldier. The unit held the position and help arrived; the medics attended to Glen's wound, and he was transported to a hospital for surgery. It is kind of hard to believe, but some three weeks after he had suffered the stomach wound he reported back to his company.

He was notified in a few weeks that he was being shipped back to the states to Ft. Sill, Oklahoma. and then was assigned to the 101st MP Co. in Germany with the job of "chasing prisoners," bringing back soldiers who had gone AWOL. Later he was transferred to Gallenhousen, Germany, where he worked in giving men advanced infantry training. In March, 1954, he was shipped home to Camp Chaffee, Arkansas for discharge, receiving an honorable discharge with no disability for his combat wound.

Glen first went back to work in Shawnee for Dr. Pepper Company. Glen left the employment of the cold drink company to go to work at the Shawnee Country Club with his father. Later, he did construction work and leaving a job in Houston, Texas, he and his wife stopped in Atoka. That was 1977 and they liked the area so much that they decided to stay. For one year he worked for county commissioner Don Loftis, then he started doing small construction jobs for individuals, plus he has always helped some of the widow women with their lawn work. You may have seen him at Mrs. Marie Ralls, Babe Wallace, Margaret Hames or others doing whatever they asked him to do.

In 1978 Glen was baptized and became a minister in the Pentecostal Church and began to preach. Through the years he has preached and helped small congregations plus has been involved in establishing new churches. Presently, Glen preaches for the Pentecostal Church of God in Wapanucka. My friend is one of those that practices what he preaches, giving all the effort that he has. I know you would agree with me that truly Glen Thomason is a patriot.

CHAPTER 40

This Pilot Survived Being Shot Down to Fly More Missions

This portrait is written by Lane Johnson about our patriot, 1st Lt. Willie W. Moore, a B-24 bomber pilot, 740th Bomb Sq., 455th Bomb Grp. 8th Air Force, World War II, based out of Italy.

I wish that I could take credit for this article due not only to the subject but also how well it was written. May I take a moment to tell you how this portrait came about? Some three weeks ago my wife answered the phone in my office and said, "There is a Thelma Johnson who would like to speak with you." When I got on the phone, she began to tell me about how much she and her husband had been enjoying our weekly writings, that she had someone about whom they thought I might be interested in writing.

I told her that we were in the process of writing the last three articles and that we were going to quit writing. She wanted me to know about her brother, Lt. Willie Moore and that we had already mentioned another brother S/Sgt. Amous Moore, B Co., 180th Infantry, 45th Division from Atoka who was killed in Italy on September 23, 1943. When she mentioned Amous, I began to get a little more interested then all at once she said, "Let me have my husband, Lane, to talk to you." After a nice conversation it was decided he would call me the next week so we would arrange to get together to talk about Willie.

The next week we had all of this heavy snow, they living in

Canadian, Oklahoma, could not get out but wanted to send me some material about her brother for me to look at and maybe meet the following week. The Johnson's mailed me a video tape of Willie and Col. Charlie Weaver, a 45th Atoka boy in both World War II and Korea, along with a draft about Lt. Moore. Once I read about Lane Johnson's brother-in-law, it was decided to publish the draft as it was written. I could tell from Lane's writings how much he admired and respected Willie Moore.

Before I received the package and letter draft, I spoke with Scott Wells, Lon Robert Fink, Jack Bonner, Olen Curry and Gilbert Baker to see if they remembered Willie Moore. They each remembered him and said he had become a bomber pilot, shot down but managed to be rescued and return to battle. By each of these men knowing about what happened, then it was just a matter of putting the balance of the article together. The following is the complete draft as written by Lane Johnson...

History teaches us that it required the combined efforts of all branches of our armed services to defeat the enemy in WWII, which included all ground forces, the air force, and the ships and submarines at sea. Among the many types of aircraft used by the U.S. and its allies in both the European theater and the war against Japan were heavy bombers, from B-25s in the first raid against Tokyo from the decks of the aircraft carrier U.S.S. Hornet, to the B-29s that dropped the A-bomb and ended the war with Japan.

Heavy bombers also played an important role in the struggle against Germany. As the fighting wore on, Hitler's ability to make war was weakened as a direct result of the relentless bombing by American and British heavy bomber planes, destroying his munitions plants, U-Boat pens, railroad yards, arms factories, oil refineries, and war supply depots. The B-17 Flying

Fortress was the pacesetter and, except for it, the war against Germany might well have been prolonged.

But in 1939, even before the U.S. entered the war, the military saw the need for a heavy bomber of even better performance and heavier bomb load than the existing B-17. The required specification was for a bomber capable of top speeds of 300 mph with a range of 3,000 miles and 35,000 feet ceiling. Thus was born the B-24. Called the Liberator, a total of 18,188 B-24's were built, more than any other aircraft before or since WWII. Although it conducted hundreds of other bombing missions, the B-24 is best remembered for its raids on the oil refineries and storage facilities in Rumania, which was the only major oil fields the Germans had access to and which supplied, on average, about 45 percent of all German petroleum. Despite heavy losses by the bombers and crews, the oil fields in Ploesti and other Rumanian locations were bombed out and made useless for the remainder of the war.

Willie W. Moore from Atoka was a B-24 bomber pilot with the 455th Bomber Group, 15th Air Force, stationed in Italy during World War II.

Born and raised in Oklahoma, Willie is a graduate of Atoka High School, class of 1938. Prior to joining the service in 1942, he served in the 45th Division of the Oklahoma National Guard. As a B-24 bomber pilot, Willie completed 55 bombing missions against the Germans during WWII. These were all high-risk missions with hundreds of allied planes and crew members lost, shot down by German anti-aircraft guns or fighter planes. On his 15th bombing mission, Willie became one of a few B-24 pilots to be shot down, rescued, then fly 40 additional bombing missions and live to tell about it. He was awarded the Distinguished Flying Cross dated July 3, 1944, and worded as follows:

"Willie W. Moore, 0-680679, First Lieutenant, 740th Bomb Sq., 455th Bomb Gp. For extraordinary achievement in aerial flight as Pilot of a B-24 type aircraft. On 21 April 1944, Lt. Moore participated in a bombing mission against vital enemy installations in Rumania. Approaching the target area Lt. Moore's formation was attacked by large formations of enemy fighter planes, resulting in severe damage to his aircraft. A shell burst in the cockpit causing wounds to Lt. Moore and the co-pilot. With the co-pilot dazed and unable to assist him and his cockpit filled with smoke, it was only by exercising outstanding skill that Lt. Moore was able to keep his aircraft under control. With two engines on fire, Lt. Moore kept his ship in formation until free from enemy attacks. He then flew his almost unairworthy aircraft back to friendly territory until his fuel supply was exhausted and he was forced to abandon his aircraft. Only after all his crew had bailed out did Lt. Moore leave his ship. By his leadership, professional skill and determination to return to safety, Lt. Moore has reflected great credit upon himself and the armed forces of the United States of America. Residence at appointment: Atoka, Oklahoma." (By Command: Major General Twining, R.E. Taylor, Colonel, GSC, Chief of Staff)".

Tail gunner S/Sgt. Robert L. Koutsky was killed by a mishap during his parachute jump. Willie Moore and all other crew members survived. Italian children led Willie and the surviving crew members together, and they were picked up later by a British army truck and American ambulance.

Said F/O Raymond C. Butler, co-pilot, who was making his first mission in this theater: "We owe our lives to the hair-trigger thinking and great flying of Lt. Willie Moore."

After being discharged from the service on September 10,

1945 at Camp Chaffee, Ark., Willie says he "high-tailed it back to Atoka" and picked up his civilian life where he had left off. He reports that he did no flying prior to WWII and has not flown an airplane since. Following his discharge, Willie and his wife, Mary, bought land in the Atoka area, stocked it with cattle, and tried ranching for a while. Deciding that wasn't what they wanted from life, they pulled up stakes and moved west to California, living and working in such California cities as Holtville, El Centro and Sunnyvale before finally settling in Waterford, where they now live and enjoy their retirement.

Willie, and the former Mary Stanphill of Atoka, have been married for over 57 years but have never forgotten their early years in Oklahoma. They make it a point to return to Atoka every year or two to attend class or family reunions and to visit their many friends and relatives. Two of Willie's brothers from Atoka, Amous and Orville Moore, also served in WWII. Amous was killed in action in the European theater. Another brother, Clarence Moore, was killed in an accident and explosion at the ammunition plant near McAlester, where he worked during the war.

In addition to the Distinguished Flying Cross, for his service in WWII, Willie earned and was awarded the Air Medal with three Oak Leaf Clusters, the Purple Heart, the ETO Ribbon with three battle stars, and a Presidential Unit Citation.

Willie Moore, Patriot, is but one of thousands that Oklahoma and all America can be proud of.

Willie Moore is living in Waterford, California, and several years ago became an Ordained Minister in the Baptist Church. His brother Amous is buried in Nettuno-Anzio, Italy cemetery along with several other boys from Atoka, they being part of 858 men from the 180th Infantry Regiment, 45th Division. Amous

Moore has a son who never got to see his father as he was born after Amous was killed.

I might also mention that Lane Johnson was a crew member of the battleship U.S.S. New Mexico which was a sister ship of the U.S.S. Mississippi that Gilbert Baker was aboard and endured several naval battles together in the Pacific during World War II.

Patriots, look around you, you may not realize it but our part of the country has served more than our fair share. Men and women willing to lay their lives on the line for each of you.

CHAPTER 41

While He Served Abroad, the FBI Thought He Was a Draft-Dodger

When I was growing up, one of the most read periodicals was the "Readers Digest" and one of my favorite articles was "the most unforgettable people that I have ever met." Our portrait this week to me is just such a person as I was held spellbound while doing the interview with him. This man happens to be none other than Robert "Bob" Christie, a man who played a dual roll for his country during World War II.

Bob is originally from Clarksburg, West Virginia, having moved from there in 1935 to Norman, Oklahoma to live with his folks and to finish his schooling. He entered the University of Oklahoma and became a member of the ROTC program, serving in what was known as "French 75 Cannon Horse Drawn Artillery Unit." It was during the time of receiving his education in order to help pay the bills that he went to work for his uncle, a oil field drilling contractor in Norman, on what is known as a Cable Tool Drilling Rig. He had to leave college, took a job with Parker Brothers and Eason Drilling Co. and worked in the Enid area until they could not get drill pipe. He then heard about Noble-Fain Drilling needing some experienced oil field hands, and he met a company man at a pool hall at 24th and Robinson in Oklahoma City. They offered him $6 per day, this seeming to him the treasury of Ft. Knox, so he accepted the employment.

Bob was first sent to Illinois by Noble then one day the

management came to him and offered him a job overseas but would not tell him where he was going; however, the money was good, and they would send his check to the bank. He accepted Noble's offer and on February 22, 1943 reported for a physical at the company's office in Tulsa. He bid goodbye to his wife and son to catch a train to New York, where he waited two weeks for a ship to take him and other oil field workers to Europe. They finally boarded the Queen Elizabeth, along with 15,000 soldiers, setting a course for Glasgow, Scotland. They crossed the Atlantic, always being watchful for the German U-Boats that had played havoc with the allied supply ships and troop transports. His crew landed in Glasgow, took a train to Edwinburg, then on to Newkirk-on-Trent, Nottingham Shire, located in the middle of England.

Shortly, they received notice that their drilling equipment was arriving at the Liverpool dock, so they took four trucks to move the equipment, as it straggled in, to an existing oil field located in the famous "Sherwood Forest." The English could not understand the moving of oil field equipment on trucks as they moved everything on rollers. As they would tear the whole rig down to the ground, the Noble and Fain-Porter Drilling Company would lay the entire rig down, then move it by using two trucks and uprighting the rig to once again start drilling another hole.

Bob's group consisted of some 46 men who worked seven days a week for a total of 84 hours. His regular pay was $1.75 per hour, then all over 40 hours was considered overtime; so they were making some pretty good money for that day and time. It wasn't as easy as it sounds, for the Germans were constantly launching air raids against England and here they were setting out in the middle, with lights on the drilling rigs to see how to work.

The rigs they were using were approximately 90-feet tall with the average depth of the well being some 2,500 feet. Most of the time they drilled on two and one-acre spacing and once they rigged up, they could drill about 1,300 feet per day, using 30-foot joints and were considered "fast hole drillers." They drilled 106 holes in a one-year period of time, and the crew left to come home in February, 1944.

Bob once again boarded a troop transport headed this time across the Atlantic for New York Harbor. When he arrived in the states, he went to Prescott, Arizona to be with his wife and son. His family had to move to Arizona as his new son had asthma and they were told the dry climate was what he needed.

Bob had no more than set his suitcase down when he found out the FBI was looking for him as he had received a draft notice while overseas that he was unaware of. Bob was immediately inducted into the U.S. Army at Ft. MacArthur, California as a private; even though he had ROTC training while attending the University of Oklahoma, he had not received a commission as an officer.

He was sent to Ft. Bragg, North Carolina for basic training. He was transported by train to New York for shipment aboard a troop transport to Europe. Already he had crossed the Atlantic twice in the last 16 months, and this was getting to be old hat for him. They were some 20 days aboard ship from New York to Oran, Africa, then on to Marseilles, France.

Once they landed in France, he was assigned to the 714th Field Artillery Battalion where the major weapon was "155 MM Long Toms" with track personnel carriers. When they first got there, it was really cold and they slept in pup tents. They received orders to go by train box cars to Thionville, France, some 300 miles to the north. It took some six days to make the trip. There was no heat in the boxcars, so when the train stopped, they tried to find pieces of coal along the side of the track to build a fire in a bucket. Neither were there any rest room facilities on board; they had one five-gallon can of water. It was so cold that their rations congealed and were almost impossible to eat. Incidentally, at one of their stops, the water can was empty, but someone found some wine and filled the can.

They were moved up to Bastogne, where they retrieved equipment that had been recaptured and moved to a recovery area. His unit, in early December, 1944, transported German POWs by truck with only one guard, while they made the German prisoners stand up packed as many as possible in the bed of the truck. Bob said that sometimes they had as many as 80 prisoners standing per load to be taken to rear-line detention camps. They also brought back civilians out of the Bastogne area, and at one time they hauled back 155 American soldiers who had deserted at Bastogne.

His unit was in Luxembourgh firing "nuisance rounds" while Bob was calling the artillery firing coordinates. When the war ended in May, 1945, he was in Germany and was transferred to work in military government at Iseneck, Germany. Bob left Germany in spring of 1946 arriving at Ft. Bliss, Texas, in April, 1946, for discharge and immediately went to his family in Phoenix.

Bob moved his family to Norman, Oklahoma, and in 1951 to Atoka and opened a business. He said they nearly starved the first two years but business finally picked up and in 1958 he founded Big Bear Construction and later other ventures.

Bob's story is very unusual in that he was probably the only U.S. citizen who played such a dual roll as both a civilian and as a soldier in the same war, on the same continent and yet having his government's law enforcement agency, the FBI, looking for him because he had not reported for the draft. Bob's interview and story is one of the most fascinating that I have had the opportunity of conducting. By the way, before I forget it, he and the group of oil field workers who went to England to help the war effort held their first reunion in 1991. I think you will agree that Bob has earned the term patriot.

CHAPTER 42

This Medic Survives D-Day to Be Wounded on Way to Berlin

So many times when we think of people involved in combat operations, we have a tendency to forget that there is one very special military occupation specialty number rarely mentioned — that number is #657.

To you that are not familiar with some military terms, in the early part of your military career, your job assignment is decided. MOS #657 is that of a combat medic. Several men from the Atoka area have served as combat medics, those being Herman Barton, Roy Mead, James Thompson, J. Jene Mungle and others, with each seeming to have had a special calling for helping others. Whenever a soldier needs medical help, whether combat or non-combat roles, the first one they call for is "medic" or "doc."

Though we may not have shown it, these guys were extra special to each of us and willing to put their lives on the line for each man in need.

We have stated the above to give you a little introduction to an Atoka patriot by the name of John Clyde Williford, rank of T/5, Medical detachment, 16th Infantry Regiment, 1st Infantry Division, affectionately called "The Big Red One." Clyde, as most people called him, grew up in Atoka, went to school here, and as some of his fellow students would tell you, "He was a big man." He was some 6'1" in height and weighed almost 250 pounds. Clyde was one of the stars of his high school football team, being an outstanding fullback and occasionally playing center.

Clyde was inducted into the U.S. Army on December 14, 1942 and reported to Ft. Sill, Oklahoma a week later. After basic training, he was sent to Ft. Sam Houston, Texas, to receive specialized training as a medic. By the middle of April 1943, he had completed his medical training and was sent to the east coast to a port of embarkation where he was assigned to the 1st Infantry Division for overseas assignment.

The "Big Red One" departed the east coast on May 9, 1943 in a convoy of troop ships headed for a landing in North Africa. They saw the land of sand and rocks on May 23, 1943 and within a week they began to prepare for yet another landing. Little did he realize that his unit, along with the 45th, 36th, 3rd and 34th Divisions would make history by becoming a part of "Operation Husky" under the command of Gen. George S. Patton's 7th Army and would storm the beaches of the island of Sicily on July 11, 1943. Once the island was taken, his entire division was transported to England on October 12, 1943 for more training. Clyde did not know that he was about to become a part of "Operation Overlord."

His unit arrived in England on November 5, 1943 and began constant infantry training for land warfare and some experience of getting in and out of small landing craft. After some seven months of hectic work, they were ordered aboard various types of landing boats and on the morning of June 6, 1944, they saw the shore line of the Normandy area of France. This was D-Day and the 1st Division along with the 2nd and 29th Infantry Divisions landed on what was to become known as "Bloody Omaha" beach. On Omaha most things that could go wrong did, the Allied air strike that was intended to eliminate the German defensive positions before the American Divisions came ashore missed its target and left the defenders largely unscathed.

Unknown to the combat troops as they steamed ashore, their beach was defended by a newly arrived and very tough German Division—the 352nd. The landing craft were shelled by expertly directed artillery fire as the small boats tried to lumber on to the beach. Many of the American amphibious tanks sank in rough water. The 1st managed to get ashore and run up the beach to the sea wall (many did not get that far) were pinned down by well-directed, accurate, small arms fire. The U.S. assigned demolition teams that were to blow an opening in the sea wall; these teams had so many casualties and loss of equipment that the situation had grown desperate, and it was necessary to call on naval vessels to fire directly on the wall so the men could get out of their entrapment on Normandy Beach.

Late in the afternoon of the first day, they were able to get off of the beach and began capturing defense positions. The cost of the blunders at Omaha Beach was frighteningly expensive as 3,881 men were dead or wounded the first day. Clyde's unit advanced into the Normandy countryside of wooded lanes and thick hedge rows that housed thousands of German snipers.

The 1st moved to Caretan then advanced towards St. Lo, where the fighting was highlighted by constant German counter attacks and the ever presence of the famed German 88mm gun that was blowing up U.S. tanks that could only travel roadways because of the wet grounds in the fields. The four weeks from the D-Day landing, the American casualties went to 10,641 killed in action and 51,387 wounded.

The first part of August, 1944, the 1st was transferred under Patton's command being made a part of the 3rd Army. Clyde's unit was a part of the Falaise Pocket Battle and on August 20,

1944, they were successful in trapping 20,000 Germans. The 1st started making the run to Berlin with Patton's 3rd Army by going into Belgium and Luxembourg. By September 12, Patton had taken Nancy and could see his way into Germany. His division managed to get into Germany and their movement was being slowed down due to a shortage of ammo, food and fuel; however they continued to move towards the German capital.

On November 18, 1944, while trying to help wounded during the course of battle, Clyde himself was wounded. His wounds were severe enough that he was sent to a hospital in England on November 26, 1944. Clyde stayed in England until March 26, 1945 then was sent back to the U.S., arriving on April 4, 1945. He was taken to Kennedy General Hospital in Memphis, Tennessee and was treated at this facility until he was discharged on June 15, 1945.

For his bravery under fire and for treating and rescuing wounded, he was awarded the Silver Star and the Bronze Star. He also wore the Purple Heart, the Eame Campaign Ribbon with four battle stars, Sicilian Campaign, African Campaign and a Bronze Arrowhead. I believe that you would call him a Patriot.

CHAPTER 43

This Medic Also Wore a Green Beret

Some 16 months ago, when we first started this series of portraits, it was my intention to write about only six patriots from this area. I had already decided who they were and to do my best to give you a little insight as to their military service, telling what they had done for this country.

All of these months later, I am finally getting around to writing about the sixth person I had in mind and the reason that he was to be the last was the very unusual experiences that he encountered while serving in the U.S. Army. Most of you know this week's subject, but I don't think that you really know what a gallant man he is. I am talking about the oldest son of Bill and "Butch" Haggard, E-5 Ransy Cooper "Ran" Haggard.

Ran was born May 28, 1943 in Atoka, Oklahoma, attended school in Durant with some college hours at Southeastern State before he moved to the Bel Monte, California area, working full time for a tree surgery company and attending San Mateo College three nights a week. In his move to California, Ran never gave any thought about notifying his draft board that he no longer lived in Oklahoma, but one day he received a letter ordering him to report to Oklahoma City on Monday morning for a physical. He contacted his draft board, and they told him to go to Oakland, California. He complied with the government's wishes and was told that he would be inducted in about 60 days. He decided that the best thing for him to do was "to go ahead and join as that was something everyone in the family had done in years past."

253

On March 15, 1964 Ran joined the army at Oakland, California and was immediately placed aboard a bus with members of Hell's Angels, men who held Ph.D.s, gang members and just about anything you can think of, becoming one big family headed for a foggy area known as Ft. Ord, California, to begin 9 weeks of basic training.

Ran had already figured out that he had to get away from some of these guys. So when a representative from the airborne jump school came in and gave a lecture the eighth week of training, Ran volunteered for parachute jump school. He was sent to Ft. Benning, Georgia in July 1964 for a four-week course. Each day began every morning at 4 a.m. with a nice brisk run, some physical training, breakfast at 6 a.m., followed by the daily grind of airborne training.

For those not familiar with airborne training, you never walk anywhere; if you are going to catch a bus to go to town, you run to the bus stop and when they open the door to let you in, you simply run up the steps. They begin to instill in you from the very first day how mean you are until you get to the point that you believe exactly what they have taught you.

From the very beginning you climb to a jump tower and begin to learn how to come out the side door of an aircraft using a cable to give you a little starting experience and some sensation of falling through the air. Gradually, the tower jumps get a little more hazardous and a little tougher, then after three weeks you look on the company bulletin board and find your name that today is your day to make your first jump.

Each man who had his name on the list would try to act brave as if there was nothing to jumping out of an airplane, but down deep inside it was only a front they were putting on. Once the aircraft got over the drop zone, the jumpmaster got the green light to go, then he would holler, "Stand-up, hookup, check your equipment, shuffle and stand in the door way." By this time each man has a little throat problem and is just a little bit antsy. You are saying to yourself, "Can I do this? Will I back out? Will the jumpmaster have to shove me out?" but all the time you are talking back to yourself, "I can't quit. I can do this. I have come through much hell to get this far." and the next thing you know the line has pushed you out of the door.

Immediately upon leaving the door of the aircraft, you begin counting 1,000, 2,000, 3,000, etc., just like you have been taught and look up to see if the chute is beginning to open. Then all at once you feel a jerk, a pull on your harness and you know that your chute is inflated as you are gliding towards the ground. Your first landing may not be perfect; however, you are all smiles saying to yourself "I've done it." You make the necessary required jumps, including a night jump and a full simulated combat exercise then on a Saturday morning you march to a parade ground where you are presented your parachute jump wings to signify that you have completed this phase of training and can now be called a "trooper."

They used to give you an overnight pass and many of the men would head for what was called "Sin City," none other than Phoenix City, Alabama, which had the reputation of having anything a G.I. wanted and a whole lot of what he didn't need. It was a tough place and many a "trooper" found out while visiting that he was not near as mean as he had been told he was. Phoenix has now been cleaned up.

After a day and night on pass, each man would report back to base and would wait for his assignment to the next unit. It was at this time that a representative from Special Forces recruiting gave the men an opportunity to join up with their outfit for special training and become a member of a very small elite group. If you could qualify, then you became what was known as a "Green Beret."

The Special Forces under President Kennedy had started a new program and about a dozen men signed up from Ran's company. They were given a series of four exams and Ran tested very high on communication skills, and he was accepted. Orders came down that he was to report to Ft. Bragg, North Carolina, and arrived there one midnight towards the last of August, 1964. He along with others who were traveling together, most of whom were going to 82nd Airborne Division, reported in to a processing center where he met a sergeant who started barking orders, "Get your gear, shut up and don't smile." Three of them, a soldier from New York, another from Chicago and Ran were held back but shortly picked up by a three-quarter ton weapon carrier to be transported to a remote RTC Area.

Their new assignment was a completely different atmosphere as they got up at 6 a.m. for breakfast. They could quit the operation anytime they wanted. (They operated under a different set of rules; if you didn't want them, then they didn't want you.) They were given new tests to see what they were the most suited for; they gave them a choice of one of five military occupations to pursue: engineering (demolition), communications, medical, all types of weapons training, or operations and intelligence training.

Ran chose the medical field to work towards a 91B45 MOS number as a combat medic; however, he was to be trained in all five phases of the requirements in order to wear the coveted green beret. He immediately began a 44-week training period starting with eight weeks of unconventional warfare training and covert operations. Then in November, 1964, he was shipped to Ft. Sam Houston, Texas, to begin his first 20 weeks of medical instruction.

He really got an eye opener when he learned that part of the course consisted of using live wounded dogs as their patients. (These dogs were first anesthetized and then given wounds in different parts of their bodies. Each medic had a dog to work on.) They expected each medic to do whatever surgery was necessary plus any treatment needed by the dog and each student was expected to be able to save the dog's life. It was the way that each was to learn battlefield surgery as where they would be working was a long way from a doctor. By the way, when the surgery was complete and the instructors were satisfied of a job well done, the dog was put to sleep.

After completing his phase of training at Ft. Sam Houston, Ran was sent for eight weeks of on-the-job experience at the Army Hospital in Ft. Campbell, Kentucky, where he was given instructions in everything from delivering babies to working in the operating room. Next, he was sent to the Great Smokey Mountains for a two-week exercise in the cold and snow.

After all of this different training, he had earned his green beret in October, 1965. Ran was sent back to Ft. Bragg, where he was assigned to the 7th Group of the 1st Special Forces Airborne and was given the red flasher emblem to wear on his beret. Shortly his unit was sent to Panama for jungle warfare training and additional instruction in simulated combat jumping from 1,200 to 1,300 feet, then four weeks of prisoner of war school.

From Panama they returned to Ft. Bragg, and Ran put in for some leave time. He called his father and told him that he would drive home, taking some five to six days to visit some old friends along the way. By the time he got home, his father said the army was looking for him, so Ran called in and was told to go immediately to Tinker Air Force Base in Oklahoma City, that a plane would be waiting.

When he arrived at Tinker, there was an Air Force Lear Jet awaiting his arrival. On board the aircraft was a full colonel, two lieutenant colonels and a major, all very unhappy because they had been waiting some two hours for takeoff due to a lowly green beret sergeant. (In that day and time the Green Hat was held to be something special.) Their plane landed at Andrews Air Force Base in Washington D.C., where he was met and taken by another plane to Polk Air Force Base, then flown to Oakland, California, where he was processed and caught a flight to Ton-So-Nouk outside Saigon, South Vietnam.

Ran was immediately assigned to IV Corps as the unit he was to work with was still being assembled. He was flown from Saigon to Nathrang, worked in a hospital for a couple of weeks, then received deployment to the B-52 Special Operations team running recon on the Laotian-Cambodian-Vietnamese border areas. Their job was to find the underground routes and tunnels used by the Viet Cong (VC) for moving men and supplies southward towards Saigon and the Mekong Delta.

Once they found the routes, the area would be saturated by bombs, then the team would go in for a view of the damage inflicted and the possibility of cleaning up any additional enemy pockets that might have survived. On occasions the team would have to be quickly removed from the area due to the number of heated fire fights. They would not have an area big enough to work as a landing zone (LZ), so the helicopter would fly over just above the tops of the jungle trees or rocks, drop out of the side door a cable with a loop at the end making a kind of a stirrup, the soldier would put his foot in the loop, then the copter would fly straight up till they had cleared the tree tops with the man holding on to the cable. Once they were clear, the aircraft would start flying off searching for a landing zone while the soldier would be holding on like "Tarzan swinging on a grapevine." Ran said, "This could get a little hairy, but it would get you out of the hands of the VC."

Ran came back to Corps Hdqrs. and was assigned to A-226 Team, II Corps, and was to be 'coptered to work with the Montagards (Mountain People) in the Central Highlands at Mai Linh near Cheo Reo, Phu Bon province about 80 kilometers southeast of Pleiky. This camp had some 1,000 to 1,200 volunteers of "Yards" (this is similar to our National Guard but they could go home anytime that they wished) who were paid by the United States government. They were organized into five companies and occasionally they also housed South Vietnamese Special Forces. (These units were not very trustworthy and bad blood ran between them and the "Yards.")

Ran found out in a hurry that the "Yards" were excellent fighters; you could trust them. If one of them were killed or wounded, you did everything possible to return them to their home so that their spirit would not "wander" for eternity. They were a very superstitious people; if you did not drink their rice wine you couldn't do anything with them. (This drinking evolved around every function - deaths, funerals, marriages, births, you name it.) They were a very religious people and would pray to their "Yangs." In short, if you did not drink with them, it was a humiliation for them.

From their base camp, team A-226 was made up of two officers, 10 enlisted men broken out in two units of six men each with all being cross-trained to do each others job. They would go out from three days to two weeks of patrol activity with constant reporting of the movement of the VC or NVA so that any necessary action could be taken by larger units or by bombing. It was during one of these patrols, this time using some of the

"Yards" operating in a valley spearheading an assault by a combination of part of the 1st Cavalry Division and the 101st Airborne Division that Ran won the Bronze Star for heroism.

Ran spent nine months in VC territory with the Montagnards and in March, 1967 he left Saigon by aircraft to McGuire Air Force Base, California for discharge. Some of the ribbons that Ran is authorized to wear are the Bronze Star, the Combat Infantry Badge, the Combat Medic Badge, the Parachutist Badge, Vietnam Campaign Medal with Device 60, National Defense Service Medal, Vietnam Service Medal, just to name a few.

Our family is extremely proud of Ran and what he has done for this country. His interview was very enlightening and this article is just a tip of the iceberg of what this young man went through. In case you didn't know it, he is my cousin and to me, if there were such a thing as rating this country's patriots, he would be at the top of my list. Thanks, Ran.

A TRIBUTE TO HER GRANDFATHER

Originally Published as a Letter to the Editor, Atoka County Times

For a long time you could turn and look in the paper to find a column entitled "Portraits of Patriots." Now you can look and it is no longer there. The man who dedicated a lot of time to that column is no longer here to write it.

I have seen many cry and many laugh as they read that column. They would read about friends and loved ones whom the writer felt should have recognition. This column was not only popular here in Atoka County, but also other counties, and even other states.

But, of all the people the man wrote about, I always felt he left out one. I feel it is my duty to recognize this man now. This man was the best, not only to his country, but to his family, friends and even strangers. This man has seen the worst of times and the best of times, and I feel this man should be included with all the others written about in the "Portraits of Patriots" because, not only did this man fight for his country, but for his family and friends.

The man I speak of is none other than the author of the "Portraits of Patriots," Sherman Bledsoe, Jr., known to everyone as "Shug."

This man did not grow up rich in money but rich in love. Though Shug was a strict father and grandfather, he was very well loved and respected. Shug was one of those people who was not afraid. He never cared what people thought of him, and he never met a stranger. He was very loyal, especially to his country, when he fought in the Korean War. His love for his country was without question.

After writing columns for the paper, he would take them to Connie Zalenski to have her go over them and type them. He would always stop her to add details to the story and tears would stream down his face while describing the situations. It made you glad for never knowing personally the extent of it.

Shug loved every man and woman he wrote about. The true respect, love and admiration for each one could not compare in words after listening to his stories.

Shug was also well loved in his community as well as in his church where, for many years, he was a preacher, song leader, teacher, deacon and elder. He devoted his life to God, and if you've never heard Shug sing praises to God, you missed the sweetest sincerity of love ever shown! God knew the condition Shug was in physically and Shug's love and fear of God is what made him the man he was.

Anyone could see the love of God Shug had just by the way he loved and cared about everyone. This man loved everyone, no matter if they were rich or poor, black or white, male or female. In his eyes and heart, they were all the same. Whether or not someone liked him, he would love them anyway.

Shug always wanted and had a way of making people feel special. He loved doing that but, most of all, he loved helping people. He did help many, but you would never hear him telling it.

Not only did he have love for other people, he also loved his wife, Thelma. He loved telling people how they "courted." I can remember him just sitting and staring at her to say "doesn't she look beautiful."

"A marriage made in heaven" is what his mother would say.

Shug raised two wonderful children to see them raise five wonderful grandchildren. This man deserved to be recognized in "Portraits of Patriots." In my eyes, he is one of the greatest grandfathers a person could ask for.

I am Melissa Bledsoe and I am one of those five grandchildren. My whole life I respected my grandfather (known by me and the other grandchildren as "Poppa"). I feared him because he was wiser and because he was usually right. But out of everything in my life, when I messed up in, he always had faith in me and would help me to strive to do better. If it were not for me wanting to please him, I feel I would not be where I am today.

So I believe my Poppa is very deserving to be a Patriot in this column. I also want to say, "Poppa, though I'm not entering the Marines like you always used to tease me about, I am still going to be the best that I can be and I know you are in Heaven, smiling down. You lived a great loving life and each and every soul which you touched I know feels the same when saying you were and still are very much loved and will always be missed and never forgotten. I love you!"

~Melissa Bledsoe
Age 17

Index

A

Adams, Franklin, 30
Alford, Travis, 189, 224, 233
Allen, David, 17, 26-28, 188
Allen, Joephene, 17, 26, 28, 188
Allen, Shirley, 133, 189
Anderson, Frank, 226
Armstrong, Alvin, 189
Armstrong, Billy, 198
Armstrong, Dean Edward, 100, 166, 182, 198
Armstrong, Fletcher, 182
Arrington, Donnie, 182
Arrington, Howard, Jr., 176, 182
Arrington, Hub, 133
Atoka County Times, 6-8, 147, 261
Atoka County Veterans Memorial, 7
Atoka High School, 8, 10, 46, 50, 70, 107, 133, 136, 168, 175, 178, 194, 240
Atoka Library, 6, 79

B

Baker, Gilbert, Jr., 111-114, 179-180, 239, 243
Baker, Jasper N., 175
Bardwell, Odis, 189, 217
Barnhill, Jim/Jimmy, 189, 218
Barrett, Bill, 97
Barton, Clyde, 188
Barton, Herman, 48, 192, 249
Barton, Tonya Bledsoe, 10
Barton, Wendy, 10
Beard, Wilbern S., 34, 48-49, 181, 232, *photo*
Belcher, Thomas, 233
Benham, Elbert, 133, 189, 191
Benham, Glenn, 189, 191
Bennett, John "Cue Ball", 34, 48, 167, 181
Berry, William A., 79
Betts, W.M., *photo*
Bickle, Burris "Buck", 177
Bisbee, Louis, 115-117
Bisbee, Pap, 115
Bisbee, Walter, 115-117
Blackburn, Houston, 22, 181, 192-193
Blackburn, Leroy D., 20-23, 193, *photo*
Blackman, Joe, 77
Blaker, Royce, 176
Bledsoe Energy Corp., 10
Bledsoe Hill, 228
Bledsoe Land & Cattle Co., 10
Bledsoe, Bill L., 11, 12, 177, 194-196
Bledsoe, Bryan Allen, 10
Bledsoe, Herman, 193-194
Bledsoe, John, 10
Bledsoe, Melissa Ann, 10, 115, 261-263
Bledsoe, Ollie May Cartwright, 9-10
Bledsoe, Scott, 10

Bledsoe, Sherman Avner, Jr. "Shug," 6-11, 120-135, 189, 197-231, 261-263, *photos*
Bledsoe, Sherman Avner, Sr., 9
Bledsoe, Thelma Lamb, 10, 119, 135, 262
Bledsoe, Tonya Alene, 10
Bledsoe's Diner, 10, 37, 51
Bloyd, William L. , 181
Boatman, Larry Neal, 100
Boggy Bottom Boys, 120-135, 172, 199
Bohannon, Edward, 169
Bohannon, Walter E., 79
Bonham, Chester, *photo*
Bonham, Marvin, 188, 191, 230, *photo*
Bonham, Olie, 189, 191, *photos*
Bonham, Orville M., *photo*
Bonifield, Wallace, 189
Bonner, Jack, 239
Bowman, Willie, 60, 120-121, 176, 189, *photo*
Bradshaw, L.A., *photo*
Brawner, Lesly, 182
Brenham, Elbert, *photo*
Brentwood, John, 173
Brown Cartwright, Daisy, 61
Brown, Edith, 231
Brown, Robert M., 47, 233
Bryant, Andrew R., 182
Bryant, Frank, Jr., 133, 189, 217
Burke, Doyce, 164, *photo*
Burkhalter, Earon, 188

Burleson, Odis Paul, *photo*
Burleson, Audie, *photo*
Burns, R. C., 177
Burrows, John, 182
Bussey, Harold, 133, 189
Bussey, William, 133
Butch, (a Korean boy), 39-40
Butler, Raymond C., 241
Butts, J.C., *photo*
Byrum, Elma Lou, 132

C

Cain, Foster & Louise, 6
Calvin, Chaney, 77
Camp, Bill, 180
Camp, Leo "Bobby Lee," 180, 189, 191, 215
Camp, Sidney A. "Sid," 122, 132, 172, 189, 191, 192, 206-207, 228-229
Capps, Larry, 53
Carnes, Ben, 17
Carpenter, Claude A., 43-44
Carr, Celia Roach, 160
Carr, Mack, 160
Carr, Morris, 160-164, 181
Cartwright, Daisy (Brown), 61
Cartwright, Jesse Billy "Slick," 60, 85-86, 137, 146, 176, 186-187, *photos*
Cartwright Bledsoe, Ollie May, 9-10
Cartwright, Roby Isabella, 8, 91, 93
Cartwright, Samuel Fulton, 60-63, 85, 86, 137-146, 176, *photos*

Cartwright Hoffelt, Knolly Ann "Shanks", 91-94, *photo*
Cartwright, Wilburn, 176
Cartwright, William Davis "Bill", 8, 91
Cartwright, Zachary Taylor, "Zack", 168-169, 175, 193, *photo*
Cates, Robert G. "Bob", 29-31, 46, 48, 176
Cates, Wendell, 176
Chaffin, Maxine, 176
Chappel, David, 113
Chatman, O.H., *photo*
Chick, Bob, 48
Chish Oktak Church, 17
Chitwood, Bob, 198
Chitwood, J.A., *photo*
Chitwood, Jack, 189, 198
Chitwood, John, 186
Chitwood, R., *photo*
Choate, Bob, 36
Choctaw "CRY", 17-19
Christie, Robert "Bob", 244-248, *photo*
Church of Christ, Lane, Oklahoma, 10
Clark, J. D. , 34, *photo*
Clark, (General) Mark, 233
Clark, R., *photo*
Clifford, Bill, 111
Coates, Buck, 153
Coats, Clyde A., 75-79, 169, *photo*
Cockrill, Grady, 215
Cole, Ditters "DAS", 6, 102, 141, 147
Cole, Ernest, 176, 181
Cole, John, 153
Cole, Neil G., 102-106
Collier, J., *photo*
Collins, Laverne, 167, 181, 193
Connell, Effie Annie, 115
Connelly, Ted, 133, 189, 217
Cook, B. R. "Red", Jr., 176, 193
Cook, Holland, 189, 191
Cook, James, 189, 191
Cook, Jay, 215
Cook, Robert, 189
Cook, Rowe, 47, 172, 175
Cook, Tim, 176
Cooksey, Lewis C., 176
Cooper, Henry, 177
Cotton, Dr. W. W. "Ol' Doc Cotton", 120, 122, 176
Cox, R. E., Jr., 181, 193
Crites, Cypus, 188
Crites, John, 182
Culverson, Larry, 182
Curry, Olen, 48 , 48, 239
Curtis, E., *photo*
Custer Lamb, Bessie Thelma, 115-119
Custer, (General) George Armstrong, 10, 115
Custer, Stephen "Steve", 115-117
Custer, William C., 115

D

Daily, Sam, 182
Dale, (a soldier), 192
Daney, J., *photo*

Darken, Gloria, 132
Dashner, Brick, 36, 37, 189, 198-199, 215
Davis, Charles E., 182
Davis, Otis O., 182
Davis, Raymond, 177
Dean, Robert C. "Doc", 33, 46, 48, 137, 146, 176
DeArmon, Opal "Shug", 176
Deaton, John C., 182
Decker, Bob/Bobby, 133, 189
DeGalle, (General) Charles, 36
DeGrazia, Bob, 133
Derrick, Randy Wayne, 100
Dobbs, Linnon, 48
Dodson, Allen, 186
Dodson, Jesse/Jess, 90, 170
Dodson, Nannie Lou, 67-68
DOK Ranch School, 186
Dole, Senator Bob, 105-106
Donaldson, Billy Marvin (Bill), 154-159, 177
Donaldson, Shuzie, 159
Dossett, John, 148
Double Springs Church, 17-18
Double X Hill, 9, 26, 216, 220, 222-230
Downs, A., *photo*
Downs, Standford, 60, 176, 191, *photo*
Dunn, Charles E., 46, 90, 170, 176, *photo*
Dunn, Paul, 170
Dunn, Ralph E., 176, *photo*
Durant, Forbes Pipkin, Jr., 100, 182
Durbin, Walter, 113

E

Eastridge, Hershel, 26, 28, 133, 189, 198, 220, 226-227
Eaves, Otis, 182
Edge, Lawrence, 181
Edge, Loyd F., Jr., 180-181
Eisenhower, (General) Dwight, 231
Embrey, W.W., *photo*
Eusey, Charles, 163-164
Evans, Benny L., 182
Evans, Danny Leo, 100, 185
Evans, Eddie, 202, *photo*
Ewing, Richard, 169

F

Farris, Larry, 51
Faudree, Marcella, 177
Fink, Lon Robert, 6, 70-74, 121, 142, 145, 147, 153, 175, 191, 199-200, 203-204, 210, 214, 218, 220, 239
Fishel, Judge Laveren, 201
Fisher, George, 32
Fitzgerald, Alfred "Hoss", 133, 189, 220
Fleet, Robert, 46-47
Flowers, Bill, 189, 218
Folsom, Bill, 189, 191
Folsom, Charles "Hagan", 133, 189, 191
Folsum, Oscar, Jr., 111
Foote, Oliver, 177
Foote, Oscar, 177, 189, 205-206

Foster, Don "Fuzzy", 133, 189
Franklin, Jesse/Jess, 90, 170
Franklin, William D., 34, 48, 182, 232
Fryer, Bob, 190
Fugate, Joe D., 176

G

Garner, Curtis W. "Cactus Jack", 32-34, 48, 82-83, 86, 89, 137, 182
Garner, Evelyn, 86, 89
Garside, Leonard, 48
Glasgow, Bob, 190, 217
Glass, Leslie, 190
Glover, John, 133, 190
Goettge, Frank, 117
Goforth, Bill, 48
Goldstein, Donald, 153
Goodson, Jim/Jimmy, 107-110, 177
Goss, Herbert, 90, 170
Greathouse, Cecil B. "Bud", 35-37, 48, 72, 180, 190, 199, 203, 214, 228-229
Green, C.N., *photo*
Griffin, William, 190
Grist, Herbert, 184-186
Grist, Jesse "Ed", 176, 190
Groves, (General) Leslie, 92

H

Hacker, Billy Bob, 198
Haggard, Bill, 253
Haggard, "Butch", 253
Haggard, Marion "Chunk", 60, 176, 189
Haggard, Ransy Cooper "Ran", 177, 253-260
Haggard-Cotner Sawmill, 17
Hale, Elzie, 205
Hall, Clyde, 176
Hall, Donald J., 100
Hall, Harold, 188
Hames, Margaret, 237
Hamilton, Kenneth, 6
Hamlin, Joe Charles, 166, 182
Hamm, Sam, *photo*
Haraway, Jack, 189, 191
Haraway, Robert "Pepper", 190, 191, 227
Harris, Billy J., 48
Harris, Robert, 133
Hayes, Paul, 46, 176
Heard, Dick, 234
Heard, T. J., 90, 170
Heck, Chris, 132
Hedges, Harold, 176
Henderson, Riley, 190, 220, 228
Hendrix, E.J., *photo*
Herrod, Billy, 190
Hess, Rudolf, 68-69
Hinkle, Clarence, 182
Hodges, Courtney, 149
Hodges, Eldon, 190
Hoffelt, Knolly Ann "Shanks" Cartwright, 91-94, *photo*
Homer, Joseph, 188
Hopson, Arnold, 177
Horn, Wilford, 176
Howard, Earl L., 182

Howard, Vincent I., 60, 176, *photo*
Huff, Bill, 152
Huff, Edna (McGee Yandell), 148-149, 152
Hunt, Charlie C., 182
Hutton, Betty, 231
Hyde, Jimmy Don, 100

J

Jackson, Ellis, 34, 48
Jackson, James S., 192, *photo*
Jackson, Linda Carol Yandell, 149, 152
Jackson, Mickey, 177
James, Matt, 10
Jarvis, Walter J., 182
Jim, Anderson, 34, 48, 182
Johnson, Chip, 220, 228
Johnson, Clifford, 190, 191
Johnson, Lane, 238-239, 243
Johnson, Thelma, 238
Johnson, Tommy, 176
Johnson, Turner Coleman, 100
Johnson, Windell, 190, 191
Jones, G.C., *photo*
Jones, Donald, 189
Jones, H., *photo*
Jones, Julis, 227
Jones, W.L., Jr., *photo*
Joyce, E.V., *photo*
Joyce, H., *photo*

K

Keeton, Claude, 188

Keith, Leonard, 190, 205, 217
Kennedy, (President) John F., 73, 196, 256
Kennedy, Larry, 176
Koutsky, Robert L., 241
Krueger, (General) Walter, 137, 138, 141

L

Lack, Floyd, 176
Lamb, Bennett Graham "Barney", 116-118
Lamb, Bessie Thelma Custer, 115-119
Lamb, Collen, 100
Lamb, Henry Allen, 116, 118
Lamb, Henry Hector, 115-117
Lamb, Robert, 100-101
Lamb Bledsoe, Thelma, 10, 119, 135, 262
Lane, Oklahoma, 8, 10, 17-18, 26, 28, 35, 38, 41, 60, 64, 66, 67, 69, 75, 78, 83, 85, 91, 92, 94, 95, 98, 107, 135, 153, 165, 178, 186, 194
Lanoy, Frank, 188
Lanoy, Henry, 188
Lawrence, Julius, 188
Lee, Hoyt, 164, 185
Lemons, John, 188
Leonard, C.E., *photo*
Lewis, Benny Joe, 50-55, 100, 182
Lewis, Bob, 50, 54
Lewis, Monica, 231

Lewis, Neoma, 50
Lillard, J. M., 140, 169
Lillard, Richard, 140
Linscott, Gordie Gene, 67-69
Linscott, Ron & Linda, 6
Linton, John, 170, 181
Locke, Charles W., Sr., 182
Loftis, Don, 237
Love, Harlan, 190
Lovinggood, Carl V., 48, 182
Lowe, Norvell "Toopie", 190
Lowe, Tommy, 112
Lowe, Thomas, Jr., *photo*
Lyles, Dubley, 181
Lynch, Cecil C., 233

M

MacArthur, (General) Douglas, 103, 113, 179, 221
Maine, Russell, 177
Maloy, Floyd E., 90, 170
Mansell, Herbert, 190
Maxey, Curtis R., 181, 182
Maxey, Walter L., 182
Mayo, Ferman, 133
McAnulty, Hal Gene, 168, 173, 181
McAnulty, Jack, 190, 191, 219
McAnulty, Oren "Smut", 190, 191
McBride, Virgil, 182
McCall, C.A. "Barney", 120-121, 177, 228
McCaskle, Fred, 122
McCasland, John "Hicky", 48, 120-135, 172, 175, 191, 198-201, 204-207, 227, *photo*

McCasland, Mark, 113
McDonald, Charles B., 153
McDonald, Ray, 186
McDougal, Dood, 182
McElroy, James L., 34
McFarland, Edward, 169
McGee (Yandell) Huff, Edna, 148-149, 152
McGee, James, 190
McGue, Jason H., 182
McGue, Ron, 51
McHenry, Wayne, 77
McKaskle, Paul, 190, 204
McKee, C.B., *photo*
McKinney, Alex, 181, 193
McKinney, Lee, 176
McLeroy, James Tilden "Jabo", 46-49, 83, 167, 181, 233, *photo*
McNally, Monroe, 51, 53
Mead, Calvin, Jr., 176, 191, 224
Mead, Roy, 48, 95-98, 167, 192, 249
Mead, William, 165
Melton, Edward, 182
Meridian, Frank, 212
Merrit, Ray, 181
Merritt, Robert, 48
Miccoli, Salvatore, 48
Middleton, (General) Troy, 151
Miller, Gus Henry "Speed Ball", 48, 78, 79, 132
Millican, Herbert, 190, 215
Millican, Louis F., *photos*
Millican, Paul, *photo*
Mills, Clifton, 48
Mills, Eual, 190

Mitchell, Bob/Bobby, 190, 218
Moffatt, George, 176
Moffatt, Hamilton "Beans," 190, 191
Moffatt, Katie, 233
Moffatt, Wallace "Bud," 133, 190, 191, *photo*
Moffatt, William D., 181, 232-233
Moffatt, W., *photo*
Monroe, Marilyn, 231
Montgomery, Conner, 176
Moore, Amous E., 182, 233, 238, 242-243, *photo*
Moore, Carl, 182
Moore, C.C., *photo*
Moore, Clarence, 242
Moore, Dwight "Russell," 190
Moore, Eugene, 182
Moore, Freddie "Sweetie Pie," 215, 227
Moore, John W., 175
Moore, Luther "Sweetie Pie," 190
Moore, Mary Stanphill, 242
Moore, Orville, 242
Moore, Willie W., 238-243, *photos*
Morgan, George, 48
Morris, Dammie, 188, *photo*
Morris, (General), 151
Morrow, Bernard G., 90, 170
Moses, Marion, 188
Muldrow, Hal, 73
Mulkey, W. J., 165
Muncy, Offie, 186
Muncy, William S., 166
Mungle, J. Jene, 249

Murphy, Audie, 35
Murphy, Pat, 85
Murray, Jack, 133
Musler, John L., 48, *photo*

N

Nanney, Bob, 188, 230
Nelson, James, 17
Nelson, Joseph "Shorty," 190, 215
New, Eldred, 181
Newson, Frank, 189
Nichols, Buck, 188, 230
Nichols, John, 18
Nichols, Lester M., 153
Nichols, Samp, 153
Nix, Bowden, 188
Norris, Harry, 58
Northcutt, Clarence, 190
Northcutt, Walter, 188
Norton, Glenn, 7
Nowlin, Frank, 188
Nuttall, R., *photo*

O

O'Jibway, Philip J., 32
Olsen, Tommy, 188
Oppenheimer, Dr. J. Robert, 92
O'Quinn, Archie, 113
Ouriel, Michael, 48
Overstreet, Harding, 182

P

Pagen, Edward E., 43-44

Parham, Don, 199
Patton, (General) George, 46, 48-49, 117, 137, 149, 231, 250-252
Payne, Onul "Cotton," 188, 230-231
Pennington, Walter, Jr., 176
Petak, Joseph, 79
Peters, Harlon, 188
Pharr, Bill, 40, 176, 178, 188
Pharr, Janet, 178
Phelps, Audie, 186
Phillips, Jesse Wayne "Jess" or "Ol' Jess," 6, 120-135, 190, 198, 220, 226, 228
Phillips, Mel, 12
Pi Kappa Alpha, 10
Piearcy, Bill, 188
Pierson, Sammy, 189
Pingleton, Bill, 176, 190, 199
Pitts, Derwin Brooks, 100
Poole, Jim/Jimmy, 133, 176
Praytor, B. E. "Bob," 133, 182, 190, *photo*
Praytor, Jimmy, 176

R

Ragsdale, Burnis, 182
Rains, C.E., *photo*
Rains, L.A., *photo*
Rains, Warren E., 182
Ralls, Joe, 186
Ralls, Marie, 237
Ramsey, Hershel, 182
Randolph, Robert, 175, 191, 211, 217, 230

Ray, Benny, 215
Ray, O. P. "Perry," 147, 190, 191, 217-218
Ray, Thomas R. "Tinker," 6, 120-135, 190, 191, 220, 226, 228
Rector, Bill/Billy, 188, 230, *photo*
Rector, Lee, 191, *photo*
Rector, Mart, 186, 188, 191, 230, *photo*
Reeves, Vernon, 175, 193
Reiger, Pliney, 81
Reynolds, Debbie, 231
Rhodes, Herman, 43-45
Rich, John, 189
Rich, Vance, 175, 228
Richardson, Bill, 190
Ridgeway, (Gen.) Matthew, 231
Ridgeway, W. R., 190, 198, 212, 217
Rigsby, A., *photo*
Roark, Tilden, 34
Roberts, Levi, 190, 220, 224, *photo*
Roberts, Steve, 188
Robinson, Calvin, 48
Rogers, Paul, 190
Rogers, William III, 190
Rollins, C.C., *photo*
Roosevelt, (President) Theodore, 15, 186
Roosevelt, (President) Franklin D., 20, 32
Rounsaville, Delbert, 136, 176
Rounsaville, Forest "Speck," 143, 176, 177

Rounsaville, Glo, 133, 143, 145, 147, 176
Rounsaville, Mittie Garner, 136
Rounsaville, Tom, 60, 61, 86-89, 103, 136-147, 169, 175, 177, *photo*
Rtoka, Chief, 13
Rush, William C. "Bill", 43, 44
Russell, L.V., *photo*

S

Salmon, A.J., *photo*
Salmon, A.W., *photo*
Sanborn, Jack, 151
Sanders, Tom, 233
Schaeffer, William "King Kong", 46
Schmidt, Felica, 122-127
Self, Billy H., 182
Sewell, Vernon, 176
Shannon, Leonard, 182
Sheffield, Leonard, Jr. 189, 198
Sheffield, Ray, 18
Sherrard, Wesley W., 38-42, 176, 177
Shields, George, 181, 182
Shields, James C., 182
Shingleton, John R., 171
Shoemake, Alonzo, Jr., 133
Shoremake, I.D., *photo*
Shrier, Harold, 185
Sico, Paul M., 233
Smith, (General) Holland, 161
Smith, James "Smitty", 230
Smith, L. G., 182
Smith, Roy, 170, 188

Smithart, Donald "Doe", 190, 191
Smithart, Willard "Wes", 190, 191
Soules, Bill, 60, 85-90, 137, 170, 176
Soules, Claudene, 85
Sprouse, Joy May, 132
Stackhouse, Lefra, 37
Stallings, E.D., *photo*
Standifer, Frank, 182
Stanphill Moore, Mary, 242
Stark, T.M., *photo*
Steele, Harold, 190, 199-200
Stowers, Matt, 186
Strain, Dan J., 182
Strickland, Hoyle, 143, 190
Strickland, James, 190
Styron, James C., 175
Sullinger, Overton, 177, 190
Sullivan, Pat, 192
Surrell, Johnny, 199
Sutherland, James Arthur, 168, 179, 182
Sutton, Clouser, 181
Sutton, Flint, 51
Swindell, Bobby Dale, 56-59, 100, 182, *photos*
Swindell, Eugene, 56, 133, 190
Swindell, Ovel & Zetta, 56

T

Tarron, C.P., *photo*
Taylor, Jim, 182
Taylor, R.E., 241
Tedford, Charlie, 182

Thomas, Casey, 36
Thomason, Glen, 234-237
Thompson, Jackie, 182
Thompson, James, 192, 249
Tidwell, Claud, 26, 28, 190, 226, *photo*
Tolar, John, 153
Tom, Benjamin, 182
Trail, Kenneth, 190
Trent, Clem, 177
Trulock, Grady, 189
Turnbull, James, 188
Turner, Alfred "Cotton", 90, 170
Turner, John Henry, 146, 167
Turner, R., *photo*
Turner, Red, 176
Turner, Wylie Clyde, 46, 175
Twining, (Major General), 241

U

Uber, L.W., *photo*
Umsted, Charles, 188, 230
U.S.S. Argonant, 179
U.S.S. Arizona, 21, 193
U.S.S. Bexar, 212
U.S.S. California, 21
U.S.S. Calvert, 46, 48
U.S.S. Chandler, 20-23
U.S.S. Dark, 163
U.S.S. Dennis, 22
U.S.S. General Hugh Gaffey, 8, 134, 208-210
U.S.S. Herring, 168, 179
U.S.S. Hope, 181
U.S.S. Hornet, 239
U.S.S. Lexington, 20

U.S.S. Minneapolis, 20
U.S.S. Mississippi, 111-114, 179, 243
U.S.S. Missouri, 179
U.S.S. Monterey, 103
U.S.S. New Mexico, 243
U.S.S. Oklahoma, 21
U.S.S. Pickens, 180
U.S.S. Pueblo, 171
U.S.S. St. Lo, 22
U.S.S. Soltis, 181

V

Vandenburg, Eddie, 188, 230, *photos*
Vietta, Albert, 190, 191
Vietta, Dominic, 176, 189, 191

W

Wainright, (General) Jonathan, 78
Walker, Gwen, 12
Walker, Jimmy "Guts", 133
Walker, LeRoy, 181
Wall, Jessie, 233
Wallace, Babe, 237
Wallace, Jesse "Pot", 190, 215
Warren, 233
Warren, D., *photo*
Watkins, Wes, 19
Watson, Doyle, 190, 191
Watson, Harley, 190, 191
Weaver, Charles G. "Charlie", 48, 175, 239
Weaver, T., *photo*

Webster, Sam, 100
Wells, (Colonel) Walter "Scott",
   6, 9, 34, 48, 61, 80-84, 86,
   99, 120-121, 134, 137, 146,
   147, 168, 176, 183, 191,
   207-231, 232-233, 239
Weston, Joe, 198
White, Claude E., 90, 170
White, Jim, 178
White, Slick, 153
White, Thomas, 179, 181
Whitman, Bill, 30, 47-48
Whitten, John David, 153
Whittington, O.L., *photo*
Willeby, Leroy, 189
Williams, Charles, 190
Williams, H.S., *photo*
Williams, James I., 90, 170
Williams, Joe, 190, 218
Williams, Lavester L., 100
Williams, Leo K., 60, 100, 153,
   176, 191, 200-206, 215
Williams, Tommy Jeff, 133,
   166-167, 190, 198
Williams, Wilbur, 177
Williams, W.F., *photo*
Williamson, Charles F. "Bud",
   24-25
Williford, John Clyde, 249-252
Wilson, Clarence "Cid", 190
Wilson, Dale "CID", 153, 173-174
Wilson, Marie, 12
Wilson, Walton "Bunt", 165-166, 171
Winkim, Blinkim, and Knod, 6,
   120-135

Winslett, James, 48
Winters, Eddie Mark, 176, 190,
   191, 199, 207
Winters, Irving, 191
Winters, Thomas "Hogjaw",
   191
Withrow, Alice, 6
Wolfe, Garvie, Jr., 182
Womble, Larry, 191
Wood, Lige P., 182
Wyatt, Billy Burr, 191
Wyrick's Lumber, 234

Y

Yandell, Albert L.C., 148-153,
   181
Yandell Huff, Edna McGee,
   148-149, 152
Yandell, Jack & Rosie, 148,
   151
Yandell Jackson, Linda Carol,
   149, 152
Yates, Doyle, 133, 191, 217
York, P. C. "Preacher", 166
York, Bill "Buffalo Bill", 48, 82
York, Paul, 48, 167

Z

Zalenski, Connie Johnston, 6,
   147, 262
Zinn, Walter Maxoe, Jr. "Mac",
   64-66